ST. ERKENWALD

A Middle English Poem

Edited with introduction, notes, and glossary
by
HENRY L. SAVAGE

ARCHON BOOKS
1972

Library of Congress Cataloging in Publication Data

Erkenwald, Saint. Legend.
  St. Erkenwald, a Middle English poem.

   (Yale studies in English, v. 72)
   Reprint of the 1926 ed., which was originally presented
as the editor's thesis, Yale, 1924.
   Bibliography: p. 88-91
   I. Savage, Henry Lyttleton, 1892-   ed.
II. Title. III. Series.
PR1968.E4 1972   821'.1   70-179571
ISBN 0-208-01136-6

First published 1926 by Yale University Press.
Reprinted 1972 with permission in an unaltered
and unabridged edition as an Archon Book by
The Shoe String Press, Inc., Hamden, Connecticut

Printed in the United States of America

TO THE MEMORY

OF

ARTHUR V. SAVAGE
LIEUTENANT 30TH INFANTRY, U. S. A.
MEZY, FRANCE, JULY 15TH, 1918

Bot for wothe, ne wele, ne wrathe, ne drede,
Ne for maystrie, ne for mede, ne for no monnes aghe,
I remewit never fro þe riȝt, by reson myn awen.

PREFACE

The present edition of *St. Erkenwald* was begun before I was aware that Sir Israel Gollancz was at work upon the same task. His edition appeared in 1922, and though its merits were many, it seemed to me that there was room for another that should deal with certain problems and phases of the poem still waiting for complete examination or discussion. Upon a number of questions of interpretation, and particularly with regard to the many cases in which he has emended the text, I have differed from my predecessor. But I am indebted, as indeed are all other students of the poem, to his edition for much light upon dark places. The debt of gratitude which scholars on both sides of the Atlantic owe to Sir Israel's assiduous study of Middle English poetry grows greater with the years that pass.

Though following the spelling of the original manuscript scrupulously in all essentials, I have made no attempt to present the form of its lettering. Abbreviations have been expanded without the use of italics to denote the abbreviated letters. Emendations are indicated by parentheses. It has been my aim to present in the footnotes to the text an account of the appearance of the manuscript and a history of emendations and suggested readings that will be complete. My practice is as follows. Words cited from the manuscript are printed in italic type, and, unless necessary for the determination of a particular reading, the common and ordinary abbreviations, well-known to scholars, have been expanded without comment. Where such necessity exists, the abbreviated letters are printed in italic, and all others in roman type. Words cited from a previous commentator also appear in italics. Where, however, a commentator has noted abbreviated letters, I have followed the convention described above: for abbreviations, italic; for all other letters, roman type. This practice has also been followed in the case of a phrase, one of whose members is a word with an abbreviated letter (cf. footnote to l. 103). In no case have I italicized abbreviations in such words as *pat, per,* and *pus.* Where one or more commentators have the same reading as the manuscript, but distinguish contractions or abbreviations by italic letters, I have sometimes, to save space, cited only the form given by the commentator.

My thanks are due to my colleagues, Professors Robert K. Root and Robert R. Cawley, for helpful advice upon a number of small particulars; to Miss Grace Lyttleton Savage, for aid in the preparation of the glossary; to the officers and staffs of the Libraries of Yale and Princeton Universities, and that of the University of Pennsylvania. To Messrs. Gruener and Ginter and to Mrs. Ingersoll of the Library of Yale University I am particularly indebted. More weighty is my debt to the editor of the *Studies,* Professor Albert S. Cook. I am obliged to him for guidance and encouragement not only in the preparation of the present edition, but also in the studies of earlier years. But my weightiest debt is to Professor Robert J. Menner. He it was who first suggested the present work, and he it has been who encouraged me in the prosecution of it, giving, whenever I asked, liberally of his time and attention. His devoted and unremitting study of the poetry of the Alliterative School has been my good fortune.

A portion of the expense of printing has been defrayed by funds at the disposal of Yale University, and for this assistance I now return thanks.

Princeton, June 14, 1926.

CONTENTS

INTRODUCTION

MANUSCRIPT

St. Erkenwald is preserved in a single paper manuscript, British Museum Harleian 2250, ff. 72b-75a. Mr. H. L. D. Ward[1] tells us that our legend is one of a group of hagiographies to be found in it. This group, which may once have formed part of a Legendary, is followed by (1) a group of 'sermons on the Feasts of Corpus Christi and SS. Philip and James' (ff. 84, 85b, col. 2) ; (2) a set of 'Instructions for priests' (f. 85) ; (3) a document containing Five Church Tales' (ff. 86b-87, col. 2). The remaining portion of the manuscript, which contains, among other religious and didactic pieces, a 'Poem on Church Festivals' (f. 1), and an abridgment, dated 1477, of the *Speculum Christiani* of John Watton (f. 50), is described at length in the *Catalogue of the Harleian MSS.*[2]

'The appearance of the hand at once suggests the period about 1470-80. It is a script hand much used in correspondence in the fifteenth century, and the general decadent character of the hand would put it later in the century. This

---

[1] *Catalogue of Romances in the MS. Dept., British Museum,* 2. 690.

[2] The manuscript and our poem are thus described by the *Catalogue of the Harleian MSS. in the British Museum* (1808) 2. 577 :

'A paper Book in folio, consisting of divers Tracts bound up together in the Order following. . . .

23 De Erkenwaldo. 72. b.

This is a Legendary Poem concerning him, written by the Hand that wrote the Legend of St. Martin before mentioned, at No. 19. This begins thus,

"At London in Englonde nozt fulle longe sythen." '

The following also describe the contents of the manuscript : *Altenglische Legenden,* ed. C. Horstmann (1875), p. xxxviii; Ward, *Catalogue of Romances in the MS. Dept., British Museum,* 2. 690, 738; C. Brown, *Register of Middle English Religious Verse* 1. 314.

is confirmed by the colophon of a tract written in a contemporary hand, f. 64b: "Explicit Speculum Christiani anno domini M° cccc^{ko} lxxvll°." There is no reason why the whole MS. should not be of this date.'[3] The first page of the legend bears the Latin title *De Erkenwaldo;* the headlines of the other pages vary, some having *De Sancto Erkenwaldo.*[4] Occasional glosses in an Italian script on the right and left margins of the pages are ascribed by Gollancz to some reader of the late sixteenth or seventeenth centuries.[5] Knigge is wrong in his statement that the text is corrupt:[6] the handwriting is clear and legible; the text fairly free from errors, and not often obscured by blots or blurrings.[7] The initial letters of the first words of lines 1 and 177 are capitalized. Since it is possible to divide the poem into two main sections, one of whch seems to end at 176, the occurrence of a large capital letter at 177 is plain indication of a desire on the part of poet or scribe to mark the conclusion of one portion of the narrative, and the opening of another.

Certain names found in the manuscript are of interest in connection with problems arising with regard to dialectal provenience and authorship. On f. 8 there is written in a

[3] I am indebted for this written description of the manuscript to the kindness of Mr. J. A. Herbert and his subordinates of the staff of the British Museum.

[4] Knigge's designation of the poem on the title-page of his dissertation as *De Erkenwalde* is erroneous. He has misread the final *o* of the proper name on the head-lines of the manuscript as *e*.

[5] *St. Erk.,* p. v.

[6] Knigge, *Die Sprache des Dichters von Sir Gawain and the Green Knight, der sogennanten Early English Alliterative Poems und De Erkenwalde* (Marburg, 1885), p. 118: 'Der Text von De Erkenwalde ist sehr verdorben.' If Knigge means by the use of the word 'verdorben' that the manuscript is badly written or full of mistakes that require emendation, he is certainly wrong. If he means that the present manuscript differs greatly from its original as regards vocabulary and spelling, he is offering a hypothesis that is incapable of final and decisive proof.

[7] Cf. the marginal notes to the text of the poem.

legal hand of the sixteenth century the following sentence, 'Ser Thomas boker has Thys boke'; on f. 71 this claim of ownership is corroborated by the following phrase, 'syr Thomas bowker mine emys.' Having been unable to trace Sir Thomas Bowker as knight, Gollancz believes that the addition of the honorary prefix was used to mark his clerical position as chaplain.[8] 'Other names are Thomas Masse (?Mosse), f. 64b,[9] and what looks like Neltho Norton, f. 75b. Some jottings are of interest, as for example against the words "How longe had he þer layne," l. 95, we find "we redyn in a boke" followed by a word or two illegible, and a reference in one of the margins of f. 75b to "Ryght reuer-rynd Sodor," before which last word is a mark resembling a Y.'[10]

On f. 76b is a marginal entry which runs as follows: 'Noverint universi per pres*entes* nos Eesebyt bothe of dunnam in the comytye of Chester in the comythe.'[11] Ward suggested that the entry might refer to a feminine member (Elizabeth) of the famous Lancashire and Cheshire family of Booth of Dunham Massey.[12] Sir Israel Gollancz, working upon this clue, found that several members of that family had been prebendaries of St. Paul's Cathedral (London), and that one in particular, Laurence Booth, a

[8] See Gollancz, *op. cit.*, p. v.

[9] In a transcript of the marginal markings of the manuscript which Professor R. J. Menner of Yale University has been kind enough to make for the present editor, the word 'esquier' occurs after the proper name, 'Thomas Masse.' The correctness of this transcription is corroborated by Ward (2. 690).

[10] Gollancz, p. vi.

[11] Gollancz, p. vi.

[12] Ward (2. 690) believes that the Elizabeth of this marginal entry refers to 'Elizabeth, dau. of George Booth and wife of Richard Sutton.' That lady was living in 1566. Gollancz (p. vi) informs us, however, that Elizabeth was a common name in the Booth family, and that there was another lady of that name who lived much before 1556.

prominent figure in the ecclesiastical and political world of
the late fifteenth century, had once been Dean of that foundation. With a connection between the West Midland
family and St. Paul's Cathedral established in this way, his
conjecture that the manuscript of this poem had once formed
part of the library of that distinguished clergyman of West
Midland birth is by no means an improbable one.[13]

In printing the text, peculiarities of the manuscript in
regard to capitalization and the division of words have been
disregarded.[14] The curl in the manuscript after final -*n* has
not been expanded as final -*e*—contrary to the practice of
Horstmann—since the present editor feels that it is a mere
flourish of the scribe's pen. *I* and *j*, *u* and *v*, have been normalized, and the ordinary abbreviations for *and, with, in,
hit, þou, þat, þer, -er, -ur*[15] expanded without italics.

SOURCES

All search for the direct source of this miracle of St. Erkenwald has hitherto proved fruitless. Four separate Latin
Vitæ of the saint exist, but none mentions any miracle per-

---

[13] Gollancz, pp. vi-vii. See also the article on Laurence Booth in
D. N. B.

[14] The following words, which I have either hyphenated or printed
as one word for the sake of uniformity, are generally written in two
parts in the manuscript:

> *aldergrattyst, alle-kynnes, avis(i)on, ay-lastande, behalve, day-
> belle, debonerte, eghe-lyddes, evermore, forgo, forþi, forwrast,
> helle-hole, hondequile, inwith, mayster-mon, mayster-toun,
> mesters-mon, moght-freten, mynster-dores, myselfe, olofte, one-
> under, oureselfe, overdrofe, today, torent, toumbe-wonder, þer-
> after, þerof, þeron, þeroute, þertille, þerto, þiselwen, uphalden,
> vayne-glorie, vouche-safe, wele-dede, werkemen, withouten.*

[15] In accordance with the practice of most of the editors of the
poems of the Cotton MS., I have consistently expanded the curl
above an *o* as *ur*. While *fōme* occurs as a substantive in 230, its
participial use is designated by the spelling *fourmyt* (46). Cf.
courte (249).

formed by him that resembles in the slightest degree the one here ascribed to him.[1]

Gollancz, who is of the opinion that there must have been a Latin original for the poem, bases his belief upon the evidence of certain phrases to be found in the *Vita* printed in Capgrave.[2] Thus the clause, *et tamen nec filum palii sepulchro superpositi naturam suam perdidit aut colorem mutavit,* he takes as a reminder of the poet's line (148) :

And ȝet his colour and his clothe has caȝt no defaute ;

and he finds a parallel to the phrase (330), *þe bryȝt bourne of þin eghen,* in a quotation taken from the *Life of St. Dunstan* (ed. Stubbs, p. 50) : *rore lacrymarum ... quas ... Sanctus quoque Spiritus. . . . ex oculorum rivulis potenter elicuit.*[3] But an examination of the *Vita* in Capgrave's collection has revealed very few Latin sentences or phrases that are translated by lines in the poem; and, furthermore, those few are found in situations in the narrative that in no way resemble the situations in the poem where their corresponding English lines occur.[4] On the other hand, where situations that are slightly similar occur in the *Vita* and the poem, certain correspondences between the phrasing of the Latin

[1] These *Vitæ* are to be found in the following manuscripts : (1) (a) Cott. Claud. A. V. ff. 135-8. Vell. small folio xii cent. (b) C. C. C. Cant. 161. 5. Vell. small folio. xii cent. (2) C. C. C. Cant. 161. Vell. small folio. xii cent. (3) (a) Cott. Tib. E. 1. ff. 116b-122. (b) Bodl. Tanner 15. Vell. folio. dbl. cols. xv cent. (4) Landsdowne 436 ff. 36b-38b. Vell. folio, dbl. cols. xiv cent. For an account of these manuscripts, cf. *Catalogue of British History* (Rolls Series) 1 (Part 1). 293-5.

[2] Capgrave's *Vita* has been taken from MS. Bodl. Tanner. 15. It is printed also in *Nova Legenda Anglie* 1. 391-405, and in *Acta Sanctorum* 12 (April 30). 789-796.

[3] Gollancz, p. 1 (note 2).

[4] Besides the parallels noted by Gollancz, these two deserve mention : 57 as a rendition of the clause, *verba de miraculo fecit ad populum;* 105 as a rendition of the clause, *ut vero rumor miraculi pervenit ad episcopum.*

and that of the English can be accounted for by the similarity
of circumstances in both accounts. In view of facts such as
these, belief in the existence of a Latin original for the poem
can hardly be warranted.

But not only is there an entire lack of evidence to warrant
the belief in the existence of a direct written original; there
is a complete dearth of information about the existence of
any oral tradition concerning this miracle of St. Erkenwald
as well.[5] No mention of this story or of any incident
whose literary elaboration might give rise to it, can be found
in the works of the monkish chroniclers who have anything
to say about the city of London or the Cathedral of St.
Paul's. With the exception of a single reference in one
work—the *Summa Prædicantium* of Bromyarde (fl. 1390)—
whose accuracy is in serious doubt, there is no mention in any
of their histories of any incident that could be connected with
our story.[6] Presumably the historians of St. Paul's and of
London would have been familiar with any legends connected
with the city's venerable foundation. Had they known of any
such wonder as the finding of a 'ferly faire tombe,' or
indeed of any miraculous or strange happening whose publication would serve to spread the fame of their cathedral more
widely, it is not probable that they would have been silent
about it.

Thus the chances of there being any story, written or oral,
about the miracle described in the poem, which could have
served the poet as a foundation for his own artistic rendi-

[5] Gerould (*Saints' Legends,* p. 238) has suggested that the story
might have been derived from some tale of the Welsh Marches, but
presents no direct evidence for the statement. His suggestion
receives some corroboration, however, from the fact that St. Erkenwald is mentioned in the Welsh *Martyrology of Gorman* (written ca.
1166-74). Cf. the *Martyrology of Gorman* (Bradshaw Soc.), ed. W.
Stokes, p. 86.

[6] The reference in question is probably an interpolation. It is found
in the printed works of Bromyarde, but in none of the extant manuscripts. For more detailed discussion, see Gollancz, pp. xxxvi-xxxviii.

tion, are scanty. The legend seems a composite, owing its strange beauty to the intertwining of a number of tales, that have been woven into complete unity by a master-hand.

In the last section, it was stated that all available evidence tended to establish the composite character of the poem. It would appear that the poet, instead of elaborating one main story, had fused together a number of stories. In this work of literary construction it is probable that he used as his source one (or more) of the chronicles which contained, as many of the mediæval histories did, a potpourri of secular and ecclesiastical history and legend.[7]

In the ensuing discussion of the sources of the story, I shall attempt to show that the poet could just as easily have culled many of the stories, which Gollancz believes could have come to him only through wide reading and an acquaintanceship with many historical and legendary works, from one work (or perhaps from several) not very different in plan and content from the *Chronica Majora* of Matthew Paris, or the *Flores Historiarum* that is based upon it.[8]

[7] Gollancz would appear to be of the opinion that our poet had a first-hand knowledge of many different histories and legends. Among the books which he supposes the author of the legend to have known are Bede's *Ecclesiastical History,* Geoffrey of Monmouth's *Historia,* and the *Historia Trojana* of Guido delle Colonne. See statements on pp. xiii, xiv, xv, xvi, xxviii, 1 of his edition.

[8] The poet himself acknowledges that his sources are chronicle-histories (44). This statement must be taken with a grain of salt; mediæval poets were fond of adducing a source for their works which subsequent research has shown to be fictitious. The earlier portion of the *Chronica Majora* which goes under the name of Matthew Paris is believed not to be his work at all. The author remains unknown, though his work was certainly written at St. Alban's Abbey, probably between 1195 and 1214. From the year 1189 to the year 1235, the *Chronica* is believed to be the work of Roger of Wendover. From 1235 to 1247 the author was almost certainly Matthew Paris, and he is also responsible for that portion of the history between 1254 and 1259. Of the *Chronica* a large

In the composition of his poem the author has interwoven five distinct pieces of narrative. These are:

I. The story of the release of a soul from hell through the agency of a righteous person still alive.

II. The story of the finding of a tomb containing a body untouched by decay.

III. The story of the founding of Troynovant by Brutus, that of the kings who succeeded him, and that of the first advent of Christianity into Britain, and of its overthrow by the Saxon invaders.

IV. The story of the arrival of Augustine in England, and of his establishment of the Roman Catholic faith, and of the subsequent episcopate of St. Erkenwald.

V. Certain legends and traditions relating to the diocese and commune of London.

We shall now examine separately each one of these five stories in the endeavor to find out how the author of the poem has made it contribute to the story as a whole.

I

The story of the release of a soul from hell through the agency of a righteous person still alive.

The majority of scholars are agreed that the story of St. Erkenwald's baptism of the pagan judge, by which means the latter was released from hell and attained to the joy of Paradise, is an adaptation of the famous legend of Trajan

number of manuscripts exist; Luard, the editor of the work in the Rolls Series, has collated no fewer than six. It is interesting to note that there is ground for the belief that one manuscript of the work was lent by the Abbey of St. Alban's to various other religious foundations, of which St. Paul's was one. Cf. the prefaces to Luard's edition of the *Chronica* in the Rolls Series. Of the *Flores Historiarum* there are, likewise, many manuscripts. In the case of one, there is good evidence for believing that it was once owned by the library of St. Paul's. Cf. preface to *Flores Historiarum* (Rolls Series), pp. xxvii-viii, and *Documents Illustrating the History of St. Paul's Cathedral* (Camden Soc., N. S. 26), ed. W. Sparrow Simpson, pp. xxix-xxx.

and Pope Gregory the Great. The story was widely known throughout the Middle Ages, and is to be found frequently in the works of theologians, historians, poets, and philosophers.[9] The earliest record of the legend of Trajan exists in a Latin *Vita* of St. Gregory, written by a monk of Whitby about 713 A.D.[10] As Gollancz suggests, Bede may have looked on this legend with suspicion, since it is inconsistent with Gregory's own words that the saints shrink from praying for the righteous pagan dead. At any rate, the story did not find its way into Bede's *Life of St. Gregory,* and hence the compilers of *Chronica Majora* knew it not. It remained unknown, at least to our modern world, until Ewald found it in the library of the monastery of St. Gall in 1886.[11]

Two other early versions of the story exist, one by Paulus Diaconus, who wrote a *Vita* of St. Gregory about 787 A.D.[12]

[9] Among the authors who refer to the story or discuss it are the theologians and philosophers, St. Thomas Aquinas (*Summa Theologica,* Pars. 3 (Supp.), Quæst. 71, Art. 5), Vincent of Beauvais (*Speculum Historiale*), John of Salisbury (*Policraticus,* Lib. 5, cap. 8) ; the historians, Bromyarde (*Summa Prædicantium,* but cf. the previous discussion of that work in this section), the anonymous author of the Middle High German *Kaiserchronik* (ed. Massmann, Quedlinburg and Leipzig, 1849, ll. 5859-6116), Godfrey of Viterbo (*Speculum Regum,* in *Monumenta Germaniæ Historica (Scriptorum)* 22. 74), and Jacobus de Voragine (*Legenda Aurea: De Sancto Gregorio*) ; the poets, Dante (*Purgatorio* 10. 73-5) and Langland (*Piers Plowman* B. 11. 137-171 ; C. 15. 192-208). Cr. also *La Légende de Trajan,* Gaston Paris, Bibliothèque de l'École des Hautes Études, Fasc. 35, 1878, and Arturo Graf, *Roma nella Memoria e nelle Immaginazioni del Medio Evo* (Torino, 1883) 2. 1-45. Neither Paris nor Graf knew of the Whitby *Vita.*

[10] *A Life of Pope St. Gregory the Great written by a monk of Whitby (probably about* A. D. *713), now for the first time fully printed from MS. Gallen 567,* by Francis Aidan Gasquet (Abbot-President of the English Benedictines), Westminster, 1904.

[11] *Historische Aufsätze dem Andenken an Georg Waitz gewidmet,* Hannover, 1886.

[12] Migne, *Patr. Lat.* 75. 56-7. Cf. also *Acta Sanctorum* 8 (March 12). 130-6.

and the other by Johannes Diaconus, who also wrote a
Vita of the same saint in the ninth century,[13] and it is
through them that the legend became known to Western
Europe.[14]

The *Chronica Majora* and *Flores Historiarum* both contain the story, but it is the version of Johannes Diaconus that
they present.[15] Its presence in these chronicles strengthens
the possibility that the poet was familiar with one or the
other (perhaps both), or with some other chronicle whose
content was not markedly dissimilar from theirs.

But the legend of Trajan's salvation is not the only form
in which the story of a deliverance from the pains and pangs
of a lower world through the prayers of a righteous person,
or through the performance of a sacramental rite, is to be
found; or in which the deliverance is gained through a reputation for justice. A story somewhat similar to the legend
of Trajan and to our own tale is told by Roger of Wendover,
supposedly the author of that portion of the *Chronica*
which covers the period of years between 1189 and 1235
A.D. In that story we are told that Henry, Bishop of
Rochester, on the Saturday before Passion Sunday in the
year 1232, announced to his congregation in his sermon that
he had thrice been shown in a vision that the souls of
Richard I, Stephen, Archbishop of Canterbury, and a chaplain of the Archbishop's, had been released from purgatory.
In his comment upon this utterance, Roger adds, after a
recital of Richard's reverence for holy things:

[13] Migne, *Patr. Lat.* 75. 104-6. Cf. also *Acta Sanctorum* 8 (March
12). 136-208.

[14] One gathers from Gollancz's discussion of the Whitby *Vita* in
his edition of the present poem (pp. xli-xlii), that he believes that
the poet of *Erkenwald* may have known of that *Vita*.

[15] The suggestion of a penalty threatened St. Gregory because
he dared pray for the soul of an unbaptized pagan does not occur in
the account given by the two chronicles, though it is to be found in
the narratives of Paulus and Johannes.

Nec illud de virtutibus magnifici regis loquentes credimus negligendum, quod statim coronatus in regem rectam semper justitiam cunctis exhibuit, pro munere nunquam judicium subverti permisit;[16]

and he further adds:

Quia jam venit tempus, de locis ut credimus, pœnalibus, excocta culparum scorria, translatus est ad regna sine fine mansura; ubi militi reposita est a rege Christo, Cui fideliter servivit, *corona justitiæ, quam repromisit Deus diligentibus se.*[17]

Less convincing, but still worthy of note, is a story told by Roger (under the date 1228), of how a certain Roger de Thony, 'vir nobilis et miles strenuus,' who had died, was adjured in the name of God by his brother to speak to him. The corpse replied, and said that his punishment could be mitigated by the performance of good works, by masses, and by alms.[18]

One will remember that St. Erkenwald is careful to say mass before he addresses the body, and that he is careful to adjure it by God to answer him. In the story just recounted, the reader will note that the corpse replies only after adjuration in the name of God, and that it acknowledges that the performance of the mass is efficacious in easing it.

Enough has now been said to show that our author could have found in some such work as the *Chronica* not only the Trajan story, but several others as well which have to do with the liberation of a soul from torment, whether of hell or of purgatory; and that, although some of them might not have been very close parallels to the story of St. Erkenwald, yet they could not but have deepened the impression which the story of Trajan and St. Gregory had already made upon his mind.[19]

[16] *Chron. Maj.* 3. 215.

[17] *Chron. Maj.* 3. 216-7.

[18] *Chron. Maj.* 3. 143-5. This story is not found in *Flor. Hist.*

[19] Cf. with the story of the miracle performed by St. Erkenwald the story of the vision of Charles the Fat told in *Chron. Maj.* (1. 419-420).

Before passing on to the second of the main divisions of
our source-material, it will be necessary to examine a certain
phase of the development of the legend of Trajan which
seems very closely connected with the poem we are studying.
This is the story of the speaking head of a pagan whose soul
had been helped by the prayer of a Christian. This story is
found often in close company with some version of the
legend of the great Roman emperor, so that there would
appear to be some bond or nexus that held the two together.
St. Thomas Aquinas is among the first to mention this story
of the speaking head. In his discussion of the question
whether the souls of the damned profit by the suffrages of
the living, Aquinas quotes a story found in one of John
Damascene's sermons (*De Defunct.*) of how St. Macharius
found a skull, and learned that it had been that of a pagan
priest, damned in hell, who had, however, been eased by the
prayer of the saint.[20]   Thence, it is interesting to note, St.
Thomas goes on to speak about the case of Trajan.

The next occurrence of the story is found in the *Commentario* of Jacopo della Lana (ca. 1326), who tells us that
in some excavations made in Rome during St. Gregory's
pontificate, there were found some bones and a tongue
'carnosa e fresca, comme fusse pure in quella ora seppellita.'
When questioned by St. Gregory, who had hurried thither-
wards, the tongue replied that it had once belonged to
Trajan, who was now in hell because he had been a pagan.
St. Gregory, much impressed, prayed for Trajan's soul, and
was told in a vision that his prayer had been heard.[21]
A story closely similar to that of Jacopo is found in the
Fiori di Filosofi once attributed to Brunetto Latini. Miss
Hibbard has called attention to the treatment of the story
of Trajan by Roger van der Weyden, in his paintings for
the Hall of Justice in the Town Hall of Brussels. These

[20] *Summa Theolog.*, Pars. 3 (Supp.), Quæst. 71, Art. 5, Obj. 4.
[21] *Commentario* (Milan, 1865), p. 201.

pictures exist now only by proxy in the great Berne Tapestry, whose weavers copied them.[22]

Perhaps the most striking parallel to these stories is the one to be discussed immediately, which is to be found in Kornmann's *Opera Curiosa,* and is quoted from Werner Rolevinck, the fifteenth-century German theologian. The story of the speaking head had obviously reached such a point of development in this version that it would take but little ingenuity or invention to expand it into the Erkenwald story.

Whether our poet found the story at this stage, or whether he helped to mould it into the form in which it occurs below, we have no means of knowing. The story runs as follows:

> Circa annum Domini 1200. in Vienna repertum fuit caput cujusdam defuncti, lingua adhuc integra cum labiis, loquebatur recte. Episcopo autem interrogante, qualis fuisset in vita, respondit: Ego eram paganus & judex in hoc loco, nec unquam lingua mea protulit iniquam sententiam, quare etiam mori non possum, donec aqua baptissimi renatus ad cœlum evolem, quare propter hoc hanc gratiam apud Deum merui. Baptizato igitur capite, statim lingua in favillam corruit & spiritus ad Dominum evolavit.[23]

II

The story of the finding of a tomb containing a body untouched by decay.

Versions of this story occur frequently in the works of mediæval chroniclers. Its wide dissemination is due to the keen interest which the man of the Middle Ages took in

[22] *Mod. Phil.* 17. 674.
[23] Kornmann, *Opera Curiosa, De Miraculis Mortuorum,* Part IV, pp. 117-8. I would here call attention to Miss Hibbard's article in *Modern Philology* (17. 669-678), in which she has pointed out an association between the proper name Erkenwald and that of the just nobleman Erkenbald, whose story appears in *Die Sagen Belgiens*

antiquarian investigation, and also to the growth of hagi-
ography; for the story is usually told in connection with
the cultus of some saint. Details such as those given in our
poem (73-92)—garments untouched by mould or rust, and
a countenance as fresh and ruddy as ever it had been in
healthy life—are common features of the tale.

Many examples of the type are to be found in the *Chronica
Majora*. Thus, when the tomb of St. Edmund was opened
preparatory to the ceremony of translating his body from
Hoxne to St. Edmundsbury, the body was found in a
state of perfect preservation:

> Sed mirum dictu contigit; nam cum corpus martyris pretiosis-
> simum ob spatium diuturni temporis putrefactum ab omnibus
> putaretur, ita integrum repertum est et illæsum, ut non solum
> caput corpori redintegratum et compaginatum, sed omnino nihil
> in eo vulneris, nihil apparuerit cicatricis.[24]

Again, when the tomb of Pallas, the son of Evander, is
opened, to the wonder of all it is found that the body 'per tot
sæcula incorruptionem servavit.'[25]

A still closer parallel is to be found in the account given
in the *Chronica* of the translation of the body of St. Edmund
of Canterbury:

> Sciendumque est, immo toti mundo prædicandum, quod totum
> corpus ejus integrum inventum est et incorruptum et odoriferum,

(Cologne, 1846). That this story was known in England is proved
by its appearance in the fifteenth century *Alphabet of Tales* (EETS.
127. 287-9). In the legend of St. Edmund Martyr one version of
the story of the speaking head occurs in *Chron. Maj.* (I. 399-400).

[24] *Chron. Maj.* I. 400. *Flor. Hist.* (I. 441) follows this account
verbatim.

[25] *Chron. Maj.* I. 511-2; *Flor. Hist.* I. 558-9 (copied verbatim from
Chron. Maj.). In connection with the account of the dissolution of
the judge's corpse (341-6), it is interesting to read the description
given in *Chron. Maj.* of the dissolution of Pallas' cadaver when
exposed to the open air: 'stillicidiis rorantibus et corpus madefa-
cientibus, communem mortalium corruptionem cognovit, nervis
fluentibus et cute soluta.'

et quod mirabilius est in mortuo, cum omnibus membris flexibile, et solet esse in dormiente; capilli ejus et vestimentum inviolatum colore et substantia.[26]

A reader of the poem cannot fail to be struck by the elaborate description which the poet gives of the marble tomb in which the dead judge was buried. Gollancz suggests the possibility of our author's having read the description of the tomb of Hector in Guido delle Colonne's *Historia Trojana,* but a closer parallel than that description is to be found in the account given in the *Chronica* of the tomb of St. Alban.[27] This should be compared carefully with the account given in the poem of the finding of the tomb, and of its handsome appearance:

> Contigit eodem anno, ut propter quasdam hiantes rimas de quibus timebatur pars orientalis ecclesiæ beati Albani, de consilio abbatis et conventus, ut firma repararetur, in Adventu Domini dissoluto tecto, muri prosternerentur. Et dum ligonibus in pavimento cementariorum ministri insisterent, per tinnitum instrumentorum et pedum strepitum perpendebant, aliquid ibi insolitum et incognitum latitare. Profundius igitur perscrutantes, invenerunt sub terra, sed non profunde, unam tumbam lapideam, satis eleganter compositam, in loco qui fuit inter altare Sancti Oswini. . . . et altare Sancti Wlstani, ubi quoque collocatum fuerat antiquum feretrum pictum, et quædam tumba marmorea cum columpnis marmoreis, qui locus et tumba dicebatur vetus tumba Sancti Albani. In ipso igitur mausoleo tumulabatur beatus Albanus. . . . In quo etiam mausoleo inventa est quædam lamina plumbea, in qua secundum antiquorum consuetudinem scriptus est hic titulus; 'In hoc mausoleo inventum est venerabile corpus Sancti Albani prothomartiris Anglorum.'

One may readily see the close correspondence between the passages illustrative of this second type of story and the descriptions in the poem. So close is that correspondence

---

[26] *Chron. Maj.* 4. 631. Cf. also the account, given in *Chron. Maj.* (1. 483), of the finding of the body of St. Ælfheah, slain by the Danes at Canterbury in 1011.

[27] *Chron. Maj.* 5. 608.

Introduction

that it seems very probable that the poet had seen several of
these passages as they were given in the *Chronica,* or in some
other book of annals that closely resembled it.[28]

III

The story of the founding of Troynovant by Brutus, that
of the kings who succeeded him, and that of the
first advent of Christianity into Britain, and of
its overthrow by the Saxon invaders.

The story of the founding of Troynovant and of the discord between Belinus and Brennius first appeared in written
form in that treasure-house which mediæval historians rifled
so frequently—the *Historia Regum Britanniæ* of Geoffrey of
Monmouth. But, while our poet uses material that undoubt-
edly was ultimately derived from Geoffrey, it is impossible
to say whether he consulted Geoffrey at first hand, or
whether he took the account of the doings of Brutus
and his successors from a secondary source, whose compiler
had in turn derived his 'matere' from the *Historia.* Gollancz
is of the opinion that the poet had a first-hand knowledge
of Geoffrey's work. He speaks of the writer's 'careful reading of Geoffrey of Monmouth and Bede's *Ecclesiastical His-*
tory,'[29] and tells us that 'the main source of our poet's knowledge was certainly Geoffrey of Monmouth's *Historia*
Britonum.'[30]

[28] The account of the translation of the body of St. Edmund is
slightly closer as a parallel to the account of the appearance of the
judge's body than the account which Bede (*Eccl. Hist.* 4. 30) gives
of the translation of the body of St. Cuthbert which Gollancz
believes to have been the source of this second type of story
(*St. Erk.,* p. 1). It should be noted that the account of the
finding of St. Cuthbert's body is also to be found in the *Chronica*
(1. 307), exactly as Bede himself tells it. The author of the *Flores*
has copied the account from the *Chronica.*

[29] Pp. xxxv-xxxvi.
[30] P. xiii.

But the assumption of such first-hand knowledge on the part of the poet, while a perfectly possible one, is too narrow. The author of *Erkenwald* might easily have learned the story of Troynovant and the kings who reigned there from many other literary sources, to say nothing of those that were purely oral. In such a matter as the determination of a literary source for an event so well-known as the story of Brutus, it would be rash to name any particular chronicle or history; for the narrative is found in a great many. Our study of the two preceding types of story has shown us the author's interest in ecclesiastical legend and dogma. The present type, and those that follow it, belong to the field of history or of historical legend. The combination of stories from these various fields into one poem certainly leads one to the belief that the author of this particular saint's legend used for his sources a chronicle which contained stories of several kinds—legendary, historical, sacred, and miraculous. Such a chronicle would in all probability closely resemble in content and style the *Chronica Majora* or the *Flores Historiarum,* for in both there is to be found that mixture of species upon which I have been remarking. A more detailed comparison for the detection of resemblances and divergences between the accounts of Geoffrey and those of the compilers of the two chronicles which we have been studying must now be made.

(*a*) *The story of the founding of Troynovant.*

This story is repeated, with some few unimportant omissions, from Geoffrey's prior account, by the *Chronica Majora,* in the very phraseology that Geoffrey uses. The *Flores* repeats the *Chronica*.[31]

(*b*) *The account of King Belin.*

Geoffrey says of Belin that he governed wisely and well,

[31] *Historia Regum Britanniæ* I. 17; *Chron. Maj.* I. 22; *Flor. Hist.* I. 25.

and implies that he enforced the code which his father Molmutius had drawn up.[32]   The *Chronica* simply remarks of the government of Belinus, that, upon his return from Italy, 'cum tranquillitate patriam tractavit,' and the *Flores* echoes the statement.[33]   Thus Geoffrey's account of the righteous and just reign of the prince under whom our judge served as justice of the Iter is much more full than that of the two chronicles, yet the simple phrase, 'cum tranquillitate,' could quite easily have given to such an imaginative poet as our author all that he desired to know about the administration of justice in King Belin's days.

(c) *The discord between Belinus and Brennius.*

The accounts of the quarrel between the two sons of Molmutius (213-5) are different (the *Flores,* as usual, is a verbatim copy of the *Chronica*), though the later writer occasionally repeats two or three successive words which his predecessor has used.[34]   I am inclined to believe that our poet would have found the clean-cut, flowing narrative of the *Chronica* more suited to his needs than the long account of Geoffrey, which covers seven chapters of his third Book.

(d) *The story of the Saxon invasion of Britain, and the downfall of Celtic Christianity.*

Of the account of the Saxon invasion of Britain which our poet gives (7-10), Gollancz has thus spoken: 'His (the poet's) references to the driving of the Britons into Wales by the Saxons, to the perversion of the folk who remained (more particularly those of London), and to the apostasy of Britain till the coming of St. Augustine, are clearly derived from Book XI, chs. viii-xii.'[35]   Here again we must be on our guard against the danger of ascribing references in the poem to particular and definite sources;

---

[32] *Historia* 3. 5-6.
[33] *Chron. Maj.* 1. 59; *Flor. Hist.* 1. 63.
[34] *Historia* 3. 1-7; *Chron. Maj.* 1. 56-8; *Flor. Hist.* 1. 60-1.
[35] P. xiii.

for the account given by Geoffrey of this event had been copied by the compilers of the two histories with only a very few changes of phrasing.[36] The further account of the destruction of the Christian monuments which is given in the *Historia Regum Britanniæ* has been taken over wholesale, with but few additions, by the two chroniclers.[37]

IV

The story of the arrival of Augustine in England, and of his establishment of the Roman Catholic faith, and of the subsequent episcopate of St. Erkenwald.

(*a*) With regard to the account given in the poem of the advent of St. Augustine (12-24), Gollancz remarks: 'When, however, our poet proceeds with the statement regarding the hurling out of the heathen idols and the dedications of the temples as churches, he is rightly transferring to St. Augustine the account given in Geoffrey concerning Lucius, the first British king to embrace the Christian faith.'[38] To assume, however, that the account, given in the poem, of St. Augustine's activity in the extinction of the heathen worship, was taken directly from Geoffrey would be a dangerous surmise. The narrative of the *Historia,* with only a few variations in its phrasing, is to be found in the *Chronica* and in the *Flores.*[39] The poet's vivid description of Augustine's 'godly, thorough reformation' need not, however, have been derived from any particular document. It might very well have followed from the expansion of the ideas contained in the prosaic sentences of Geoffrey, or still more probably have owed its existence to the activity of the poet's own vivid imagination.

(*b*) In connection with the history of the introduction of

[36] *Chron. Maj.* I. 250; *Flor. Hist.* I. 279-80.
[37] *Chron. Maj.* I. 251; *Flor. Hist.* I. 280.
[38] Pp. xiii-xiv.
[39] *Historia* II. 12; *Chron. Maj.* I. 255-6; *Flor. Hist.* I. 284-5.

Christianity into England, it is important to note that in the
Chronica (but not in Geoffrey's *Historia*) is to be found the
account of St. Erkenwald's episcopate.[40] The narrative is
derived not from Bede, but from William of Malmesbury's
Gesta Pontificum,[41] though William admittedly borrowed the
facts for his account from Bede's *Ecclesiastical History.*

V

Certain legends and traditions relating to the diocese and commune of London.

References to landmarks in or near London show that the
poet was familiar with some of the traditions of the city of
London. Whether this familiarity was gained by first-hand
knowledge of the actual traditions of the old city or whether
it was gleaned from the 'crafty cronecles' which he claims
as the sources of the story, we have no means of knowing.
An examination of his references to the conversion of various Saxon temples into Christian churches will show him
to have been no mean antiquary.

(*a*) 'Þat ere was of Appolyn is now of Saynt Petre' (19).

Here, as Gollancz has noted, there is a reference to an
old tradition of a temple of Apollo being converted into a
church dedicated to St. Peter. Gollancz cites references to
this tradition in the *History of Westminster Abbey* of John
Flete, a monk of that foundation from 1420 to 1465.[42] The
Chronica mentions the fact of there being a temple of
Apollo in the New Troy,[43] as does Geoffrey of Monmouth,[44]

_____

[40] *Chron. Maj.* I. 297-8; *Flor. Hist.* I. 331. The author of the
Flores, as is his wont, has taken over the account of the *Chronica.*
   [41] *Gesta Pontificum* (Rolls Series), pp. 142-4.
   [42] P. xv.
   [43] *Chron. Maj.* I. 29. The *Chron. Maj.* (I. 461) also speaks of a
church of St. Peter at Westminster that was built by Mellitus, one
of the early bishops of London.
   [44] *Historia* 2. 10.

but this temple is not mentioned in connection with the worship of the Saxons.[45]

(*b*) 'Mahon to Saynt Margrete oþer to Maudelayne' (20). As Gollancz has noted, the reference to St. Margaret may have been prompted by the preceding reference to Westminster, since the parish church of Westminster was dedicated to St. Margaret.[46] As for the reference to St. Mary Magdalen, Mr. Wilberforce Jenkinson informs us that within the group of buildings which composed Westminster Abbey there was a chapel dedicated to that saint.[47]

c) 'Þe Synagoge of þe Sonne was sett to oure Lady' (21).

Gollancz, in his discussion of the instances in which pagan temples were converted into churches, identifies the 'Synagoge of þe Sonne' with the temple of Minerva Sul at Bath (Aquæ Solis), on whose site the Church of St. Mary de Stabula—St. Mary Stall—is said to have been erected.[48] He finds further confirmation for his belief in the account given in Geoffrey's *Historia* (2.10), in which it is said that Bladud, the legendary founder of Bath, made hot baths in the city, and dedicated them to Minerva. This account is also found in the *Chronica*[49] and in the *Flores*.[50]

(*d*) 'Jubiter and Jono to Jhesu oþer to James' (22).

---

[45] Flete's account of the destruction of Christianity, and the worship of Apollo by the Saxons, is as follows: 'Rediit itaque veteris abominationis ubique sententia; a sua Britones expelluntur patria; immolat Dianæ Londonia, *thurificat Apolli suburbana Thorneia*' (quoted from Gollancz, p. xvi). For further information about the early history of Westminster Abbey, cf. Dart, *Westmonasterium* (1742) I. 2-5, and *History of the Abbey Church of St. Peter's, Westminster* (London, 1812) I. 1-19.

[46] P. xvi. (There were throughout London and Westminster a number of churches dedicated to St. Margaret.)

[47] *London Churches before the Great Fire* (1917), p. 72.

[48] Pp. xvi-xix.

[49] *Chron. Maj.* I. 28-9.

[50] *Flor. Hist.* I. 34-5.

Of this line Gollancz says, 'the mention of Jupiter and Juno, as yielding to Jesus or James, has no definite significance, and the seeming identifications are due to alliterative effect.'[51] I find, however, in the 1807 edition of Holinshed's *Chronicle*,[52] mention of a temple dedicated to Jupiter in the city of London.

(*e*) The chief heathen temple of London, the 'Temple Triapolitan,' was dedicated, so the poet tells us, to a 'maghty devel.' Gollancz believes this god to have been the Saxon Woden, whom the Romans identified with Mercury, and cites from Geoffrey's *Historia* (6.10) the speech of Hengist before Vortigern, where the same identification is made.[53] The speech of Hengist is also to be found in the *Chronica*[54] and in the *Flores*.[55]

Sufficient evidence, I think, has been adduced to warrant one in the belief that the poet used as his source some large chronicle containing a number of narratives regarding the early history of Britain and the establishment of the Christian faith in England, and a number of legends concerning local English saints and the greater saints of the Church Universal. That this chronicle was the *Chronica Majora*, or its slavish repeater, the *Flores Historiarum*, is by no means improbable; though it is quite possible that the source was some lost or undiscovered work in which the various stories were bound together in a closer nexus, and in which the descriptions resembled more nearly those in the poem than those of the two chronicles so often referred to. Moreover,

---

[51] Pp. xix-xx.

[52] I. 237.

[53] Pp. xx-xxiii. Tacitus (*Germania*, cap. 9) tells us that the Germans 'deorum maxime Mercurium colunt, cui certis diebus humanis quoque hostiis litare fas habent.'

[54] *Chron. Maj.* I. 189.

[55] *Flor. Hist.* I. 216.

the assumption of such a source in no way weakens the possibility of the influence of popular oral tradition upon the mind of the poet. But our study should have shown us more than the mere probability that our poet's sources were contained in one manuscript, instead of many. Whether our author derived his 'matter' from one book or several books, however, does not alter the fact that he had to fuse a number of stories into unity. Of the skill with which he has done this there can be no question. He has removed from the old stories with which he dealt all the elements that would by their remaining have marred the power and beauty of the work as a whole. If his work is a mosaic, it is one in which no lines of demarcation are visible. Like many poets of his time and school, he is distinguished by poetic force and fire, by a high sincerity and earnestness, and by a deep religious zeal; but he is distinguished from them by the possession of one quality which he shared with Chaucer alone—an almost perfect mastery of the materials of his art.

DIALECT

The determination of the particular dialects in which many of the alliterative poems were written has been, and still is, a matter of some difficulty. Even in the *Pearl* and *Sir Gawain*, where the presence of rhyme lends an aid to the researches of the student that is lacking in many another poem, it has been found impossible to place the origin of the poems within any but the most general provincial limits. Yet despite the difficulties confronting those who have sought to determine the dialects of these two poems, scholars seem fairly well agreed that the speech in which their poet wrote them down was that of the Northwest Midland.

With regard to the dialectal characteristics of *Erkenwald* there has been no such agreement. Knigge, who published the first, and by far the best, extended study of the poem in

1885, believes that its dialect is that of the poems of the
Cotton MS., i. e. West Midland, though he finds in it also
traces of the East Midland speech.[1]   Gollancz, who tells us
that 'our poem is in the same hand as the main part of the
manuscript, the contents of which, whatever their origin,
are in the Northern dialect,' presumably intends those words
to apply to *Erkenwald*.[2]   Hulbert is of the opinion that the
authors of *Winner and Waster, Piers Plowman,* and *Erkenwald,* were men who had lived long in London, if not Lon-
doners born and bred; and he explains their use of the
alliterative measure and vocabulary in the following words:
'the writers of these poems preferred not to use the speech of
the capital, but instead used a language which had for its
basis perhaps some particular dialect (which was possibly
traditionally associated with alliterative verse), altering it
probably in the direction of their own native dialect.'[3]

This uncertainty of scholarly opinion, however, may find
some excuse when one remembers the existence of a number
of facts that render difficult a definite decision upon the
question of the dialect of *Erkenwald*.   In the first place, as
Hulbert has well said, the writers of alliterative poetry were
'sophisticated authors, who read French romances and Latin
prose, knew courtly customs, certainly used archaic words
and probably old-fashioned forms.'[4]   One who studies the
dialect of a poem of this school should ever remember this
fact: that his author was a skilled literary craftsman, who
borrowed or adopted French or Latin forms with considerable freedom, and who was therefore in all probability perfectly capable of doing the same in the case of English forms.
Secondly, as regards this particular poem, the connection
it has with London, the chief city of the East Midlands,
should not be overlooked.   While a connection of this sort

[1] *Die Sprache,* pp. 1-14 *passim,* 118.
[2] *St. Erk.* p. v.
[3] *Mod. Phil.* 19. 12.
[4] *Ibid.,* p. 12.

affords no special ground for believing that the dialect of the original manuscript was East Midland, it has still a certain bearing upon the dialect of the poem, and cannot be dismissed entirely. Thirdly, the spread of a *Gemeinsprache* at the time at which the poem was copied down in the form in which we now have it, would render difficult precise ascriptions of the language in which it is written to this or that locality.

Yet despite the factors that make difficult any decision, it is still possible to come to more or less definite conclusions about the dialect of the manuscript, and, from the knowledge thus obtained, to some determination of the locality in which the poem was copied. In it some East Midland characteristics are to be found, and a larger number that are Northern; more pronounced, however, are those that belong to the West Midland. Since scholars have hitherto been unable to come to any decision about the dialect of the manuscript or that of the original poem, it will be necessary to examine their statements, and in some cases to correct them in the light of new evidence.

The following peculiarities, phonological and morphological, are distinctively Northern:

PHONOLOGICAL.

(1) OE. $\bar{a}$ + $\jmath$ generally appears as *aw: awen*, 235.[5]

(2) OE. *hw-* appears as *qu-*.[6]

(3) OE. $\bar{a}$ + *w* appears rarely as *au,* instead of *ǫu: saule,* 273; *unknawen*, 147.[7]

---

[5] Cf. Luick, *Historische Grammatik der Englischen Sprache* (Leipzig, 1920), § 402 (2).

[6] Morsbach, *Mittelenglische Grammatik* (Halle, 1896), § 6.

[7] Luick, § 373 (e).

(4) OE. *ā* appears twice as *a: halde*, 42, 166 (but *holde*, 232, 249).[8]

MORPHOLOGICAL.

(1) The 2d and 3d persons singular of the present indicative end in *-es*.[9]

(2) The plural of the present indicative ends in *-es* or in *-en(-e): heldes*, 196; *leves*, 176; *wondres*, 125; *repairen*, 135; *leven*, 183; *ryve*, 262.[10]

(3) The present participle ends in *-ande*.[11]

(4) One contracted form appears: *bitan*, 28.

The following peculiarities, phonological and morphological, are distinctively Midland:

PHONOLOGICAL.

(1) OE. *a + ng* appears as *o + ng: longe*, 1, 95, 157, 175; *longen*, 268.[12]

(2) OE. *ŏ* appears as *o*, and not as *u, ui, oi: bode*, 181; *boke*, 103; *body*, 76, 94.[13]

(3) OE. *ȳ* generally appears as *e* or *i(y): kidde*, 222, 254; *fulfille*, 176; *myrthe*, 350.[14]

---

[8] Morsbach, §§ 6, 7.
[9] Morsbach, § 6.
[10] *Ibid.*, § 6.
[11] *Ibid.*, § 6.
[12] Luick, § 367 (note 1).
[13] Luick, § 406; Wyld, *Short History of English* (London, 1914), § 207 (3).
[14] Luick (§ 287) says of this characteristic: 'Es stellt sich heraus, das ae. ȳ auf dem nordhumbrischen Gebiet und in einem grossen Teil des östlichen Mittellandes, in Lincoln, Norfolk und in angrenzenden Strichen durchaus zu ĭ geworden war.'

(4) OE. *ā* of various sources generally appears as *o* instead of *a: bones,* 346; *clothe,* 82, 148, 259, 263, 266; *dole,* 6; *holy,* 4, 127; *lore,* 264; *ston,* 47, 219.[15]

(5) OE. *ā + w* generally appears as *ǫu: biknowe,* 221; *crowes,* 71; *knowe,* 74, 263; *row,* 52; *soule,* 279, 293, 300, 305, 328.[16]

(6) OE. *ǣr* appears as *er* instead of *ar,* as in the North: *ere,* 19, 24.[17]

(7) OE. *sc* in stressed or unstressed position appears as *sh* or *sch.*[18]

MORPHOLOGICAL.

(1) The plural of the present indicative ends often in *-en(-e): soupen,* 336.[19]

(2) The preterite of weak verbs often preserves its personal endings: *herghedes,* 291; *wroghtyn,* 301.[20]

The reader can readily see that the dialect of the poem is a mixed one, containing some traits peculiar to the Northern, and others savoring of the Midland dialect. Disregarding at present the question whether the poem is East or West Midland, we may explain this mixture of dialectal peculiarities that belong to the two major linguistic areas, that of the North and that of the Midlands, upon one of three possible grounds:

(1) The poem may have been written in the North, and copied by a Midland scribe.

(2) The poem may have been written in the Midlands, and copied by a Northern scribe.

(3) The poem may have been written in a region where Northern and Midland forms were intermingled, i. e. in the North Midlands.

[15] Morsbach, § 7.
[16] Luick, § 373 (e).
[17] Morsbach, § 7.
[18] *Ibid.,* § 7.
[19] *Ibid.,* § 7.
[20] *Ibid.,* § 7.

The first of these peculiarities is extremely unlikely. The morphological traits of the manuscript tell heavily against the assumption that the scribe wrote in an out and out Midland speech. Though it is true that *-en* endings for the present plural are more numerous, yet *-e* and *-es* endings are not lacking. The distinctive Midland endings for the present singular are entirely absent. The present participle nowhere has the Midland termination *-ende* (*-inge, -ynge*). *Qu* stands as the representative of OE. *hw*. All these particulars are well defined Northern characteristics, and their presence in the manuscript is sufficient to dispose of the assumption that the scribe wrote in a pure Midland dialect. The second possibility cannot be so easily disposed of. The presence of the Northern morphological examples just cited may be due to a Northern scribe, who copied an original written in the Midland dialect. Yet the case for such a possibility would be greatly strengthened if the Northern forms were introduced in a less regular and consistent manner. Their presence side by side with many Midland traits tells against the assumption that the scribe was a Northern man who copied a Midland poem. Moreover, the vocabulary of *Erkenwald* is distinctly not a vocabulary that one would expect to find in a purely Midland document. It is nearer to the vocabulary of the poems of the alliterative group of the Northwest Midland than to that of any work whose origin is not from that quarter.

The third assumption, then, appears the most probable. The poem contains both Northern and Midland traits, because it was copied down (or composed) in a region where such traits were to be found existing side by side, i. e. in the North Midland area. Hence the existence of examples of Northern, besides more numerous examples of Midland phonology. Hence the appearance of OE. $\bar{a} + w$ as *ǫu* of the Midlands in the majority of cases, instead of Northern *au*. Hence the appearance of Northern inflectional endings in the present singular, instead of Midland endings. This assumption is strengthened by the occurrence of similar admixtures in other documents that are known definitely to be of the North Midland regions, for example in *Handlyng Sinne,* in *Purity,* and in *Gawain.*[21] Our study of the dialect of *Erkenwald* has now brought us to the point at which we may say that it appears fairly certain that the poem was not written in the Northern dialect, but that it was, in all probability, composed in some place which possessed a mixed Midland and Northern dialect.

But if the poem were composed in the North Midland dialect, in what part of the North Midland dialectal area was it composed? Was it written in the Eastern or in the Western portion of that particular region? The question is an important one, for it bears upon the further question of whether or not *Erkenwald* is to be included in the works of the *Gawain*-poet. The evidence of the manuscript certainly shows West Midland characteristics predominant. That is in accord with the results of Knigge's examination of the poem, though he admits that he found in it slight traces of the East Midland dialect.[22] The following traits are distinctively East Midland:

PHONOLOGICAL.

(1) OE. $\breve{e}o$ appears as *e* in the greater number of cases: *derke,* 117, 294; *erthe,* 45.[23]

(2) OE. $\breve{y}$ appears in the majority of cases as *y* or *i:* *fyrst,* 197, 331; *myrthe,* 350; *spyr,* 93.[24]

---

[21] For a study of the phonology and morphology of *Handlyng Sinne,* Boerner's study, *Die Sprache Roberd Mannyngs of Brunne* (Halle, 1904), is invaluable. Boerner's doctoral dissertation, *Die Sprache Roberd Mannyngs of Brunne* (Halle, 1903), is chiefly concerned with an examination of the metre of the poem.

[22] *Die Sprache,* p. 118: 'Spuren der östlich-mittelländischen Dialecte sind bemerkbar.'

[23] Luick, § 357, note 1.

[24] Luick, § 287.

(3) OE. $a + n(m)$ is occasionally written $a + n(m)$ instead of $o + n(m)$: *name*, 28, 195; *wan*, 301.[25]

As against the traits just cited, which indicate the possible influence of East Midland speech, there must be placed the following which speak for the West Midland dialect:

(1) OE. $\breve{y}$ appears sometimes as *u*: *burde*, 260; *busmare*, 214; *gurdille*, 80; *gurden*, 251; *lures*, 328; *luste*, 162; *murthe*, 335.[26]

(2) OE. $a + n(m)$ is written in the majority of cases $o + n(m)$: *bone*, 243; *con*, 156; *mon*, 4, 163, 206, 240; *mony*, 11, 153, 220; *nome*, 152, 318.[27]

(3) OE. *ĕo* appears sometimes as *o*: *glow*, 171.[28]

MORPHOLOGICAL.

(4) *ho* appears as the pronoun for the nominative feminine singular of the third person. This form is used in every case where it could occur grammatically, in 274, 279, 308, 326.[29]

(5) *þai* (from ON.) appears as a pronominal form, together with the native forms, *hor, hom*.[30]

(6) The present participle ends in *-ande*.[31]

[25] *Ibid.*, § 367.
[26] *Ibid.*, § 287, note 3; Menner, *Publ. Mod. Lang. Assoc.* 37. 505-9.
[27] Menner, *Publ. Mod. Lang. Assoc.* 37. 509-11.
[28] Menner, *Publ. Mod. Lang. Assoc.* 37. 511-3; Luick, § 357. I believe also that *love* (34) is a case in point. But as several other explanations of the word are possible, I refrain from introducing it as evidence of West Midland provenience; see also the notes on *ʒorde* (88) and *glotte* (297).
[29] Menner, *Publ. Mod. Lang. Assoc.* 37. 513-4.
[30] Menner, *Pur.*, p. lix; see also the article by the same author in *Publ. Mod. Lang. Assoc.* 37. 523.
[31] Though this termination is found in some texts of the Northeast Midlands, *Handlyng Sinne*, for instance, it has been recognized as distinctive rather of the West Midlands than of the East Midlands. Cf. Morsbach, § 7, note.

The first four traits cited above are regarded as definite and sharp West Midland peculiarities. Their evidence is more weighty than that of the three East Midland traits, for it is impossible to say whether the first two stand out as examples of East Midland influence, or whether they are due to the influence of the *Gemeinsprache,* which may well have normalized some of the West Midland forms at the time that the manuscript was transcribed. In view of this last possibility, and of the evidence presented by the distinctive West Midland characteristics, Knigge's statement seems hardly too strong: the examples of East Midland dialectal influence are little more than traces. As it stands, then, in the manuscript, the poem seems without doubt to be written in the Northwest Midland dialect.

But in the case of *Erkenwald,* as elsewhere in mediæval literature, one is confronted by the baffling problem of transcription. There still remains a possibility that the poem was written in the East Midlands, and copied by a West Midland scribe. A final decisive answer to this possibility is, of course, impossible, but evidence that speaks against it is not wanting. The importance of the vocabulary in a question of this sort cannot be overlooked. The vocabulary of *Erkenwald* is, for our present intent and purpose, practically that of *Gawain* and the other poems of the *Pearl*-poet.

Although Trautmann's statements as to similarities of vocabulary between *Erkenwald* and the poems of the Cotton MS. were a little too extreme, his main thesis stands: the vocabulary of the legend is substantially the same as that of the *Gawain*-group.[32] To mention no other instance, the word *nourne,* which occurs nowhere else outside of the works of the *Gawain*-poet, is found in *Erkenwald.* One who compares the glossary of the legend with those of such

[32] *Angl. Anz.* 5. 23-4. Cf. also the valuable thesis of Kullnick, *Studien über den Wortschatz in Sir Gawayne and the Grene Knyʒt* (Berlin, 1902).

typical Northeast Midland texts as *Handlyng Sinne* or *The
Earl of Toulouse,* works not very far removed from our
poem as regards phonological and morphological traits, cannot fail to be struck by the fact that it contains many words
not found in them. On the basis of its vocabulary, *Erkenwald* must be grouped with the four poems of the *Gawain*-
author; it is closer to them in this respect than to any other
poem or body of poems in Middle English. In the light of
this test, there is no reason why we should not believe the
dialect of the manuscript to have been the dialect of the
original poem.

Certain differences between the manuscript of *Erkenwald*
and that of the four poems of the *Pearl*-poet, as regards
phonology, orthography, morphology, may here be noted.

Vowels.

(1) The Harleian MS. has *i* for *y* (the usual representative of OE. *i* in the Cotton MS.) : *blis,* 340,
345.
(2) The Harleian MS. has *e* for *i* (the usual representative of OE. ON., ĭ; OF. *i* in the Cotton MS.)
wehes, 73; *Ser,* 108.
(3) The Harleian MS. has *ou* for *au* (the usual representative of OE. ēow in the Cotton MS.) : *routhe,*
240; *trouthe,* 13, 184.
(4) The Harleian MS. has the spelling -*ie* for -*ye* or -*y*
(the usual spelling for OF. -*ie* in the Cotton MS.) :
memorie, 44; *mysterie,* 125.
(5) The Harleian MS. has the spelling *u* for *o, oe* (the
usual spelling of OF. *ue* in the Cotton MS.) : *dul,*
246; *dulfully,* 309.

Consonants.

(1) There are apparently no instances of *g* that follows
a nasal becoming *k,* either medially or finally in this

poem. There are a number of instances of the change, however, in *Purity*.

(2) Medially between vowels the scribe of the Harleian MS. writes *th* (where the scribe of the Cotton MS. writes *þ*) : *sothe,* 170, 197.

(3) The scribe of the Harleian MS. employs *sh* as the representative of OE. *sc* more frequently than does the scribe of the Cotton MS., who uses *sch* (or *sh*): *shapen,* 88; *shuld,* 42, 54.

(4) *Erkenwald* and *Pearl* employ exclusively the adverbal termination *-ly* (ON. *-liga*), whereas in the other poems of the *Gawain*-poet that termination varies with *-lych* (OE. *-līce*).

(5) The scribe of the Harleian MS. uses the spelling *cch* in preference to *ch, chch* (the usual representative of OE. *cc* in the Cotton MS.) : *tecche,* 85; *lacche,* 316.

(6) The scribe of the Harleian MS. writes *on* for *oun* (the usual representative of OF. *o + n* in the Cotton MS.) : *resones,* 52, 267; *procession,* 351.

(7) There are no cases of *tz* for *z* in *Erkenwald*.

(8) The scribe of the Harleian MS. uses the spelling *gh* in preference to *w* or *ʒ*, to represent the consonant in the OE. combination *a + g* (*aw, au, aʒ* are the spellings employed by the Cotton MS.) : *laghe,* 34, 187, 200 (but *lawe,* 216, 268).

INFLECTION.

The following inflectional characteristics are all to be found in the four works of the *Gawain*-poet.

Nouns. The plural of nouns generally ends in *-es* (*-s*). Some plurals occur that lack the ending: *ʒere,* 208, 210 (but *ʒeres,* 11). Relics of the OE. weak declension are to be found: *eghen,* 194,

311. The genitive case of nouns sometimes has no ending in the singular: *Fader*, 318.

Verbs. The infinitive ends in *-e*, more rarely in *-en*. The endings of the present indicative are 1 sg. *-e*, 2nd and 3rd sg. *-es;* plural, *-es, -en* (more rarely *-e*). The preterite 2d sg. sometimes ends in *-es: herghedes*, 291 ; *hentes*, 291. The present participle always ends in *-ande;* the past participle of strong verbs in *-en*.

Before concluding this study of the dialect of *Erkenwald*, we must ascertain whether the conclusions reached tell for or against the theory that the poem is the work of the *Pearl-*poet. On the basis of the dialectal evidence that we have just surveyed, there is better reason for believing that the poem may have been written in the speech of the Northwest Midland area than in any other. The grammatical inflections of the nouns, adjectives, and verbs differ little from those found in the manuscript of the Alliterative poems. Though there are a large number of differences between the two manuscripts as regards phonology and orthography, these may be accounted for by the fact that the Harleian MS. was written at a very much later date than the Cotton MS., when orthographical practice was beginning to change. A number of instances bear out this view: (1) Medially between vowels or between voiced vowels and *r* the Harleian MS. has *th*, more rarely *þ;* the Cotton MS. *þ*, more rarely *th*. (2) No examples of *tz = z* (*s*), as in *watz*, occur in the Harleian MS. (3) *Gh* in the Harleian MS. corresponds to *ʒ* of the Cotton MS. (4) Guttural *g* is written sometimes as *w* in the Harleian MS., as in *sorowe*, 305, 309, 327. Knigge remarks[33] that *w* is a later spelling.

---

[33] *Die Sprache*, p. 68. Though superseded, perhaps, in some cases, Knigge's excellent work is still indispensable to the student of Middle English alliterative poetry.

The results of our study confirm the belief of Knigge. In our present state of knowledge about the dialect of the poem, the weight of linguistic evidence is in favor of the theory of a common authorship for all five poems.

METRE AND ALLITERATION

The alliterative verse which flourished in the Northern and Midland counties from the fourteenth to the early years of the sixteenth century is probably not the result of an attempted revival of the Old English alliterative measure on the part of poetically inclined antiquarians. Its authors, by the care they take to preserve verse-patterns which are very closely related to the Old English types, to maintain the most salient features of the Old English alliterative scheme, and to retain the sharply marked mid-line pause, seem not so much to be trying to imitate an art that was dead, as to be endeavoring to carry over into their own days a poetic practice long sanctioned by tradition.[1]

But though one set of general principles may govern both the Old English and the Middle English alliterative verse, the passage of time and the ever-changing habits of speech produced marked differences between the two forms. One of the most important of these differences is that caused by the loss of the enjambement which is so striking a feature of Old English poetry. This loss has made of the Middle English alliterative line a rhythmical unit, and has also caused a weakening of the strict character of the alliteration, for-

---

[1] Regarding the belief entertained by Moorman (*Interpretation of Nature in English Poetry: Quellen und Forschungen* 95. 105) that the *Gawain*-poet had read, or was otherwise familiar with, the sea-pictures presented by the Old English *Exodus*, Menner (*Pur.*, pp. xlii-xliii) says: 'Not a jot of evidence has as yet been presented that either the *Gawain*-poet or any of his contemporaries was familiar with Old English poetry, or could even read a single line of it.'

merly used as a device for marking the unity and individuality of the line in which it occurred.

Such changes as these, with others that affected word-stress and vowel-quantity, modified the Old English half-line types. Though some remained unchanged, or suffered slight curtailment, others disappeared almost entirely.[2] Two different theories are held concerning the form of the Middle English (and Old English) line. The supporters of the one believe that the Middle English alliterative long line had four primary stresses, two in its first half and two in its second half. The supporters of the other believe that this line is one of seven stresses, four of the seven being found in the first half-line.[3] According to the first-mentioned theory, the first four lines of *Erkenwald* would be read thus:

At Lóndon in Énglònde noʒt fulle lónge sýthen
Sythen Críst suffride on crósse, and Crístendome stáblyde,
Ther was a býschop in þat búrghe, bléssyd and sácryd:
Saynt Érkenwòlde, as I hópe, þat hóly mon hátte.[4]

It is probable that the final syllable of the alliterative line, often a weak *e,* was pronounced; though it is true that at the time of the greatest flowering of the alliterative school,

---

[2] Cf. Luick, in Paul's *Grundriss der Germ. Phil.,* 2d ed., 2. 2. 163.
[3] The four-stress theory has the support of Sievers, Skeat, Schipper, Luick, Deutschbein, and Thomas. The seven-stress theory has the support of Trautmann, Kaluza, Rosenthal, Kuhnke, Fischer, Leonard, and Croll. Kuhnke, however, holds that each half-line has four beats, and not three. Rosenthal assumes for the half-line 'Zwei haupt- und ebenso viele Nebenhebungen.' Both schools allow the presence of secondary accents (*Nebenhebungen*) in the alliterative line, but most of the upholders of the seven (eight)-stress theory regard such stresses as true time-marking stresses.
[4] Since the supporters of the seven-stress theory are not unanimous in their belief that the Middle English alliterative line is one of seven stresses solely (and not eight), I refrain from giving a scansion of the first four lines of the poem according to the seven-stress theory. The absence of such a scansion, however, implies no disrespect for their views.

weak *e* at the end of words had become, or was becoming
silent. Luick is of the opinion that the desire on the part
of the poet to preserve an archaic style may have led to the
retention of this sound in the reading of the verse, at least
at the end of the line.[5]

The alliteration in *Erkenwald* is generally on the two
stresses of the first half-line, and on the first stress of the
second half-line. The presence of only one alliterating word
in the first half-line is not found in this poem.[6] As in
nearly all poems of the school, alliteration is becoming much
more frequent and elaborate, as it becomes less indispensable
to the structural form of the line. The author of *Erkenwald,* like his poetic brethren, crowds his lines with subtle
and unexpected alliterations. Sometimes double alliteration
is to be found.[7]

---

[5] *Grundriss der Germ. Phil.,* 2d ed., 2. 2. 165. Gollancz (p. 19),
noting apparently that a large number of lines in *Erkenwald* end with
a final weak *e,* has suggested that the last words of the following
lines might once have had a final *e,* though they do not now have it:
6, 27, 37, 118, 144, 174, 210, 212, 232, 241, 242, 257, 272, 326, 328,
336. While the possibility of the loss of final *e* in the case of those
particular words is one to be considered at all times, the lines as they
now stand are in no need of emendation for purposes of scansion.
Most of them fall under one of the metrical types which Luick
(*Grundriss der Germ. Phil.,* 2d ed., 2. 2. 163, 165) gives. Thus the
second half of l. 6 is a regular example of Luick's A[1] type.

[6] It is doubtful whether alliteration appears in the second half of 29.

[7] Several lines are to be found in which the alliteration, added either
accidentally or for ornament, prevents one from citing the particular
line as one in which parallel, or transverse, or inclusive alliteration
exists. Thus the poet would appear to be trying for parallel alliteration in 221 (perhaps also in 300) :

      The bisshop biddes þat body : 'Biknowe þe cause';

for transverse alliteration in 34 (and in 61) :

      At love London toun, and the laghe teches;

for inclusive alliteration in 308 :

      Longe er ho þat soper se, oþer segge hyr to lathe.

In the use of alliterative sounds and sound-combinations
the poet of *Erkenwald* shows no great divergences from the
practice of his contemporaries. Vowel alliteration occurs in
33, 108, 118 (complete), 211, 295 (complete). Alliteration
of vowels with the *h* that precedes the vowel is found in 4,
17, 40, 90, 127, 137, 196, 198, 208, 232, 339. Alliteration of
f with *v* occurs in 53, 144, 169. Alliteration of *w* with *wh*
occurs in 185, 186.[8] Our author seems careful to observe
one practice which is also characteristic of the poems of the
Gawain-group—that of making *sk, sp, st,* alliterate only with
words that have the same consonant combinations.[9]

In 1891 Kaluza called attention to the fact that certain
groups of poems of the alliterative school were capable of
being divided into stanzas of four lines, or of lines whose
number was a multiple of four.[10] Kaluza's suggestion that

---

[8] Tolkien-Gordon (*Sir Gawain and the Green Knight,* p. xxiii)
note that this alliteration is in contrast to the practice of the *Dest. of
Troy,* where *wh* (OE. *hw*) alliterates with *qu* (OE. *cw*). For this
reason they believe that *Gawain* was composed further south than the
Dest. of Troy.

[9] Ll. 2, 132 are exceptions to this practice of not alliterating *st* with
s, and *sp* with *s. Sh* alliterates with *s* in 129. *Cl* alliterates with *k*
in 140. Knigge (*Die Sprache,* p. 8) notwithstanding, there are no
examples of *excused-scape, expouned-speche* alliteration in this poem.
K alliterates with *qu* in 74. Schumacher (p. 207) cites 276 as an
example of *g-ʒ* alliteration. Luick (*Angl.* 11. 584-5) notes the following peculiarities in the metrical structure of certain half-lines of
Erkenwald: (1) cases of second half-lines which vary between A
and C types, 5, 44, 51, 61, 254; (2) cases of second half-lines with a
preceding prepositional adverb, 167, 349; (3) a case of weak cæsura,
167; (4) occurrence of a D type, 258 (first half-line). So close do
the metrical practices and habits of the poet of *Erkenwald* appear to
those of the *Gawain*-poet, that Luick regards them as one and the
same person, and adds at the conclusion of his study: 'Die zuweisung
dieser legende an unseren dichter erscheint als kaum zweifelhaft.'

[10] *Engl. Stud.* 16. 169-180. For Kaluza's division of *Erkenwald* into
eight-line stanzas, see pp. 174, 179. See also the brief statement on
stanzaic form in alliterative poetry which Luick gives in Paul's
Grundriss der Germ. Phil., 2d ed., 2. 2. 167.

the authors of the alliterative school intended to divide their
poems into sections has been substantiated in the case of the
Gawain-poet: in *Pearl* and *Gawain* the scribe has indicated
by a mark the different stanzas; in *Purity* and *Patience*,
while many of the marks that indicate a four-line division
are obliterated, enough are still visible to indicate that the
poet intended his poems to have quatrain division.[11]   In
1913 Gollancz applied the quatrain division to *Patience*.   In
1921 appeared his edition of *Cleanness*, and in 1922 his
edition of the present poem, both with the quatrain-arrangement.   The present editor agrees with Gollancz that a
stanzaic arrangement renders a poem that is apparently
monotonous 'altogether more vivid and lighter in structure,'[12] and on the strength of what seems such obvious
intention on the part of the *Gawain*-poet and other poets of
the alliterative school to break up their works into stanzas,
has divided the poem into quatrains.[13]

Such a division not only provides for the vividness that is
to be gained by observance of the logical pauses in the course
of the narrative and in the flow of the speeches, but brings
out also the major transitions of the story.   In this way those
stanzas that would naturally form the prologue, and those
that would form the *dénouement* (with the several sections
that logically intervene between the two) fall into their

[11] See Gollancz, preface to *Patience* (1913) and *Facsimile Repro-
duction of Cotton Nero MS. A. x* (*EETS*. 162 (1923)): p. 8;
Menner, *Pur.*, p. xliii; Emerson, *Mod. Lang. Notes* 31. 2-4.

[12] Preface to *Patience*.

[13] While the manuscript of *Erkenwald* contains no marginal marks
that indicate any attempt at stanzaic arrangement, there remains
always the possibility that a hypothetical original manuscript might
have had them.   The large ornamental capital letters at 1 and 177 are
plain indication of some sort of major division.   Natural and logical
pauses in the sense of the story require that the following stanzas do
not have four lines: stanza 30 (117-121); stanza 38 (150-154);
stanza 41 (163-168).

proper places, so that the resultant stanzaic arrangement indicates the skilful and artistic composition of a true artist, one who knew how to work from the whole to the part.

AUTHORSHIP

I

The poet of Erkenwald and the other poems of the alliterative school.

The legend of *St. Erkenwald* takes its place among that group of alliterative poems which flourished in the western counties of England three hundred years after the Norman Conquest. The brief period of some seventy or eighty years which saw the rise, flowering, and decay of the school, was sufficient time for the perfection of a distinct poetic technique, but hardly long enough for the development of poetic individuality among its various poets. We find, therefore, among the poems of the school so great a similarity of expression in verse-form and vocabulary as to make the attribution of a particular poem to a particular author or locality a very difficult matter to determine. Nor has this difficulty been lessened by the methods which students or admirers of the poems have adopted when they wrote about them. Misled by similarities of vocabulary and of style, they have been over-hasty in attributing to one poet several poems whose similarities are often only those of a common vocabulary and practice. Yet even among poems in which the personality of the author is so vague and shadowy as it is in those of this school, some distinctions as to style and authorship are possible.

The earliest poems of the school are certainly the two shorter *Alexander* fragments, *Joseph of Arimathie,* and *William of Palerne.* Their composition took place at a time too early for the author of our legend to have been writing, and their few cases of alliterative parallelism are insufficient to prove definitely that the author of *Erkenwald* knew of them, though it is, of course, quite possible that he did. Very scanty also are the cases of alliterative parallelism between *Erkenwald* and the group of poems published by Professor Amours in 1897 for the Scottish Text Society— *Awntyrs off Arthure, Golagros and Gawayne, Pistill of Susan,* and the *Buke of the Howlat.*[1] To supplement this scarcity of parallel passages one should note the more frequent and numerous occurrence of peculiarities of the Northern dialect as against those of the West Midland in the poems of the Scottish group. The paucity of evidence of this kind makes it difficult to believe that there is any connection between the group and the present poem. The more numerous alliterative parallelisms between the *Destruction of Troy* and *Erkenwald* make possible some sort of connection between those two poems,[2] but their differences as regards metrical structure, vocabulary, and style make impossible the assumption of a common authorship. The poet of *Erkenwald* is more careless in his observance of the laws of alliterative verse; his vocabulary contains a number of important words not to be found in the *Destruction of Troy;* and his style is more clean-cut, and suffers much less from the 'expletives' and conventional expressions so frequently used by the other poet.

The employment of the same criteria, tests as to vocabulary, metrical structure, and the use of *Flickwörter,* would distinguish *Erkenwald* and *Morte Arthure* as the work of different authors. Particularly distinctive in a comparison between the two poems would be the practice of the poet of *Morte Arthure* of grouping several lines together by the same alliteration. As for the *Sege of Jerusalem,* the lack of

---

[1] *Scottish Alliterative Poems* (Scottish Text Soc., 1897), ed. F. J. Amours, 2 vols.

[2] See notes to this edition, *passim.*

similarity as to vocabulary and alliterative phrasing renders the likelihood of a relationship between it and *Erkenwald* rather faint.[3] Although there are quite a number of cases in which the *Wars of Alexander* repeats alliterative combinations employed by our legend, these resemblances could be sufficiently accounted for by the supposition that the poet of the *Wars* borrowed alliterative forms from his predecessors.[4] Furthermore, the style of his poem is so unlike that of *Erkenwald* in its use of conventional expressions, and in the frequency with which the author pads out his line with some such stereotyped expression as, 'þe writt me recordis,' that it is quite impossible to believe that one and the same author could have written both poems. Different also are the two poems in verse-technique, for the author of the *Wars* has a peculiarly characteristic trick of running the same alliteration through a number of lines. Moreover, even if these stylistic difficulties could be set aside, the late date which Hennemann assigns for the *Wars* would militate strongly against the theory of a common authorship.[5]

It is not impossible that our author knew of the two poems, *The Parlement of the Three Ages* and *Winner and Waster*. The latter was written some thirty years before the year in which scholars have supposed the legend to have been com-

[3] Menner (*Pur.*, p. xxii (note 3)), however, believes that the author of the *Sege* was acquainted both with *Morte Arthure* and with the works of the *Gawain*-poet.

[4] For a discussion of the stylistic peculiarities of the *Destruction of Troy, Wars of Alexander, Sege of Jerusalem, and Morte Arthure,* cf. Trautmann, *Angl.* I. 120 ff.; Reicke, *Untersuchungen über den Stil der Mittelenglischen Alliterierenden Gedichte Morte Arthure, The Destruction of Troy, The Wars of Alexander, The Siege of Jerusalem, Sir Gawayn and the Green Knight* (Königsberg, 1906); MacCracken, *Publ. Mod. Lang. Assoc.* 25. 507-534.

[5] *Untersuchungen über das Mittelenglische Gedicht 'Wars of Alexander'* (Berlin, 1889), pp. 30-6. Hennemann has proved the assumption of a common authorship for the *Wars* and the poems of the *Gawain*-poet an impossibility.

posed,[6] and the fact that it displays its author's knowledge of London life is worthy of note. Yet the assumption that the poet of *Erkenwald* and the author of either of the two poems were one and the same person is hardly a probable one. Similarities in phrasing are not strikingly abundant, and the rapid narrative flow of the legend is very different from the balanced speeches of the formal and orthodox debate- and vision-types, under which species the two poems are to be classed.[7] Absent also from the earlier poems is that repose and dignity that characterize the legend.

The late date which Hanford and Steadman assign to *Death and Life*—before 1450—would make impossible the supposition of common authorship for it and our legend.[8] But the occurrence of not a few alliterative phrases in one

[6] For a discussion of the date and authorship of *Winner and Waster,* see Gollancz's preface to his edition of *Wynnere and Wastoure* (London, 1920); Hulbert, *Mod. Phil.* 18. 31-40; Steadman, *Mod. Phil.* 19. 211-220; 21. 7-14. Gollancz assigns the poem to the year 1352-3, and is of the opinion that *The Parlement of the Three Ages* is by the same hand. Steadman (*Mod. Phil.* 21. 7-14), however, produces evidence that renders the theory of a common authorship dubious.

[7] Manly (*Camb. Hist. of Engl. Lit.* 2. 42-6) is certain that there is some connection between the two poems and *Piers Plowman.* Among the poems which he takes to have been influenced by the latter are *Peres the Ploughmans Crede, Jacke Upland, Crowned King, Death and Life, Scottish Field.* While it is worthy of remark that the legend of Trajan has been treated in both *Piers Plowman* and our story, yet the influence of the great allegorical poem upon the legend is not markedly apparent. The latter belongs rather to the poems of the *Gawain*-group than to those patterned after the allegory. The author of *Death and Life,* however, is apparently familiar with the poems of both groups.

[8] Hanford and Steadman, *Death and Life (North Carolina Studies in Philology* 15. 231-2). These editors render untenable the view of Miss Scamman ('The Alliterative Poem: Death and Life': *Radcliffe Studies in English and Comparative Literature* 15. 96) that the poem was composed as late as 1503.

poem that are closely paralleled in the other, and the solemn
and devout spirit which breathes in lines of the later work,
make possible the assumption that its writer was influenced
by the work of his gifted predecessor. This likelihood
is strengthened by certain resemblances and parallelisms
between the two poems. Passages in the elder poem are
paralleled in the later, and paralleled so closely that one
cannot but accuse the author of *Death and Life* of having
copied from the saint's legend. Thus the brief account of
the temptation of Adam and Eve to be found in *Erkenwald*[9]
would seem to be imitated in *Death and Life*,[10] and the
account of the Harrowing of Hell found in *Erkenwald*[11] is
expanded in the later poem.[12] In view of the fact that
Menner has already shown that the poet of *Death and Life*
knew the works of the *Gawain*-poet,[13] these evidences of his
borrowing from the legend are of great interest, since they
indicate that a connection between our poem and the alliterative poems of the *Gawain*-group is most probable.

The parallel passages and similarities of style which exist
between *Erkenwald* and those poems which preceded it, are
not sufficiently weighty to enable one to state definitely that
the poet of the legend borrowed much from any of them.
He must have been familiar with the works of his predecessors, but how deeply he knew them, or how much he was
influenced by them, there is no means of knowing. That he
was known by the authors of the *Destruction of Troy* and
the *Wars of Alexander* is probable; for in those poems turns
of phrase which he uses occur more frequently than in any
other subsequent alliterative poems, except *Death and Life*.
But the legend is too short, and its lines too free from

[9] Ll. 294-8. Cf. also *Pur.* 240-8.
[10] Ll. 269-73.
[11] Ll. 289-300.
[12] Ll. 421-9.
[13] *Pur.*, p. xxvi.

mannerisms, to warrant any very definite conclusions as to how widely it was known by the poets of the alliterative school. Its metrical structure, its vocabulary, the evidence of numerous close parallel passages, and, more than all else, the spirit in which it is written, all link it more closely with the poems of the *Gawain*-group than with any others that we have considered.

II

Other possible works of the author of Erkenwald.

The name mentioned most frequently in connection with the authorship of *Erkenwald* is that of the *Gawain*-poet. As early as 1881 Horstmann, in his preface to the reprint of the story,[14] expressed his belief that the legend was to be grouped with the four poems of the Cotton MS. Since that date a body of evidence has been slowly accumulating that has tended, on the whole, to strengthen the belief of those who would add *Erkenwald* to the works of the *Gawain*-poet.[15] It is worth noting, moreover, that this body of

[14] *Altenglische Legenden* (Heilbronn, 1881), p. 266.

[15] Horstmann's opinion was adopted in the following year by Trautmann (*Angl. Anz.* 5. 23-5) ; in 1885 by Knigge (*Die Sprache des Dichters von Sir Gawayne and the Green Knight,* pp. 4-10) ; in 1889 by Luick (*Angl.* 11. 584-5) ; in 1893 by Brandl (Paul's *Grundriss der Germ. Phil.,* 1st ed., 1893, 2. 663). Gollancz, who in his first edition of *Pearl* (p. xlv, note 2) expressed his doubt, has now become a convert to the possibility of a common authorship (*St. Erk.,* pp. lvi-lxii). Osgood (*Pearl,* p. xlix, note 5) is of the opinion that one poet wrote *Erkenwald* and *Pearl,* and Gerould (*Saints' Legends,* p. 237) admits that the assumption is a possible one. In 1924 R. W. Chambers (*Essays and Studies by Members of the Engl. Assoc.* 9. 65-6) expressed the belief that the author of *Erkenwald* was also the author of *Gawain.* C. F. Brown (*Publ Mod. Lang. Assoc.* 19. 126, note 2) and J. T. T. Brown (*Huchown of the Awle Ryale and his Poems,* Glasgow, 1902, pp. 15-6) doubt the possibility of a common authorship, the latter basing his belief upon metrical grounds solely. Tolkien-Gordon (*Sir Gawain and The*

evidence has been growing at a time when various scholars were finding a good deal of evidence that tended to disprove the common authorship of a number of alliterative poems. In order to present as clearly as possible the results that have been reached concerning this question, I shall summarize the evidence that previous scholars have gathered, examine it critically, and, where possible, add further evidence that I believe should be considered.

I. VOCABULARY.

Trautmann[16] pointed out that the vocabulary of our legend is very similar to that of the four poems of the *Pearl*-poet. He gave a list of 52 words to be found in *Erkenwald* which are more frequently used in the same sense by the *Gawain*-poet than by the other poets of the school.[17] Of those 52 words, he believed that 8 were common only to *Erkenwald* and the four poems of the Cotton MS.; but an examination of NED. reduces that number to 5.[18] Further examination

Green Knight, Oxford, 1925, p. xviii) admit that there is 'a strong similarity' between the workmanship of the legend and that of the four other poems, but do not find that similarity 'so close as between the four poems themselves,' and therefore regard the possibility of common authorship as 'very dubious.'

[16] *Angl. Anz.* 5. 23-4.

[17] The following words Trautmann believed to be specially characteristic of the five poems we have been considering (the 8 words which he believed common to the legend and the poems of the *Gawain*-group are treated in the note below): *Avay,* 174; *bigripe,* 80; *brayde,* 190; *breve,* 103; *burde,* 260; *busmare,* 214; *clos,* 55; *debonerte,* 123; *ditte,* 116; *folwe,* 318; *fulsen,* 124; *glent,* 241; *glisne,* 78; *gynge,* 137; *hathel,* 198; *helle-hole,* 291; *heere,* 339; *japes,* 238; *laite,* 155; *lathe,* 308; *lave,* 314; *layne,* 179; *lethe,* 347; *lodely,* 328; *lome,* 149; *loves,* 349; *lures,* 328; *metely,* 50; *mynne,* 104; *mynte,* 145; *nait,* 119; *note,* 38, 152; *reken,* 135; *ronke,* 11; *slent,* 331; *spakly,* 335; *spyr,* 93; *stable,* 274; *stadde,* 274; *tome,* 313; *to wale,* 73; *witere,* 185; *wothe,* 233; *ʒepely,* 88.

[18] The following words Trautmann believed common only to *Erkenwald* and the poems of the *Gawain*-group: *baythe* (ask), 257;

of NED. serves also to reduce the value of certain words and expressions which Trautmann adduced as evidence of common authorship. Of his original list of synonyms for the word 'go,' synonyms which he believed could not be found outside of the *Gawain*-poet, there are none which cannot also be found in the works of other alliterative poets of the period. Of the three synonyms for 'say' which Trautmann gave, two are to be found only in the poems under discussion, the expression *louse wordes* and the word *nourne*.[19] The occurrence of the word *helle-hole* (291) deserves notice. It occurs in *Purity* as well, but in none of the other alliterative poems written at that time (1350-1400). Its occurrence in *Death and Life* is quite evidently an echo of the *Gawain*-poet's prior use. Thus it can be seen that, while the value of Trautmann's findings has been somewhat reduced by the appearance of the later volumes of the NED. and the progress of scholarship, yet the test of vocabulary indicates an unusually close connection between the five poems, and has strong affirmative bearing on the possibility of a common authorship.

2. ALLITERATION.

Trautmann's belief in a common authorship is unjustified in so far as it is based upon tests by means of alliteration;

blysnande, 87; *glew* (call, pray), 171, but see note to that line; *glode*, 75; *refete* (refresh), 304; *roynyshe*, 52; *teme*, 15; *thryvandly*, 47. Of these, *refete* is found in the Scottish *Legends of the Saints* (*Legends of the Saints* (Scottish Text Soc., 1906) 2. 415, ll. 294-5); *teme* in *Dest. of Troy* 3306; *thryvandly* in *Wars of Alex.* 3747. For *glode* see note on 75; cf. also *Wars of Alex.* 1334.
[19] Trautmann believed that the following synonyms were to be found only in the five poems under discussion: for 'go,' *helde* (137), *skelt* (278); for 'say,' *warpe wordes* (321); for 'man,' *tulke* (109); though he notes the occurrence of *tulke* in *Dest. of Troy*. But *helde* occurs in *Wars of Alex.* 3201, *skelt* in *Dest. of Troy* 1089, 6042, cf. note on 278; *warpe wordes* in *Dest. of Troy* 2683; *tulke* in *Wars of Alex.* 752, 2258.

for many of the phenomena which he regarded as distinctively characteristic of the four poems and of the saint's legend are also to be found in other alliterative poems.[20] One peculiarity of the *Gawain*-poet is not to be found in *Erkenwald,* the alliteration of *expoun* with *sp.*[21] On the other hand, one should note that there is no wide divergence between the alliterative manner of *Erkenwald* and that of the *Gawain*-poet. Our author shares with that poet the habit of alliterating unstressed syllables, and shows also his apparent reluctance to rhyme only like vowels.[22]

3. PHRASEOLOGY AND SIMILAR PASSAGES.

One who would point out parallel passages between any two alliterative poems of the period must be on his guard against citing those that are similar only because they contain alliterative commonplaces, such as 'mon upon molde,' 'hent harmes.' But even after all such similarities as those above have been laid aside, a great many parallelisms between *Erkenwald* and the poems of the Cotton MS. still remain. Furthermore, these seem so closely connected with regard to the circumstances in which they occur in the particular narratives, and to the meanings they convey, that one cannot,

---

[20] The similarities of verse-structure which led Trautmann to believe them indicative of a common authorship are no true test. Verse-structure is markedly homogeneous throughout all the alliterative poems of the period. Moreover, his tests cover only the first 300 lines of the poems he examined. From what has just been said, it follows that the arguments based on the evidence of the poet's metrical practice which J. T. T. Brown (*Huchown of the Awle Ryale and his Poems* (Glasgow, 1902), pp. 15-6) has advanced against a common authorship are equally invalid.

[21] Fischer, *Die Stabende Langzeile in den Werken des Gawain-Dichters* (*Bonner Beiträge zur Anglistik,* 1901), pp. 41-2; Schumacher, *Studien über den Stabreim in der Mittelenglischen Alliterationsdichtung* (Bonn, 1914), pp. 120-1.

[22] Schumacher, pp. 26-8, 49, 55-6.

I think, refuse to recognize the existence of a close connection between *Erkenwald* and the works of the *Gawain*-poet. Slight changes in the wording of one passage as compared with another should not blind us to the similarities that lie beneath them both. The *Gawain*-poet is too pronounced an artist ever lamely to repeat an alliterative phrase until it becomes stereotyped and flat.

The passages here presented have different values as evidence for common authorship. Some may be explained as reminiscences of past phrases which the author found helpful or pleasing. Others may be due to an author's unconscious tendency to repeat the words and phrases that were used to paint a similar situation in an earlier work. Of such similar passages only the more important and striking are given below. Others that have value as evidence are to be found in the notes.[23]

Erkenwald	*Gawain*
40 Harde stones for to hewe.	789 Of harde hewen ston.
192 Þurghe sum lant goste.	2250 Þat me gost lante.

Erkenwald	*Patience*
171 Bot glow we alle opon Godde.	164 Bot vchon glewed on his god.
176 If ȝe hym frende leves.	404 ȝif we hym God leuen.
192 See above under parallels with *Gawain*.	260 Þat any lyf myȝt be lent.
283 Maȝty Maker of men.	482 A! þou maker of man.
304 Þer richely hit arne refe-tyd þat after right hungride.	19 Þay ar happen also þat hungeres after ryȝt.

[23] The following parallels are cited in the notes: *Erk.* 80, *Gaw.* 2395; *Erk.* 92, *Gaw.* 244; *Erk.* 181, *Gaw.* 852; *Erk.* 15, *Pat.* 316; *Erk.* 92, *Pat.* 186; *Erk.* 78, *Pearl* 165; *Erk.* 246, *Pearl* 642; *Erk.* 290, *Pearl* 646, 705; *Erk.* 311, *Pearl* 807; *Erk.* 15, *Pur.* 9; *Erk.* 30, *Pur.* 1447; *Erk.* 98, *Pur.* 1201; *Erk.* 219, *Pur.* 1523; *Erk.* 246, *Pur.* 1329; *Erk.* 268, *Pur.* 1066.

Erkenwald	*Pearl*
195-6 Þe name þat þou nevenyd has and nournet me after Al heven and helle heldes to, and erthe bitwene.	441-2 Þat Emperise al heuenȝ hatȝ, & vrþe & helle in her bayly.

Erkenwald	*Purity*
294-8 Dwynande in þe derke dethe, þat dyȝt us oure fader, Adam, oure alder, þat ete of þat appulle. Þat mony a plyȝtles pepul has poysned for ever. ȝe were entouchid with his tethe, and take in þe glotte, Bot mendyd with a medecyn, ȝe are made for to lyvye.[34]	241-8 Bot þurȝ þe eggyng of Eve he ete of an apple, Þat enpoysened alle peplez þat parted fro hem boþe, For a defence þat watz dyȝt of Dryȝtyn selven, And a payne þeron put and pertly halden. Þe defence watz þe fryt þat þe freke towched, And þe dom is þe deþe þat drepez uus alle. Al in mesure and meþe watz mad þe veng(a)-unce, And efte amended wyth a mayden þat make had never.

Erkenwald	*Purity*
337 And þer a marcialle hyr mette with menske aldergrattest.	91 Ful manerly wyth marchal mad for to sitte.
161 Towarde þe providens of þe Prince þat Paradis weldes.	195 Þat þat ilk proper Prynce þat paradys weldez.
245 And for I was ryȝtwis and reken, and redy of þe laghe.	294 Ful redy and ful ryȝtwys, and rewled hym fayre.

[34] Cf. *Pearl* 637-660 for a similar passage.

291 Quen þou herghedes helle-
   hole and hentes hom
   þeroute.

1179 He herȝed up alle Israel,
   and hent of þe beste.

332 Ryȝt now to soper my
   soule is sette at þe table.

1763 Seten at her soper.

It would, however, be dangerous to bring forward a claim of common authorship for our legend and the four other poems simply on the ground of close parallelism of expression. Resemblances such as these may be taken as indicative, not so much of common authorship, as of imitation by one poet of another. Our study of the relationship of the legend to the other poems of the school has shown us that such imitation was not an infrequent practice among the several poets. Menner has presented evidence of the borrowing of the phraseology of the *Gawain*-poet by the poet of the *Wars* and by the author of *Death and Life*,[25] and the present editor has called attention to the repetition by the latter poet of certain words and situations in *Erkenwald*. In view of such a tendency towards imitation among the makers of these poems, it is possible to explain correspondences between this legend and the works of the *Gawain*-poet in just this way.

Yet those who would thus explain such parallelisms of phrasing must take into account also the fact that the five poems under consideration were in all probability written at dates not far removed from one another. All of them could quite easily fall within the compass of a single lifetime. Such contiguity between the several dates of composition does not exist with regard to the cases in which the *Wars of Alexander* and *Death and Life* repeat the phrasing of the *Gawain*-poet: for the former was written between 1400 and 1450,[26] and the latter probably a short time before the date last mentioned;[27] so that an outside limit of some 100

[25] *Pur.* pp. xxiv-xxvii.

[26] Wells (*Manual of the Writings in Middle English*, p. 103) says 'of date 1400-1450 or about 1450.'

[27] Hanford and Steadman, *Death and Life*, pp. 231-2.

years probably exists between the composition of *Patience* and the dates of those two poems. Probabilities such as these militate against the belief that the resemblances between *Erkenwald* and the four other poems of the Cotton MS. are explicable by the assumption that one poet copied from another; for the diffusion of manuscripts in mediæval England, generally speaking, required time, and the known examples of such imitation occur, as we have seen, between poems whose dates of composition are separated by many years.

If, then, imitation by one poet of another is an inadequate explanation of the many resemblances between *Erkenwald* and the works of the *Gawain*-writer, one can account for them in only two other ways, both of which recognize the fact of a close connection between all five poems. It is possible that these similarities are due to some disciple or pupil of the *Gawain*-poet, who, thoroughly imbued with his master's spirit, had very cleverly caught his master's style.[28] But it is more likely that they are due to the fact that all five poems are the work of one author.

4. STYLE.

Several structural and stylistic mannerisms characteristic of some of the poems of the *Gawain*-group are not noticeably apparent in *Erkenwald*.[29] However, the shortness of the poem would have to be considered by any critic who is inclined to stress the fact of their infrequency or non-appear-

---

[28] Gollancz in his early edition of *Pearl* (p. xlv, note 2) thinks that the legend was written by an 'enthusiastic disciple' of the *Gawain*-poet. In his late edition, however, he admits the possibility that the *Gawain*-poet may have been the author of the legend (p. xlv).

[29] The following mannerisms characteristic of the style of the *Gawain*-poet are not found in our legend: (1) the device of concluding the poem with much the same phraseology with which it is begun; (2) use of absolute construction with *and* (see Menner, *Pur.*, p xviii) ; (3) fondness for beginning a line with *for*.

ance. In a longer poem their occurrence might have been more frequent. Moreover, there is always the possibility that the transcriber of the Harleian MS. reduced the number of mannerisms peculiar to the poet of *Purity* in the interests of uniformity of structure.

The poem is more condensed than *Pearl*, as one might quite reasonably expect; for in one poem the author is telling a story, and in the other, at least for the greater part of the time, he is engaged in carrying on a debate. The structure of the saint's legend is smoother than that of *Gawain* or that of *Purity*. From the broken utterance and obscurities of the latter poem it is quite noticeably free.[30] Shifts in sentence-structure, a characteristic that is marked in *Purity* and rare in *Patience,* are rare also in *Erkenwald*. There is to be found in the poem but one case of the pleonastic pronoun (269); in the first 300 lines of the following poems, the proportions run thus: *Pearl* 3, *Gawain* 1, *Patience* 0, *Purity* 2, *Wars of Alexander* 3.[31] The use of the historical present is rare in *Erkenwald* and *Pearl,* slightly more marked in *Gawain* and *Purity,* and abundant in *Patience* and the *Wars of Alexander*.[32]

---

[30] Cf. notes to ll. 21, 32, 42, 167, in Menner's edition of *Purity*.

[31] The pleonastic pronoun is to be found in the following lines of the poems under discussion: *Pearl,* 41, 201, 256; *Gaw.,* 53; *Pur.,* 111, 150; *Wars of Alex.,* 56, 96, 122. Occurrence of the pleonastic pronoun in *Pearl* is often to be explained by the demands of metre.

[32] The historical present is to be found in the following lines of the poems under discussion: *Erkenwald,* 33, 34, 35, 131, 177 (twice), 191, 221, 222, 257; *Pearl,* 75, 77, 79, 98, 125, 128, 177, 191; *Gaw.,* 8, 9, 10, 11, 12, 14, 104, 106, 110, 112, 136, 221 (twice), 250; *Pur.,* 74, 75, 109, 111, 129, 150 (twice), 154 (twice), 279, 280, 295; *Pat.,* 89 (twice), 93, 97, 98, 99 (twice), 101, 102 (twice), 103, 105 (twice), 106, 107, 108, 137, 141, 152, 153 (twice), 155, 225, 230, 241, 242, 251, 253 (twice), 269, 273 (twice), 277 (twice), 278, 280, 293, 296, 297; *Wars of Alex.,* 47, 53 (twice), 55, 56, 57, 58, 59, 64, 77, 78 (twice), 79, 80, 111, 113, 120 (twice), 121, 122, 123 (twice), 125, 126, 131, 132, 133, 135 (twice), 140, 143, 145, 149, 151, 153, 155, 156, 161

It may be seen then, that the stylistic dissimilarities between *Erkenwald* and the four works of the unknown poet of the West Midlands, while noticeable, are comparatively unimportant. Some of them would seem to be capable of explanation on the ground of the peculiar and distinctive requirements of story and situation. Furthermore, even among the four poems of the *Gawain*-group, there are stylistic dissimilarities. For example, the use of the historical present is strikingly marked in *Patience,* and infrequent in *Pearl* and *Gawain.* On the other hand, several stylistic tricks and mannerisms that have been noted by scholars and critics as peculiarly characteristic of the *Gawain*-poet are to be found in the legend.[33]

One of these stylistic mannerisms is a certain habit of paraphrasing 'Lord' or 'God' by means of a relative clause. As Menner has remarked, these paraphrases are more detailed and more elaborate in the works of the *Gawain*-poet than in other alliterative homilies and romances.[34] Of such paraphrases no less than four occur in the poem, though Knigge cites only one.[35] The examples given below are divided

(twice), 163, 166, 220, 224 (twice), 225, 234, 241, 265, 266, 267 (twice), 286. Only the first 300 lines of each poem have been examined. The *Gawain*-poet would appear to be more careful in his use of this tense than many of his fellow-poets. In *Purity* he employs it wherever vividness and colour are necessary for the description of a scene or action: thus it is often to be found in the account of the Man in Foul Clothes (125-160). In *Patience* it occurs frequently in the account of the shipwreck. The occurrence of this tense in such scenes leads me to believe that its use was not unintentional, and that the poet employed it wherever he thought it might lend something to the vividness and reality of the scene he was describing.

[33] An important characteristic which our poem seems to share with *Purity* and *Patience* is the division into quatrains. For more detailed discussion of this peculiarity of structure, the reader is referred to the section dealing with the metre of the poem.

[34] *Pur.,* pp. xvi-xviii.

[35] *Die Sprache,* p. 6. Knigge uses this mannerism as an argument for considering *Erkenwald* a part of the corpus of the *Pearl*-poet.

into groups in order to bring out similarities in phraseology;
these noted by Knigge are indicated by (K.) :

(a) *Erk.* 161 þe Prince þat Paradis weldes. (K.)
    Pat. 225 þe prynce þat prophetes seruen.
    Pur. 195 Þat þat ilk proper Prynce þat paradys weldez.
    644 þo men þat my3tes al weldez.

(b) *Erk.* 267 þe riche Kynge of reson, þat ri3t ever alowes.
    Pur. 17 þe Kyng þat al weldez.

(c) *Erk.* 192 hym þat al redes.
    Pur. 1528 hym þat alle goudes gives.

(d) *Erk.* 272 He . . . þat loves ry3t best.
    275 He þat rewardes uche a renke.
    Pur. 31 he þat flemus uch fylþe fer fro his hert.

Another trick of style, to which Schmittbetz seems first to
have alluded, the substantive use of the adjective, occurs in
lines 116 and 138.[36]

Under the heading of style may be included the argument
brought forward by Miss M. Carey Thomas, based upon the
habit of the *Gawain*-poet of grouping similes in clusters of
two.[37] Of the three similes to be found in this poem one
example of this practice occurs. In so short a poem this
one example is noteworthy.

Hitherto we have been noticing the outward marks of
similarity that exist between our legend and the four poems.
But similarities in vocabulary and metrical usage, resemblances as regards the mere outward mechanics of style,
would count for little, were we to find *Erkenwald* notably

[36] 'Das Adjektiv in "Sir Gawayn and the Grene Kny3t"' : *Angl.* 32.
359-369.
[37] *Sir Gawayne and the Green Knight*, p. 12. In *Pearl*, 15 out of
35 comparisons occur in groups; in *Pur.*, 14 out of 24; in *Pat.*, 3 out
of 7; in *Gaw.*, 6 out of 19; see Menner, *Pur.*, p. xix. Another point
made by Miss Thomas (pp. 10-11) may be mentioned here: the fact
that in *Patience, Pearl*, and *Gawain* is employed the device of closing
the poem with approximately the same words with which it is begun.
This device, however, is found neither in *Purity* nor in *Erkenwald*.

inferior to the other poems as a work of art. If the literary powers of our author are not on the same high plane as those of the *Gawain*-poet, the theory of a common authorship must be regarded as extremely dubious. It is precisely upon this point that the supporters of that theory base one of their strongest claims. As a literary artist, the poet of *Erkenwald* must hold high rank. Particularly skilful has been the construction of the story. The legend falls naturally into three parts, a prologue (1-33), a middle (33-177), and a conclusion (177-352). This conclusion is capped by a startling and dramatic *dénouement*. As in the case of *Sir Gawain*, the problem before the author involved the careful ordering of the several parts of the story, that a dramatic outcome might be secured. As in the case of *Sir Gawain*, one feels, after a perusal of the tale, that the problem has been solved. Though the descriptive passages in the poem are neither so extensive nor so rich in details as those that are to be found in the poems of the Cotton MS., yet our author is gifted with the seeing eye. His descriptions of the appearance of the tomb and of the apparel of the judge, if brief, are sharp and clear, and evince their creator's mastery of the *mot juste*.[38] In sheer narrative interest, *Erkenwald* is in no way inferior to *Gawain* or *Patience*. In the legend, as in the other poems, there is the same care on the part of the writer to preserve the even flow of the story, the same care to subordinate the details of the narrative to its final *dénouement*, the same care to avoid the repetition of stock conversations or wordy debates, a sin of which the authors of the *Wars*, the *Destruction of Troy*, and the *Morte Arthure* are too frequently guilty.

Evidence gained from æsthetic and artistic appreciation is

[38] To obtain an idea of the conciseness and adequacy of our poet's word-pictures, the description of the tomb of the judge (45-52) should be compared with the long drawn out and diffuse description of the tomb of Hector in *Dest. of Troy* (8733-66).

frequently vague and inconclusive in a question of disputed authorship, yet a study of literary gifts and aptitude has its place in a survey of an author's style. Thus much can be said, however, that to the other similarities and correspondences that exist between the five poems there must be added this further one: that they are alike in the skill with which they have been constructed, and in the power and beauty of style with which they have been written.

In conclusion, it can safely be said that the evidence deduced from this survey of the vocabulary of the saint's legend, of its author's use of alliteration, and of the style in which he wrote, confirms the belief of those who regard him as identical with the *Pearl*-poet. A number of the stylistic traits which characterize that author are to be found also in our legend, while certain practices and mannerisms habitual with other poets of the school are lacking. If there are any who believe that so short a piece as our legend hardly provides sufficient evidence on which to base a claim for a common authorship for all five poems, they overlook the fact that the brevity of the poem is in favor of the defenders of common authorship: if there is so much evidence in so short a poem, it is likely that a longer one would furnish more.

III

The relationship of the poem to the City of London.

Any discussion of the authorship of the legend must take into consideration the question of how such a poem as *Erkenwald*, written as it is in the characteristic and approved manner of the North and West, and differing in vocabulary and dialect from the poetic usage of the metropolis, should have had a London setting. Chaucer's good-natured allusion to the poetic practice of his western contemporaries is well-known,[39] and might lead one to suppose that alliterative verse

[39] Cf. *Parson's Prologue* 42-3, and Skeat's notes on those lines.

found no very warm appreciation among the higher classes in London. Yet evidence to be gleaned from references in other alliterative poems would not confirm the belief of any one who supposed that western poets were men who wrote in a remote rural backwater, unruffled by the winds of passing events. The authors of *Winner and Waster, Piers Plowman,* and *Richard the Redeles,* certainly had no provincial outlook.[40]

William, the supposed author of the *Vision of Piers Plowman,* knew London well. He tells us that he and his wife, Kit, dwelt in Cornhill,[41] and he refers no less than four times to St. Paul's Cathedral or to clergymen connected with that foundation.[42] Nor was the author of *Winner and Waster* ignorant of the metropolis. His five hundred and four vigorous lines show his familiarity not only with the political events of his day, but also with the low life that went on in Cheapside, Bread Street, and the Poultry.

The preceding examples, displaying the knowledge of London and its life which other alliterative poets possessed, all go to establish the fact that there is nothing unusual or out of the way in the poet of *Erkenwald* showing a familiarity with the life of the metropolis. It is not necessary to assume that because the maker of our legend shows such an acquaintance with London, he must have been a mere redactor, who put into alliterative verse a story of London originally written in the East Midlands.[43] In writing about

[40] Osgood (*Pearl,* p. liii) says of the author of *Pearl:* 'At the same time he was a person who had enjoyed great advantages. His reading, both religious and secular, shows this. Nor is it likely that such reading could have been acquired in the remote Northwest of England.'

[41] C. 6. 1-4.

[42] C. 12. 56; C. 16. 70; B. 10. 46; B. 13. 65. Skeat (*Parson's Prologue* 43, note) tells us that *Piers Plowman* had become extremely popular in London, especially among the lower classes.

[43] The poem contains a few dialectal traits of the East Midlands; cf. section dealing with the dialect of the poem. Whether their

London, our poet was doing nothing out of the ordinary, for several of his predecessors or contemporaries had also written poems in which the life of the city, or the historical events happening there, had figured prominently.

How the author of *Erkenwald* came to a knowledge of the capital city we have no means of knowing. It is quite possible that he may never have seen it, and that his knowledge of London was derived from books or from oral tradition. On the other hand, it is equally possible that he knew the city thoroughly. He may have visited it on a pilgrimage, drawn to the town by the great preparations that were being made by the clergy for the celebration of the anniversary of the translation of St. Erkenwald's body; for such an event might well have a peculiar interest for a man of our author's devout and reverent spirit. Whether he derived his knowledge from hearsay or from actual residence, we cannot say. But it must be borne in mind that the knowledge of London which he displays cannot be used as prima-facie evidence that he was not a native of the West of England.

IV

Theological opinions of the poet.

We pass now to the application of another test of some importance. Professor C. F. Brown, who is the author of a most interesting and suggestive article on the theological views of the *Pearl*-poet,[44] has advanced certain views as to that writer's position with regard to the body of doctrine that was held by the Church of the fourteenth and fifteenth centuries. The question, then, naturally arises whether his

presence be due to scribe or author is uncertain. Even if they could be traced back to the author, their number and importance are less than the number and importance of the dialectal traits characteristic of West Midland localities.

[44] 'The Author of the Pearl, considered in the Light of his Theological Opinions': *Publ. Mod. Lang. Assoc.* 19. 115-153.

views on the religious tenets of the *Pearl*-poet raise any objections to the theory of a common authorship, which its defenders must be prepared to meet.

Brown finds the 'atmosphere' of *Erkenwald* quite different from that which is to be found in *Pearl, Purity,* and *Patience.* 'In the *Legend of Erkenwalde,*' he tells us, 'there is legendary material in abundance. The "Limbus Patrum" and the "Harrowing of Hell" are especially prominent. It is in such striking contrast in this respect to *Pearl, Cleanness* and *Patience* that I find it difficult to regard it as the work of the same author. The whole atmosphere of *Erkenwalde* is different from that of the other three poems.'[45]   Brown, therefore, would have us regard the poet of *Erkenwald* as one whose attitude towards religious matters was the reverse of that of the poet of *Pearl*—'ecclesiastical' rather than 'evangelical.'

A superficial study of the religious opinions of the author of the legend might lead one to the belief that he had in matters of dogma and doctrine a liberal bias. His story is a *rifacimento* of a legend that had long lingered on the borders of orthodoxy. St. Gregory the Great, who figures so prominently in the legend of Trajan, had himself stated that the saints shrink from praying for the unbelieving righteous dead, for they fear that their petitions for those who must suffer eternal punishment will be made of none effect before the countenance of the just Judge.[46]   Furthermore, one who reads the account of the baptism of the pagan justice might well suspect the orthodoxy of a person who thought that tears were valid water of baptism, in opposition to the opinion of many doctors and theologians of the Church.[47]

[45] *Ibid.* 19. 126, note 2.
[46] *Moralia (Patr. Lat.* 76. 739).
[47] From the earliest period of Christianity, water was regarded as the true and proper substance of baptism. St. Thomas, in allowing the use of certain other substances that had a water component, but were not *aqua pura,* is adopting a liberal point of view. The opposite

Deeper examination, however, shows that the poet can hardly be stamped as a liberal on the ground of his religious views. Tested by the cardinal principles of Catholic belief, as they are set forth by St. Thomas Aquinas, a theologian and doctor greatly reverenced and quoted by churchmen of the fourteenth and fifteenth centuries, the poet's tenets would be found orthodox. If there are any who see in our poet's reworking of a version of the legend of Trajan's salvation evidence of an unorthodox *Tendenz,* they must reconcile their view with the decision of St. Thomas to the effect that the miracle was within the bounds of orthodox belief.[48]

The question of whether the only valid water of baptism is *aqua pura* the Angelic Doctor carefully examines, and

opinion is held by Hugo of St. Victor (*De Sacramentis* 2. 6. 14: Migne, *Patr. Lat.* 176. 460; *Summa Sententiarum* 5. 10: Migne, *Patr. Lat.* 176. 136) and St. Bonaventura (*Scriptum D. Bonaventuræ Card. Ac. Doct. . . . in Quatuor Libros Sententiarum Petri Lombardi* (Rome, 1569): *De Sacramentis* (Lib. 4, Distinct. 3), pp. 66-8). The Church of Rome at the present time forbids the use of tears as valid water of baptism; cf. *Catholic Encyclopedia: Baptism* 6.

[48] *Summa Theolog.,* Pars 3 (Supp.), Quæst. 71, Art. 5. The legend is frequently referred to in the writings of the mediæval period in England. It is often mentioned by Gower. Wyntoun also tells the story in his *Original Chronicle* (Scottish Text Soc. 3. 286-296). An interesting discussion of the story is found in the B- (11. 132-171) and C- (13. 71-99) versions of *Piers Plowman.* The author of the B-version of the story speaks out very boldly, declaring that (150-1)

> Nou3t thorw preyere of a pope but for his pure treuthe
> Was that Sarasene saued as seynt Gregorie bereth witnesse.

The author of the C-version is evidently unwilling to lay down so rash an assertion, for the lines quoted above are not found in his account. Both authors, however, are agreed in minimizing the import-ance of the celebration of the mass as a means of aiding the deliver-ance; cf. B. 11. 145; C. 13. 85. Other references to the possibility of Trajan's salvation are to be found in B. 12. 275-290 and C. 15. 205-214. The treatment of this point of doctrine by the conservative poet of *Erkenwald* is more guarded and careful. He lays stress upon the performance of mass before the bishop proceeds to the tomb. It

concludes finally that any watery substance is proper,
provided that it have not lost the essential quality of water—
a decision broad enough to embrace sea-water or tears.[49]
Narrower decisions may have since been handed down by
church councils on many theological questions which St.
Thomas examined, but at the time that the poet wrote they
were still in the future. Whatever he may now appear, our
poet was then neither schismatic nor heretic.[50]

   With this opinion Brown is in thorough agreement. He
finds the poet of *Erkenwald* quite orthodox in his religious

would seem that deliverance came not so much because of the judge's
righteousness, as by a manifestation of God's free grace. The legend
seems based upon a theme which *Pearl* seeks to drive home:

> For þe grace of God is gret innoghe.

Furthermore, the story is of a nature to impress upon its hearers
or readers the absolute necessity of the sacrament of baptism for
salvation. This difference between the attitude of the author(s) of
Piers Plowman and that of the poet of *Erkenwald* upon the problem
of the salvation of the righteous heathen has also been noted by
Chambers ('Long Will, Dante, and the Righteous Heathen': *Essays
and Studies by Members of the Engl. Assoc.* 9. 50-69). It might be
noted in passing that Trevisa, in his translation of Higden's *Poly-
Chronicon* (Rolls Ser.) 5. 7, brands the legend of Trajan as an
idiot's tale, though elsewhere in that work (6. 197) he refers to it
as if he attached a certain amount of credibility to it.

   [49] *Summa Theolog.*, Pars 3, Quæst. 66, Art. 4.

   [50] L. 279 appears to me to furnish evidence of the poet's belief in
the orthodox doctrine of the inequality of heavenly rewards. To
Brown the poet of *Pearl* seems to dissent from the orthodox view and
to hold to the heretical view of Jovinian (cf. Jerome, *Adversus
Jovinianum:* Migne, *Patr. Lat.* 23. 222-351), namely, that in heaven
the reward was the same for all. J. B. Fletcher, in his article on the
allegorical significance of *Pearl* ('The Allegory of the Pearl': *Jour.
Engl. and Germ. Phil.* 20. 17-8), has proved, I think, quite clearly
that the poet held no such doctrine. Gollancz finds the attitude of
the poet of *Pearl* thoroughly conservative. While he believes that
Brown has made 'some interesting and valuable observations on the
relationship of the poem to the theology of the time,' he is 'convinced
that the poem is not primarily associated with questions of contemporary theology' (*Pearl* (1921), p. xlvi, note 1).

beliefs, a man who accepted the teaching of the Church, regardless of whether that teaching contained legendary or apocryphal elements—matter without proper scriptural warrant. Different, however, are his views regarding the poet of *Pearl*. He finds him, to be sure, an earnest Catholic; but he finds also a sharp distinction between the unquestioning acceptance of ecclesiastical legend, and the respectful attitude towards ecclesiastical dignitaries and services which characterize the author of *Erkenwald,* and the 'evangelical' attitude of the author of *Pearl*. So marked does he find this distinction to be, that he doubts any possibility of common authorship for the two poems.

Professor Brown has called our attention to a noteworthy fact about the work of the *Pearl*-poet—its almost complete lack of the legendary and apocryphal matter which is so common in other devotional and homiletic literature of the time. Particularly noticeable does he find this absence of legendary and apocryphal material from *Patience* and *Purity*. In *Purity,* for example, he finds only five instances of the occurrence of this material.[51] But in *Erkenwald* only four instances of the occurrence of such material are to be found.[52] It cannot, therefore, be argued that the author

[51] These are: The description of the Fall of the Angels (203-234); the story of the disobedience of Lot's wife (820-8); the account of the wonderful properties of the Dead Sea and of the Apples of Sodom (1013-48); the description of the wonders that attended the birth of the Saviour (1078-88); the account of Christ's miraculous breaking of the bread (1101-8).

[52] These are: (1) the legend of Trajan; (2) the reference to the Harrowing of Hell (291-2); the reference to the Limbus Patrum (292); (4) the account of the recalling of the dead judge to life. I have not included in this list the poet's use of the story of Brutus and the founding of Troynovant, since that was probably derived from some book which our author regarded as a *bona fide* historical work; cf. the use of this story in *Gawain* 1-24. Nor have I included the account of the Christianizing of Britain and the conversion of the pagan temples into churches, since those stories also would probably

of *Erkenwald* could not have written *Purity,* because his
story is too full of legendary material, when a larger amount
of such material is actually to be found in the homiletical
poem.

Regarding the first example of legendary material that he
lists—the description of the Fall of the Rebel Angels—
Brown remarks: 'It is a question whether this legend should
be classed as apocryphal, inasmuch as it established itself in
the church at an early date and was a direct outgrowth of
certain passages in the Scriptures themselves.'[53]   But a similar case could be made out for the legends of the Harrowing
of Hell[54] and the Limbus Patrum.[55]   Each had 'established
itself in the church at an early date';[56] each is an 'outgrowth
of certain passages in the Scriptures themselves.'   At the
time of the composition of the poems under discussion, both
legends had become well established parts of Catholic dogma,
and are to be found discussed as parts of the body of orthodox belief in the *Summa* of St. Thomas Aquinas, and in the
writings of many other patristic and scholastic commentators.   If, then, the legend of the Fall of the Rebel Angels
is to be received as non-legendary material, so also ought
the legends of the Harrowing of Hell and the Limbus
Patrum.   Moreover, the question might well be raised
whether the legend of Trajan should not be similarly
classed, since it also had become a part of Catholic tradition.

In the course of his definition of the attitude of the author

be regarded, not as legendary, but as historical.   It must be remem-
bered that when we speak of 'legendary material,' we are speaking
from a modern point of view.   What we regard as 'legendary
material' the poet may have regarded as historic fact.

[53] *Publ. Mod. Lang. Assoc.* 19. 124.

[54] Cf. *Summa Theolog.,* Pars 3, Quæst. 52.   This legend is based
upon the following biblical texts: Psalms (Vulg.) xxiii. 7, 9;
Zachariah 9. 11; Acts 2. 24; Philippians 2. 10; Colossians 2. 15.

[55] Cf. *Summa Theolog.,* Pars 3 (Supp.), Quæst. 69, Artls. 4-7.
This legend is based on I Peter 3. 18-20.

[56] Cf. note on 291.

of *Pearl* towards religious matters, Brown gives several
further reasons for his belief that the attitude of that writer
was 'evangelical rather than ecclesiastical.' 'Holy Church,'
he tells us, 'is not once mentioned, nor the benefits to be
gained from the prayers and merits of the saints;'[57] and he
goes on to say that still more significant than the poet's
silence about Holy Church and the saints, is his disregard
of patristic authority and tradition. All these observations
of Brown are in large measure true, but they are almost
equally true of *Erkenwald* as well. In that poem there are
no references to 'Holy Church,' no mention of patristic
writers, nor appeals to their authority.[58]

It can be seen, I think, that as regards the manner in
which traditional material is employed, there is no difference
between *Erkenwald* and the four poems of the *Pearl*-poet.
In the absence of reference to the authority of theologians,
homilists, and patristic writers the five poems are also alike;
and, furthermore, all five are animated by the same deep
religious faith and feeling. Moreover, in the light of the

---

[57] *Publ. Mod. Lang. Assoc.* 19. 140. Mention of the merits of
prayers to the saints and the miracles performed by them is indeed
very rare in the poems of the Cotton MS., but Brown is in error when
he says that the poems make no mention of the benefits to be derived
from saintly intercession. The author of *Pearl* (383-4) distinctly
acknowledges his dependence upon them:

> Bot Crystes mersy & Mary & Jon,—
> Þise arn þe grounde of alle my blysse.

Cf. also *Gawain* 753-762, where Sir Gawain beseeches aid of Christ
and the Virgin.

[58] While *Erkenwald* is to be classed as a saint's legend, it is quite
free from many of the conventional characteristics of that literary
type. It is concerned with the performance of a single miracle, and
makes no attempt to recount the whole course of the saint's life and
his numerous miracles. It gives no catalogue of cures wrought by his
relics. It has no final invocation or address, as many of the legends
have, nor any conventional benediction. The interest of the author
seems rather to be centred on the theological problem raised in the
poem, than on the excellences and merits of St. Erkenwald.

views which Fletcher has advanced regarding the allegorical
character of *Pearl,* it is no longer possible, I think, to regard
its author as any other than an orthodox son of the Church.[59]

A further consequence of the acceptance of Fletcher's
views is that distinctions as to the poet's orthodoxy, or lack
of it, that are based upon the amount of apocryphal material
he uses, or the presence or absence of references to theological writers, are not of great value. In the matter of
religious belief, then, there appears to be nothing to hinder
us from regarding the poet of *Erkenwald* and the poet of
Pearl as one and the same person. Whoever he was, he
appears to have been a devout Catholic, who accepted without
question the body of dogma which the Church laid down
for the faithful, and felt no wish to stray beyond the limits
of her doctrine and liturgy.

But it would be a mistake to conclude that because our
poet's opinions were orthodox and conservative, he was therefore a gloomy bigot. Such the poet of *Pearl* and *Gawain*
could not have been. His poem forbids us to think of him
as any other than a man of quick and warm human sympa-
thies. 'His theological utterance is of a kind proceeding
rather from a personal than a professional impulse.'[60] In
telling his story he has been influenced more by the lines
which I think that he wrote

> Hit is a dom þat neuer God gaue,
> Þat euer þe gyltleȝ schulde be schente,[61]

than by a desire to glorify a saint. For the legend reopens
a case that had formerly been decided adversely. Theologians before the time of Aquinas had been fairly well agreed
that the lot of those who did not hold the faith was eternal
damnation. Against this dark background of ecclesiastical

[59] *Jour. Engl. and Germ. Phil.* 20. 17-8.
[60] Osgood, *Pearl,* p. li.
[61] *Pearl* 667-8.

opinion the poet's warm and ready sympathy for struggling humanity shines out the more brightly. His reaction, as Osgood has said, is nearly always personal; and thus it comes about that he feels more for the poor dumb beasts and the innocent women and children of Nineveh than for the prophet of God, more for the little girl who had gone to dwell in heaven than for the angelic orders therein, more for the pagan judge than for the saintly bishop of 'love London toun.'

DATE

I

It is impossible to fix an exact date for the poem. While the evidence to be gained from a study of the style and language indicates that it was written during the latter half of the fourteenth century, the poem itself yields no clue as to the exact time at which it was composed. It seems safe, however, to believe that it could not have been written much before 1386, the year in which Robert de Braybroke, Bishop of London, issued a pastoral letter establishing the two commemorative days of Saint Erkenwald as feast-days of the first class.[1] In this document the bishop deplored the neglect into which the days of the Conversion and Commemoration of St. Paul, and those of the Deposition (April 30th) and Translation (November 14th) of Saint Erkenwald had been allowed to fall, and ordered that they should thereafter be kept as feasts of the first class by the clergy and laity of his diocese. To those observing them in a fitting and solemn manner, 'vere pænitentibus, contritis, et confessis,' he granted an indulgence of forty days.[2] In

[1] Knigge (*Die Sprache,* pp. 9-10) first suggested the connection between the poem and the events of the year 1386.
[2] The bishop's *Monitio* is quoted in Wilkins' *Concilia* (3. 196-7). Two points in it are worthy of notice: (1) the two days commem-

view of these facts, it is reasonable to suppose that the author of the legend wrote his poem with the same end in view as that of the bishop—the promotion of a deeper respect for the memory and merits of one of the early bishops of London.

It is almost unnecessary to remark, however, that this historic event is, after all, valuable only as circumstantial evidence for the dating of the poem, and that it in no way fixes a definite time of composition. It is possible that the legend might have been written some two or three years earlier than the date of the episcopal letter, or the events which resulted from its publication. It may have been composed with the idea of aiding Bishop Braybroke's efforts to arouse in London a warmer devotion to the great patron of the metropolis. In such an event, it could hardly have been written a very long time before 1386. Yet in view of the fact that the bishop complained of a lack of veneration for the days consecrated to the saint, it would seem more probable that the poem was not written before 1386. For if it is in any way to be connected with the revival of interest in the cultus of St. Erkenwald, it was more likely to have been written at a time when the tide of popular devotion was running at the full, than at a time when it had reached its lowest ebb. If such an assumption seem reasonable, it would be safe to assign the composition of the poem to 1386, or to a year not very much later than that date.

orative of St. Erkenwald are to be kept with as much solemnity as those in honor of St. Paul, the patron-saint of the cathedral; (2) those days are to be kept sacred in the future. I append that part of the document which illustrates these two points:

> De consilio et assensu decani et capituli dictæ nostræ cathe-dralis ecclesiæ, festa conversionis et commemorationis ipsius apostoli; necnon etiam dies depositionis et translationis sancti Erkenwaldi supradicti, cum veneratione et solennitate debitis, sicut sacrum diem dominicum, ab universis christicolis nostrarum civitatis et diœcesis decrevimus de cætero celebrandas.

II

The assumption that the legend was composed ca. 1386 would in no way conflict with the belief that it might have been written by the *Gawain*-poet;[3] for the very earliest date suggested for the beginning of the literary career of that gifted artist is one at the middle of the century, and most scholars are of the opinion that his literary activity covers the forty years between 1360-1400.[4] Knigge and Gollancz, the only critics who have discussed at any length the question of the date of the saint's legend, although they differ as to its place in a sequence of the works of the *Gawain*-poet, are agreed in their belief that it was one of his latest. Knigge, adopting the views of Miss Thomas as to the chronological order of the works of the *Gawain*-poet, believes it to have been the last that issued from his pen.[5] In his latest edition of *Pearl* (1921), Gollancz seemed inclined to agree with the German scholar that the saint's legend came after the four other poems, though he differed from his views on the question of their chronological order.[6] In his edition of

[3] The problem of authorship is discussed in the preceding section.

[4] Bateson (*Pat.*, p. xxx) would assign *Gawain* to the middle of the fourteenth century, on the basis of the descriptions of costumes found therein, unless 'the author was now withdrawn from the world, and was describing habits which had just passed out of date' (p. xxxi).

[5] *Die Sprache*, p. 10. According to Miss Thomas (*Sir Gawayne and the Green Knight*, Zürich, 1883, p. 33) the chronological order of the poems is: '*Pearl* before *Gawain; Gawain* c. 1375-7:—*Cleanness* 1378-80, and *Patience* after *Cleanness*.' Brandl (*Grundriss der Germ. Phil.*, 1st ed. 2. 661-3) agrees with this view, though he adds to the four poems ascribed to the *Gawain*-poet *Erkenwald* as his final work.

[6] Cf. *Pearl*, p. xl: 'From among all these poems only one can be singled out as being possibly by the author of "Pearl." On the strength of diction, metre, and other characteristics, the anonymous alliterative poem of "Erkenwald," though it lacks the peculiar intensity of "Cleanness" and "Patience," may be an early or very late work, unless we have here an imitation by an enthusiastic disciple.'

the present poem, however, he contented himself with the
mere statement that the poem was 'not earlier than the
companion poems, *Cleanness* and *Patience*.'[7]

To the present editor the poem appears to be more closely
linked with *Pearl* and *Gawain* than with the two homilies.[8]
Its story, which treats of a theological problem already discussed in *Pearl,* would seem to link it with the elegy;[9] while

Cf. also p. xlv: 'If, late in life, he wrote the poem on "Erkenwald,"
the great Bishop of London, whose magnificent shrine was the glory
of St. Paul's Cathedral, and whose festival Bishop Braybroke
re-established in the year 1386, it would seem that the poet may have
found occupation in the City of London, in some secular office,
allowing him leisure for poetry or theology or philosophy, or other
intellectual exercise.' Gollancz's views as to the date and chronological order of the four poems of the *Gawain*-poet are to be found on
p. xxxvi of his latest edition of *Pearl.*

[7] P. lvii.

[8] The connection between *Erkenwald* and these two poems as
regards theme (a theological question) and form (a narrative which
teaches by implication rather than by homiletical exhortation) seems
to support the views of Osgood (*Pearl*, pp. xlix-l), Bateson (*Pat.,*
pp. xi-xxii), and Menner (*Pur.,* pp. xxvii-xxxviii), all of whom
place *Pearl* and *Gawain* after the homiletical poems. To Gollancz
(*St. Erk.,* p. lvi) the present poem, 'in its plan, its vocabulary, its
general style and method, and its quatrain arrangement, recalls
Cleanness and *Patience*.' He is correct as regards the matter of
quatrain-arrangement, which he was the first to adopt. In the absence
of other evidence, the probability of quatrain-arrangement is a
valuable help in the dating of the poem. As for the matter of plan,
the plan of the legend—narrative pure and simple, not written for
the inculcation of any particular virtue—seems to recall *Gawain*
rather than the homilies. The test of vocabulary is no sure one on
which to base such decisions. The poems probably do not differ
widely enough from one another for us to come to any very decided
conclusions on this point. Gollancz calls attention in a note to the
word *norne,* which occurs three times in *Cleanness* and four times in
Gawain. This is the only test of vocabulary that he gives.

[9] Ll. 673-684 of *Pearl* declare that two classes of people shall be
saved: (1) the righteous and (2) the innocent. In the elegiac poem,
the salvation of the innocent is chiefly discussed. A particular class

the skill displayed in the conduct of the narrative, and the literary finish of its execution, remind the reader strongly of the 'jewel of English mediævalism,' *Sir Gawain and the Green Knight*.[10] So keen is its author's interest in the great problems of human frailty and error, of human aspiration and effort, so mature and developed is his style, that one seems forced to the conclusion that the legend is nearer in point of time to *Pearl* and *Gawain* than to *Patience* and *Purity*. If such be the case, it is to be assigned to the end, rather than to the beginning, of the literary career of the *Gawain*-poet.

of innocent persons receives the poet's attention—little children, who, though baptized, have been unable to perform good works because of an early death. In the legend, the question under discussion is the salvation of a righteous man who has never been baptized. It is important to note that in both poems the discussion is based upon verses 3 and 4 of Psalm xxiii (Vulgate).

[10] I cannot agree with the statement of Gollancz (*St. Erk.*, p. lx) that the poem seems 'to be the work of a hand that was losing its cunning.'

ST. ERKENWALD

TEXT

ABBREVIATIONS

F. = J. Fischer, *Bonner Beiträge zur Anglistik* 11. 64.

G. = Gollancz, edition of 1922 (for full titles, see Bibliography).

H. = Horstmann, *Altenglische Legenden*, Neue Folge, pp. 265-274.

Holt. = Holthausen, *Anglia Beiblatt* 34. 17-8.

K. = Knigge, p. 63.

NED. = *New English Dictionary* (s. v. *sperel*).

S. = Schumacher, pp. 87-8, 184.

T. = Trautmann, *Anglia Anzeiger* 5. 24.

DE ERKENWALDO

At London in Englonde noȝt fulle longe sythen
Sythen Crist suffride on crosse, and Cristendome stablyde,
Ther was a byschop in þat burghe, blessyd and sacryd:
Saynt Erkenwolde, as I hope, þat holy mon hatte.

In his tyme in þat toun þe temple aldergrattyst　　　　5
Was drawen doun þat one dole to dedifie new,
For hit hethen had bene in Hengyst dawes,
Þat þe Saxones unsaȝt haden sende hyder.

Þai bete oute þe Bretons, and broȝt hom into Wales,　　9
And pervertyd alle þe pepul þat in þat place dwellide.
Þen wos this reame renaide mony ronke ȝeres,
Til Saynt Austyn into Sandewiche was sende fro þe pope.

Þen prechyd he here þe pure faythe and plantyd þe trouthe,　13
And convertyd alle þe communnates to Cristendame newe;
He turnyd temples þat tyme þat temyd to þe develle,
And clansyd hom in Cristes nome, and kyrkes hom callid.

He hurlyd owt hor ydols, and hade hym in sayntes,　　　17
And chaungit chevely hor nomes, and chargit hom better:
Þat ere was of Appolyn is now of Saynt Petre;
Mahon to Saynt Margrete oþer to Maudelayne.

Þe Synagoge of þe Sonne was sett to oure Lady;　　　　21
Jubiter and Jono to Jhesu oþer to James;
So he hom dedifiet, and dyght alle to dere halowes,
Þat ere wos sett of Sathanas in Saxones tyme.

---

1 *At:* with large rubricated initial letter: MS. *sythen;* H. sythen*e*; G. (*tyme*).—13 MS. *þen*, but with *e* added above the line.—14 MS., H. *cri*st*en*dame; G. reads as *cri*st*en*d*e*rame, and emends to Cristendame.—15 A horizontal line below *m* of *tem*yd.—23 MS. *hom;* H. home*; G. note (?)'omit "hom."'—24 MS., H. *sett;* G. note (?)*sete.*

Now þat London is nevenyd hatte þe New Troie;   25
Þe metropol and þe mayster-toun hit evermore has bene.
Þe mecul mynster þerinne a maghty devel aght,
And þe title of þe temple bitan was his name;

For he was dryghtyn derrest of ydols praysid,   29
And þe solempnest of his sacrifices in Saxon londes;
Þe thrid temple hit wos tolde of Triapolitanes;
By alle Bretaynes bonkes were bot othire twayne.

(I)

Now of þis Augustynes art is Erkenwolde bischop   33
At love London toun, and the laghe teches;
Syttes semely in þe sege of Saynt Paule mynster,
Þat was þe temple Triapolitan, as I tolde are.

Þen was hit abatyd and beten doun, and buggyd efte new,   37
A noble note for þe nones, and New Werke hit hatte.
Mony a mery mason was made þer to wyrke,
Harde stones for to hewe with eggit toles;

Mony grubber in grete þe grounde for to seche,   41
Þat þe fundement on fyrst shuld þe fote halde;
And as þai m(u)kkyde and mynyde, a mervayle þai founden,
As ȝet in crafty cronecles is kydde þe memorie.

For as þai dyȝt and dalfe so depe into þe erthe,   45
Þai founden fourmyt on a flore a ferly faire toumbe;

25 Above *a* of *hatte* an Arabic 1; below the word a horizontal line; on
the left margin the gloss reads 'was called.'—29 Above first *y* of *dryghtyn*
an Arabic 2; on the left margin 'L, master' appears.—30 MS. *saxon;*
H. Saxon*e;* G. *Saxon;* G. note (?)*Saxone.*—34 MS. H., G. *loue;* G. note
(?)*l(e)ue;* Holt. suggests *lēue.*—35 First *e* of *semely* obscured by blot,
but still legible.—37 Above *u* of *buggyd* an Arabic 3; on the left margin
the gloss reads 'builded.'—43 MS. *makkyde;* H. makkyd*e;* G.
m(u)kkyd*e.*—45 MS., H. *dyȝt;* G. note suggests *deghit,* 'digged': *to* of
into written above line.—46 Above *e* of *ferly* an Arabic 2; on the left
margin the gloss reads 'wonderful.'

Hit was a throghe of thykke ston, thryvandly hewen,
With gargeles garnysht aboute, alle of gray marbre.

Thre sperle(s) of þe spelunke þat sparde hit olofte   49
Was metely made of þe marbre and menskefully planede,
And þe bordure enbelicit with bryȝt golde lettres;
Bot roynyshe were þe resones þat þer on row stoden.

Fulle verray were þe vigures, þer avisyde hom mony;   53
Bot alle muset hit to mouthe: and quat hit mene shulde,
Mony clerke(s) in þat clos, with crownes ful brode,
Þer besiet hom aboute noȝt, to brynge hom in wordes.

Quen tithynges token to þe toun of þe toumbe-wonder,   57
Mony hundrid hende men highide þider sone.
Burgeys boghit þerto, bedels ande othire,
And mony a mesters-mon of maners dyverse.

Laddes laften hor werke and lepen þiderwardes,   61
Ronnen radly in route with ryngande noyce;
Þer commen þider of alle-kynnes so kenely mony,
Þat as alle þe worlde were þider walon within a hondequile.

Quen þe maire with his meynye þat mervaile aspied,   65
By assent of þe sextene, þe sayntuare þai kepten;

47 Above *n* of *thryvandly* an Arabic 4; on the left margin opposite 48, I distinguish this much of the gloss: 'artificialy = e'; four (or five) blurred letters follow 'e.'—49 MS., H. *Thre;* G. *The:* MS. *sperle* (or *spert*(?)), the last letter of the word has a horizontal stroke that indicates either final *e* or the cross stroke of *t;* H. sperl*is;* H. note *spertis*(?); G. spe(k)*e:* MS., H., G. *spradde;* NED. *sparde*(?): the last three letters of *sperle* are underlined; on left margin two words with = between them, one has seven letters, the fourth being 'e'; the other five(?) letters, the first looking like 'L,' and the second being 'r.'—52 A horizontal line below *n, y, s, h* of *roynyshe.*—55 MS., G. *clerke;* H. erroneously clerk*e;* H. note clerk*is*?; F. *clerkes.*—61 Above *þ* and second *e* of *lepen* Arabic 1; the gloss on the right margin reads 'ran.'

Bede unlouke þe lidde, and lay hit byside;
Þai wolde loke on þat lome quat lengyd withinne.

Wyȝt werkemen with þat wenten þertille;   69
Putten prises þerto; pinchid one-under;
Kaghten by þe corners with crowes of yrne;
And were þe lydde never so large, þai laide hit by sone.

Bot þen wos wonder to wale on wehes þat stoden,   73
That myȝt not come to knowe a quontyse strange;
So was þe glode within gay, al with golde payntyde,
And a blisfulle body opon þe bothum lyggid,

Araide on a riche wise in rialle wedes: 77
Al with glisnande golde his gowne wos hemmyd,
With mony a precious perle picchit þeron,
And a gurdille of golde bigripide his mydelle;

A meche mantel on lofte with menyver furrit,   81
Þe clothe of camelyn ful clene, with cumly bordures;
And on his coyfe wos kest a coron ful riche,
And a semely septure sett in his honde.

Als wemles were his wedes, withouten any tecche,   85
Oþer of moulynge, oþer of motes, oþir moght-freten,

67 MS. *unlouke: u* added above the line.—68 Opposite this line on the
right margin of the MS. is a sentence of five words written in a mediæval
script; the second looks like 'est'; the third is 'mea'; the fourth looks
like 'boni'; the initial letter of the first word is a large ornamental 'I';
this letter, with its flourishes at top and base, extends from 61 to 70.—
69 Above *y* of *wyȝt* an Arabic 2; on the right margin the gloss reads
'skilful.'—70 MS., H., G. *prises;* F. *prikes* 'brecheisen.'—72 *lydde* blotted and
written out on left margin by same hand.—74 MS., H. *to to knowe;* G. *to
to-knowe;* F. *for to knowe.*—76 MS., H. *bothum;* G. *both(um).*—82 MS.
originally had *glene* for *clene,* but *g* has been crossed out and *c* written
above by the same hand.—85 MS., G. *tecche;* the first *c* resembles an *i,*
hence H. reads *teiche:* opposite 82, 83, 84, 85 on the right margin of the
MS. some words in a mediæval script that are indistinguishable; the
writing begins opposite 85, and is canted diagonally upward from that line.

And als bry3t of hor blee in blysnande hewes,
As þai hade 3epely in þat 3orde bene 3isturday shapen;
And als freshe hym þe face and the fleshe nakyde,   89
Bi his eres and bi his hondes þat openly shewid
With ronke rode as þe rose, and two rede lippes,
As he in sounde sodanly were slippide opon slepe.

Þer was spedeles space to spyr uch on oþer   93
Quat body hit my3t be þat buried wos ther;
How longe had he þer layne, his lere so unchaungit,
And al his wede unwemmyd;—þus ylka weghe askyd:

'Hit my3t not be bot suche a mon in my(n)de stode longe;   97
He has ben kynge of þis kithe, as couthely hit semes
He lyes dolven þus depe; hit is a derfe wonder
Bot summe segge couthe say þat he hym sene hade.'

Bot þat ilke note wos noght, for nourne none couthe,   101
Noþer by title, ne token, ne by tale noþer,
Þat ever wos brevyt in burghe, ne in bok(e) notyde,
Þat ever mynnyd suche a mo(n), more ne lasse.

Þe bodeworde to þe byschop was broght on a quile,   105
Of þat buriede body al þe bolde wonder;

88 Above *þ* of *3epely* an Arabic 3 (2 over the second *e* has been erased);
on the right margin the gloss reads '(finely) skilfully': MS., H., G.
3orde; Holt. suggests *3erde.*—89 MS. hym; H. hyn (= in); G. hym.—
93 MS., H., G. *space;* F. *speche:* above *y* of *spyr* an Arabic 2; on the
right margin the gloss reads 'ask': MS. *uschon;* H. *vsch* one; K. *vch;*
G. *vschon;* Holt. suggests *uchon.*—94 After *hit* the word *hade* appears in
the MS. with two lines of erasure drawn through it.—95 Above first *e* of
lere an Arabic 2; on the right margin the gloss reads 'cheek': opposite
95 the words 'we redyn in a boke' are followed by two illegible words.
Both legible and illegible words are written in a mediæval script.—97 MS.,
H. *myde;* G. my(n)de.—98 A horizontal line below kithe.—99 A horizontal
line below *derfe.*—103 MS., H. Þat euer wos; G. Þat wos: MS., H. burghe;
G. b(rut): MS. boko; H., G. bok(e); H. note bokis(?).—104 MS. more
more; H. mone more; G. mo(n) more; a plain case of dittography.

Þe primate with his prelacie was partyd fro home;
In Esex was Ser Erkenwolde, an abbay to visite.

Tulkes tolden hym þe tale with troubulle in þe pepul;   109
And suche a cry aboute a cors crakit evermore,
The bischop sende hit to blynne by bedels and lettres,
Ande buskyd þiderwarde bytyme on his blonke after.

By þat he come to þe kyrke kydde of Saynt Paule,   113
Mony hym metten on þat meere, þe mervayle to telle;
He passyd into his palais and pes he comaundit,
And devoydit fro þe dede and ditte þe durre after.

Þe derke nyȝt overdrofe, and day-belle ronge;   117
And Ser Erkenwolde was up in þe ughten ere þen,
Þat welneghe al þe nyȝt hade na(i)tyd his houres,
To biseche his Soverayn, of his swete grace,
To vouche-safe to revele hym hit by avis(i)on or elles: 121

'Þaghe I be unworthi,' al wepande he sayde,
Thurghe his deere debonerte, 'digne hit, my Lorde,
In confirmynge þi Cristen faithe, fulsen me to kenne
Þe mysterie of þis mervaile þat men opon wondres.'   125

And so longe he grette after grace, þat he graunte hade,
An ansuare of þe Holy Goste, and afterwarde hit dawid.

109 MS., H. *wt;* G. (*&* þe).—111 MS., H., G. *to blynne by bedels;* F. *to blynne bedels.*—116 MS., H. *dede;* G. *d(outh)e:* above *i* of *ditte* an Arabic 1; on the left margin the gloss 'shutte.'—117 MS. ou*er drofe;* G. ou*er*-drofe; H. has mistaken the curl of the stroke designating -*er* abbreviation for the flourish that is merely scribal, and reads on*e* drofe.—119 MS., H. welnegh*e;* G. wel negh*e:* MS. *nattyd;* H.. G. *na(i)tyd:* a horizontal line below -*tyd* of *nattyd.*—121 MS. *a vison;* H. a vis(i)on*e;* G. *a-vis(i)on.*—123 MS., H. *his;* G. (þi).—124 Above *e* of *fulsen* an Arabic 2; on left margin a gloss reads 'help Fylstan,' the letters after *n* of 'Fylstan' I cannot decipher.—127 Below *i* of *dawid* a line; a gloss on the right margin reads 'it was day.'

Mynster-dores were makyd opon, quen matens were songen;
Þe byschop hym shope solemply to synge þe heghe masse.   129

Þe prelate in pontificals was prestly atyride;
Manerly with his ministres þe masse he begynnes
Of Spiritus Domini for his spede, on sutile wise,
With queme questis of þe quere, with ful quaynt notes.   133

Mony a gay grete lorde was gedrid to herken hit,
As þe rekenest of þe reame repairen þider ofte,
Tille cessyd was þe service, and sayde þe later ende;
Þen heldyt fro þe autere alle þe heghe gynge.   137

Þe prelate passide on þe playn—þer plied to hym lordes—
As riche revestid as he was, he rayked to þe toumbe.
Men unclosid hym þe cloyster with clustrede keies;
Bot pyne wos with þe grete prece þat passyd hym after.   141

The byschop come to þe burynes, him barones besyde;
Þe maire with mony maȝti men and macers before hym;
Þe dene of þe dere place devysit al on fyrst
Þe fyndynge of þat ferly, with fynger he mynte.   145

'Lo, lordes,' quoþ þat lede, 'suche a lyche here is,
Has layn loken here on loghe, how longe is unknawen;

128-9 *s* of *songen* obscured by smudge; second and third strokes of *m*
and first stroke of *a* of *masse* also obscured.—130 MS. *pontificals* with *fi*
added above the line.—139 A horizontal line under the last three letters of
rayked; above *y* of that word an Arabic 1; on the left margin the gloss
reads 'went'; opposite this line and 140 on the right margin some illegible
words appear in a mediæval script.—140 MS. *gloyster,* but *c* has been
written above the first letter of the word, apparently by the same hand.—
142 Over *u* of *burynes* an Arabic 3; on the left margin the gloss reads
'grave,' after which a comma and an indistinguishable word follow.—146
Here, as elsewhere, I have read the abbreviation as *quoþ,* not *quod:* above
c of *lyche* an Arabic 4; on the left margin the gloss read 'body.' On the
right margin, some indistinguishable letters in a mediæval script slant from
this line diagonally upwards and towards the right.

And ȝet his colour and his clothe has caȝt no defaute,
Ne his lire, ne þe lome þat he is layde inne.   149

Þer is no lede opon lyfe of so longe age
Þat may mene in his mynde þat suche a mon regnyd,
Ne noþer his nome ne his note nourne of one speche;
Queþer mony porer in þis place is putte into grave,   153
Þat merkid is in oure martilage his mynde for ever.

And we have oure librarie laitid þes longe seven dayes,
Bot one cronicle of þis kynge con we never fynde.
He has non layne here so longe, to loke hit by kynde,   157
To malte so out of memorie, bot mervayle hit were.'

'Þou says soþe,' quoþ þe segge þat sacrid was byschop,
'Hit is mervaile to men, þat mountes to litelle
Towarde þe providens of þe Prince þat Paradis weldes,   161
Quen hym luste to unlouke þe leste of his myȝtes.

Bot quen matyd is monnes myȝt, and his mynde passyde,
And al his resons are torent, and redeles he stondes,
Þen lettes hit hym ful litelle to louse wyt a fynger   165
Þat alle þe hondes under heven halde myȝt never.

—149 Above *m* of *lome* an Arabic 5; on the left margin the gloss is illegible.—150 On the right margin, midway between the end of the line and the margin of the MS., some illegible letters in a mediæval hand.—151 MS. *amon;* H. a mon*e;* G. *a mon.*—155 H. reads *laitid;* G. reads *lattid,* and emends to *la(i)tid.*—156 MS. *cronicle;* abbreviation for *ro* added above line makes a loop like that of *l, n* looks like *u,* hence H. reads *clucle, i* and *n* appearing almost merged; G. *cronicle;* F. *cluue* 'anhaltpunkt.'—161 *þ* has been crossed out before *þat:* above *d* of *weldes* an Arabic 6; the gloss on the left margin reads 'posseses.'—163 Below *matyd* a horizontal line; above the *a* of that word an Arabic 8; the gloss on the left margin reads 'frustrated'; below that word another gloss that I cannot decipher.—164 A horizontal line below the last five letters of *redeles;* above the second *e* an Arabic 7; on the left margin there is a gloss of two words, the first is 'without,' the second looks like 'counsel.'

Þere as creatures crafte of counselle oute swarves,
Þe comforthe of þe creatore byhoves þe cure take.

And so do we now oure dede, devyne we no fyrre; 169
To seche þe sothe at oureselfe, ȝee se þer no bote;
Bot glow we alle opon Godde, and his grace aske,
Þat careles is of counselle and comforthe to sende.

(Anande) þat, in fastynge of ȝour faithe and of fyne bileve, 173
I shal avay ȝow so verrayly of vertues his,
Þat ȝe may leve upon longe þat he is lord myȝty,
And fayne ȝour talent to fulfille, if ȝe hym frende leves.'

(II)

Then he turnes to þe toumbe and talkes to þe corce; 177
Lyftande up his eghe-lyddes, he loused suche wordes:
'Now, lykhame, þat þ(us) lies, layne þou no lenger!
Sythen Jhesus has juggit today his joy to be schewyde,

Be þou bone to his bode, I bydde in his behalve; 181
As he was bende on a beme, quen he his blode schedde,
As þou hit wost wyterly, and we hit wele leven,
Ansuare here to my sawe, councele no trouthe!

Sithen we wot not qwo þou art, witere us þiselwen, 185
In worlde quat weghe þou was, and quy þow þus ligges,

168 MS., H. cure; G. c(re at) ure.—171 A horizontal line below the last two letters of glow; on the right margin the gloss 'look' appears: MS., H. glow; T. glew; G. gl(e)w; Holt. suggests glew.—172 MS., H. &; G. (vs).—173 MS., H. &; G. (Anande).—177 Then; with large rubricated initial letter.—179 Above m of lykhame an Arabic 1; on the right margin the gloss reads 'body': MS., H. þou; G. þ(us): MS. has ne altered to no.—181 MS. bone: originally bode, but d has been crossed out and n written above it.—182 A horizontal line below n and d of bende.—184 to blurred in MS., but still to be deciphered. The blur which covers this word extends over certain letters in 185, 186, 187.—185 o and t of wot covered by the blur noted in footnote to 184: w of þiselwen blurred.—186 First part of w of weghe covered by blur: þow written above line in a different hand (G. Erk. p. 18).

How longe þou has layne here, and quat laghe þou usyt,
Queþer art þou joyned to joy oþer juggid to pyne.'

Quen þe segge hade þus sayde, and syked þerafter,   189
Þe bry3t body in þe burynes brayed a litelle,
And with a drery dreme he dryves owte wordes
Þurghe sum lant goste lyfe of hym þat al redes:

'Bisshop,' quoþ þis ilke body, 'þi bode is me dere,   193
I may not bot boghe to þi bone for bothe myn eghen;
Þe name þat þou nevenyd has and nournet me after
Al heven and helle heldes to, and erthe bitwene.

Fyrst to say the þe sothe quo myselfe were: 197
One þe unhapnest hathel þat ever on erthe 3ode,
Never kynge ne cayser ne 3et no kny3t nothyre,
Bot a lede of þe laghe þat þen þis londe usit.

I was committid and made a mayster-mon here,   201
To sytte upon sayd causes. Þis cite I 3emyd,
Under a prince of parage of paynymes laghe,
And uche segge þat him sewide þe same faythe trowid.

Þe lengthe of my lyinge here, þat is a lewid date;   205
Hit(is) to meche to any mon to make of a nombre:

187 *a* of *has* blurred.—190 M.S., H. *brayed;* G. *bray(þ)ed:* a horizontal line below the last two letters of *brayed.*—192 MS. su*m* lant goste lyfe; H. follows MS.; G. s(*um*) lyf(ly) goste lant; F. *goste of lyfe;* Holt. *lyf(es) goste:* a horizontal line below *t* of *lant:* S. *lyfe of þe lorde þat al redes.*—193 *þis* written above the line: MS., H., G. *boode.*—195 MS. to *þe;* H. *To þe;* G. *Þe.*—198 The last four letters of *hathel* underlined.—203 A horizontal line which starts above *þ* of *prince* extends to second *a* of *parage:* above second *a* of *parage* an Arabic 2; on the right margin the gloss reads 'parentage.'—205 MS., H. *lewid;* G. *l(app)id.*—206 MS. *hit to meche;* H. *Hit(is) to meche;* G. *Hit to m(ut)he:* h of *meche* is blurred: a long horizontal line over *o* and *m* of *nombre;* H. reads noumbre; G. *nombre;* cf. same word in 289.

After þat Brutus þis burghe had buggid on fyrste
Noȝt bot (aght) hundred ȝere þer aghtene wontyd—

Before þat kynned ȝour Criste by Cristen acou⸱ ⸱e   209
(Þre hundred) ȝere and þritty mo, and ȝet threnen aght,
I was (o)n heire of an oye(r) in þe New Troie,
In þe regne of þe riche kynge þat rewlit us þen,

The bolde Breton Ser Belyn—Ser Berynge was his brothire— 213
Mony one was þe busmare boden hom bitwene
For hor wrakeful werre, quil hor wrathe lastyd.
Þen was I juge here enjoynyd in gentil lawe.'

Quil he in spelunke þus spake, þer sprange in þe pepulle   217
In al þis worlde no worde, ne wakenyd no noice,
Bot al as stille as þe ston stoden and listonde,
With meche wonder forwrast, and wepid ful mony.

The bisshop biddes þat body: 'Biknowe þe cause,   221
Sithen þou was kidde for no kynge, quy þou þe croun weres.
Quy haldes þou so heghe in honde þe septre,
And hades no londe of lege men, ne life ne lym aghtes?'

'Dere ser,' quoþ þe dede body, 'devyse þe I thenke.   225
Al was hit never my wille þat wroght þus hit were;

207 Above the first *g* of *buggid* an Arabic 2; on the right margin the
gloss reads 'builded.'—208 *b* of *bot* has been altered from *f:* MS., H. *fife;*
S. *eighte;* G (*aght*).—209 Above *e* of *kynned* an Arabic 3; on the right
margin the gloss reads 'was born.'—210 MS., H. A. þousand*e;* G. (*Þre
hundred*).—211 MS. *an heire of anoye;* H. an*e* heire of anoye; G. (o)n
eir*e* of an oye(r) : a horizontal line below the first three letters of *anoye.*—
214 Above *m* of *busmare* an Arabic 4; on the right margin a gloss reads
'reproach.'—220 A horizontal line drawn below the third, fourth, and fifth
letters of *forwrast.*—222 MS. crou*n* or *cron,* if one regards the curl at
the end of the word as a mere flourish; as in many cases in this poem,
it is difficult here to distinguish between *u* and *n;* G. *cron;* H. incon-
sistently reads crou*n,* cf. his ton*e* (5), don*e* (6), ston*e* (219).

I wos deputate and domesmon under a duke noble,
And in my power þis place was putte altogeder.

I justifiet þis joly toun on gentil wise,   229
And ever in fourme of gode faithe, more þen fourty wynter.
Þe folke was felonse and fals, and frowarde to reule;
I hent harmes ful ofte to holde hom to riȝt.

Bot for wothe, ne wele, ne wrathe, ne drede,
Ne for maystrie, ne for mede, ne for no monnes aghe,
I remewit never fro þe riȝt, by reson myn awen,
For to dresse a wrange dome, no day of my lyve.

Declynet never my consciens, for covetise on erthe,   237
In no gynful jugement no japes to make,
Were a renke never so riche, for reverens sake,
Ne for no monnes manas, ne meschefe, ne routhe.

Non gete me fro þe heghe gate to glent out of ryȝt,   241
Als ferforthe as my faithe confourmyd my hert;
Þaghe had bene my fader bone, I bede hym no wranges,
Ne fals favour to my fader, þaghe felle hym be hongyt.

And for I was ryȝtwis and reken, and redy of þe laghe,   245
Quen I deghed, for dul denyed alle Troye;

227 On the left margin of the MS. opposite this line a mark like capital
C without its lower part; close behind it a large capital *Y* or Þ whose
blurred vertical stroke extends downwards in a diagonal direction to 229:
b of *noble* blurred.—229 Two thick strokes extend diagonally upwards from
the first word of this line towards the left extremity of the page.
Behind them, and canted slightly backward a large capital Y or Þ whose
upper portion is a little above 229, and whose lower portion a little below
230. This letter is nearer the left edge of the leaf than the one opposite
227.—231 On the left margin of the MS. some words written in a mediæval
script occupy the space between 231 and 235. I cannot decipher them.
MS. *felonse* or *felouse;* H. *felouse;* G. *felonse.*—233 *o* of *bot* blurred, but
still legible.—241 A horizontal line below the second, third, and fourth
letters of *glent.*—243 *e* of *wranges* slightly blurred.—244 *y* of *hongyt*
slightly blurred; only cross stroke of *t* visible.—245 A horizontal line below
e and *n* of *reken.*

Alle menyd my dethe, þe more and the lasse;
And þus to bounty my body þai buriet in golde;

Cladden me for þe curtest þat courte couthe þen holde,   249
In mantel for þe mekest and monlokest on benche;
Gurden me for þe governour and graythist of Troie;
Furrid me for þe fynest of faithe me withinne.

For þe honour of myn honeste of heghest enprise   253
Þai coronyd me þe kidde kynge of kene justises,
Þ(at) ever wos tronyd in Troye oþer trowid ever shulde;
And for I rewardid ever riȝt, þai raght me the septre.'

Þe bisshop baythes hym ȝet, with bale at his hert,   257
Þaghe men menskid him so, how hit myȝt worthe
Þat his clothes were so clene: 'In cloutes, me thynkes,
Hom burde have rotid and bene rent in rattes longe sythen.

Þi body may be enbawmyd, hit bashis me noght   261
Þat hit thar ryve ne rote ne no ronke wormes;
Bot þi coloure ne þi clothe, I know in no wise
How hit myȝt lye by monnes lore and last so longe.'

'Nay, bisshop,' quoþ þat body, 'enbawmyd wos I never,   265
Ne no monnes counselle my clothe has kepyd unwemmyd;
Bot þe riche Kynge of reson, þat riȝt ever alowes,
And loves al þe lawes lely þat longen to trouthe;

251 A horizontal line below *r, d, e, n,* of *gurden:* MS., H. þe *gouernour*
&; G. for *gouern*(ance þe).—252 MS. *me winne;* H. *me wt-inne;* G.
(þer) *withinne.*—254 Below *n* and final *e* of *bene* a horizontal line; over
final *e* an Arabic 1; a gloss on the right margin reads 'stout (stoute?).'—
255 MS. þ*er;* H. þ*at;* G. þ*(at):* MS., H. *wos;* G. *was:* MS., H., G.
trowid euer; F. *tronid be.*—258 A horizontal line below *r* and *t* of *worthe.*
A gloss of four words on the left margin whose first word looks like 'be';
a comma follows 'be,' and then the phrase 'coᴗ to pas.'—260 A horizontal
line below *tt* and final *-es* of *rattes.*—262 The third letter of *ryve* may be
read as *n;* H. *ryue;* G. *ryne:* MS. originally read *route,* but *u* has been
crossed out; H. believes that *fede* may be lacking before *no:* MS., H., G.
ne no; F. *be no.*

And moste he menskes men for mynnynge of riȝtes,   269
Þen for al þe meritorie medes þat men on molde usen;
And if renkes for riȝt þus me arayed has,
He has lant me to last þat loves ryȝt best.'

'Ȝea, bot say þou of þi saule,' þen sayd þe bisshop.   273
'Quere is ho stablid and stadde, if þou so streȝt wroghtes?
He þat rewardes uche a renke as he has riȝt servyd
Myȝt evel forgo the to gyfe of his grace summe brawnche;

For as he says in his sothe psalmyde writtes: 277
"Þe skilfulle and þe unskathely skelton ay to me."
Forþi say me of þi soule, in sele quere ho wonnes,
And of þe riche restorment þat raȝt hyr oure Lorde!'

Þen hummyd he þat þer lay, and his hedde waggyd,   281
And gefe a gronynge ful grete, and to Godde sayde:
'Maȝty Maker of men, thi myghtes are grete!
How myȝt þi mercy to me amounte any tyme?

Nas I a paynym unpreste, þat never thi plite knewe,   285
Ne þ(e) mesure of þi mercy, ne þi mecul vertue,
Bot ay a freke faitheles þat faylid þi laghes,
Þat ever þou, Lord, wos lovyd in? Allas, þe harde stoundes!

I was non of þe nombre þat þou with noy boghtes   289
With þe blode of thi body upon þe blo rode;
Quen þou herghedes helle-hole and hentes hom þeroute,
Þi loffynge, oute of Limbo, þou laftes me þer.

269 MS., G. *moste;* H. *more*: below first *e* and *n* of *menskes* a horizontal
line; above *m* an Arabic 2; on the left margin a gloss reads 'honours.'—
271 A horizontal line below the last three letters of *renkes*.—273 MS., H.
sayes; G. *say*.—275 A horizontal line below the last four letters of *renke*.—
278 A horizontal line below *o* and *n* of *skelton*.—286 MS., H. *þi;* G.
þ(e).—289 *o* of *nombre* has horizontal line above it.—291 A line drawn below
the last six letters of *herghedes*.—292 MS. *þi;* H. *Þi;* G. *Þ(e)*: MS., H.,
G. *loffynge;* Holt. suggests *leffynge*: MS. *ne;* H., G. *me*. I believe that the
scribe intended the stroke joining *n* and *e* to count as a third stroke.

And þer sittes my soule þat se may no fyrre,   293
Dwynande in þe derke dethe, þat dyȝt us oure fader,
Adam, oure alder, þat ete of þat appulle
Þat mony a plyȝtles pepul has poysned for ever.

Ȝe were entouchid with his tethe, and take in þe glotte,   297
Bot mendyd with a medecyn, ȝe are made for to lyvye:
Þat is fulloght in fonte, with faitheful bileve;
And þat han we myste alle merciles, myselfe and my soule.

Quat wan we with oure wele-dede þat wroghtyn ay riȝt,   301
Quen we are dampnyd dulfully into þe depe lake,
And exilid fro þat soper so, þat solempne fest,
Þer richely hit arne refetyd þat after right hungride?

My soule may sitte þer in sorow and sike ful colde,   305
Dy(m)ly in þat derke dethe, þer dawes never morowen,
Hungrie inwith helle-hole, and herken after meeles,
Longe er ho þat soper se, oþer segge hyr to lathe.'

Þus dulfully þis dede body devisyt hit sorowe,   309
Þat alle wepyd for woo, þe wordes þat herden;
And þe bysshop balefully bere doun his eghen,
Þat hade no space to speke, so spakly he ȝoskyd,

---

293 The second letter of the word *soule* is very much blurred, but it is still legible: *ne* is very much smudged; I believe the scribe corrected *ne* to *no*; H. *no*; G. *n(o)*.—295 Second *a* of *adam* written above *m*.—297 MS., H. *tethe*; G. *te(c)he*: MS., H. *take*; G. *t(o)ke*: MS., H. *glotte*; H. note *glette*(?); G. *gl(e)tte*: a horizontal line below the last three letters of *glotte*.—298 First stroke of *m* of *medecyn* blurred.—300 *e* of *we* almost illegible.—302 *e* of *þe* written directly over the first letter of that word because of blot after *þ*: *d* of *depe* covered by a blot.—303 MS., H. *exilid*; G. *exiled*.—306 Ms. *dynly*; H. *Dymly*; G. *Dy(m)ly*.—307 MS. *hungrie*; G. *Hungrie*; H. misreads as *Hungre*.—308 A horizontal line below the last three letters of *lathe*; above *e* an Arabic 2; on the right margin a gloss reads 'invite.'—311 *h* and *o* of *bysshop* covered by a blot; *h*, however, legible.—312 A short pen-stroke below *a* and *k* of *spakly*.

Til he toke hym a tome, and to þe toumbe lokyd,   313
To þe liche þer hit lay, with lavande teres:
'Oure Lord lene,' quoþ þat lede, 'þat þou lyfe hades,
By Goddes leve, as longe as I my3t lacche water,

And cast upon þi faire cors, and carpe þes wordes: 317
"I folwe þe in þe Fader nome and his fre Childes
And of þe gracious Holy Goste";—and not one grue lenger.
Þen þof þou droppyd doun dede, hit daungerde me lasse.'

With þat worde þat he warpyd, þe wete of eghen   321
And teres trillyd adoun, and on þe toumbe lighten;
And one felle on his face, and þe freke syked.
Þen sayd he with a sadde soun: 'Oure Savyoure be lovyd!

Now herid be þou, heghe God, and þi hende Moder,   325
And blissid be þat blisful houre þat ho the bere in!
And also be þou, bysshop, þe bote of my sorowe,
And þe relefe of þe lodely lures þat my soule has levyd in!

For þe wordes þat þou werpe, and þe water þat þou sheddes, 329
Þe bry3t bourne of þin eghen, my bapteme is worthyn;
Þe fyrst slent þat on me slode slekkyd al my tene;
Ry3t now to soper my soule is sette at þe table.

For with þe wordes and þe water þat weshe us of payne   333
Li3tly lasshit þer a leme loghe in þe abyme,
Þat spakly sprent my spyrit with unsparid murthe
Into þe cenacle solemply þer soupen alle trew;

---

313 A horizontal line below *o* and *m* of *tome.*—316 H. expands as *goddis:*
below the last four words of *lacche* a horizontal line; on the right margin
a gloss reads 'take.'—319 H. 'grue ? Ms. undeutlich'; but the word is
clearly legible.—321 MS. *þe wete of eghen;* H. þe wete of eghen*e;* G. *(of
his) wete eghen.*—322 MS., H. *& teres;* G. *(Þe) teres.*—328 A horizontal
line below the last three letters of *lodely* and all five letters of *lures.*—
329 MS., H., G. *werþe;* Holt. suggests *worþe* (?).—330 A short pen-stroke
below *bourne;* on the right margin the gloss reads 'fountain, water.'—331
A horizontal line below the last three letters of *slent.*—334 A short stroke
over *h* of *loghe;* MS., H. *loghe;* G. reads loghee and emends to *loghe.*

And þer a marcialle hyr mette with menske aldergrattest,   337
And with reverence a rowme he raȝt hyr for ever.
I heere þerof my heghe God, and also þe, bysshop,
Fro bale has broȝt us to blis, blessid þou worthe!'

Wyt this cessyd his sowne, sayd he no more;   341
Bot sodenly his swete chere swyndid and faylide,
And alle the blee of his body wos blakke as þe moldes,
As roten as þe rottok þat rises in powdere.

For as sone as þe soule was sesyd in blisse,   345
Corrupt was þat oþer crafte þat covert þe bones;
For þe ay-lastande life, þat lethe shalle never,
Devoydes uche a vayneglorie, þat vayles so litelle.

Þen wos lovynge oure Lorde with loves uphalden;   349
Meche mournynge and myrthe was mellyd togeder;
Þai passyd forthe in procession, and alle þe pepulle folowid,
And alle þe belles in þe burghe beryd at ones.

337 A horizontal line extending from below the first *e* of *menske* to the
g of ald*e*rgrattest.—339 A short pen-stroke below *ee* of *heere;* above those
two letters an Arabic 2; on the right margin a gloss reads 'praise.'—340
Holt. suggests the insertion of *þat* before *has*.—349 Holt. suggests the insertion of *of* after *lovynge*.

NOTES

1-2. In reality St. Erkenwald was not consecrated Bishop of London until 675 (or 676) A. D. (see *Dict. Chr. Biog.* 2. 177-9). The statement contained in these lines is one of several anachronisms to be found in the poem. Other instances occur at 38, 65.

3. byschop . . . burghe. A common alliterative expression: 'þat was a bisshop of the burghe,' *Dest. of Troy* 4491; 'þat was þe bischop in þat burȝe,' *Wars of Alex.* (Ashmole MS.). 1172.

5. For another instance of the application of the term to a Christian church, cf. *Richard the Redeless,* prol. 3-4:

> In a temple of the trinite the toune euen amyddis,
> That Cristis chirche is cleped amonge the comune peple.

5-6. The poet seems to imply that the 'temple aldergrattyst,' originally heathen, had been later dedicated to Christian worship, only to undergo a perversion at the hands of the pagan Saxons. In Augustine's episcopate this temple had been dedicated a second time to Christian worship, and consecrated to St. Paul (35). At the time that St. Erkenwald was bishop, part of the temple was being torn down to be replaced by a new structure (6). There are several sources whence the poet might have derived his knowledge regarding the attitude of the Church towards buildings formerly dedicated to heathen divinities. He might have read the account given in *Chron. Maj.* (1. 129) of the first conversion of Britain under King Lucius: 'Templa, quæ in honore plurimorum deorum fundata fuerant, uni Deo ejusdemqve sanctis dedicaverunt, diversisque ordinatorum cœtibus expleverunt.' He may, as G. believes, have known of Pope Gregory's letter to Mellitus concerning the heathen temples in England (*Eccl. Hist.* 1. 30). It is quite possible, however, that his knowledge was derived from common oral tradition.

6. Note the abrupt change from passive to active voice.

7. in Hengyst dawes. *Chron. Maj.* (1. 196) gives a vivid account of the overthrow of British Christianity by Hengist and his Saxons:

> Invadebant undique cives, quasi lupi oves, quas pastores deseruerunt; ecclesias et ecclesiastica omnia ad solum usque destruebant, sacerdotes juxta altaria trucidabant, sacras scripturas igne concremabant, super sanctorum martyrum sepulturas cumulos terræ congerebant; viri religiosi, qui ab hac clade evadere potuerunt, speluncas et terrarum concavitates, nemorosa

loca atque deserta, montium quoque et collium præruptα, cum
sanctorum reliquiis petierunt.

8. Unsaʒt. 'Warlike.'

11-12. Cf. *Chron. Maj.* I. 255:

Anno gratiæ DXCVI., qui est annus centesimus quadragesimus
septimus ex quo Horsus et Hengistus fratres venerunt in Britanniam ut eam sibi subjugarent, missus est servus Dei Augustinus
a beato Papa Gregorio in Britanniam ut barbaræ genti Anglorum
verbum Dei prædicaret; qui, pagana superstitione cœcati, totam
Christianitatem deleverant in illa parte insulæ quam habebant.

Sandewiche. Bede (*Eccl. Hist.* I. 25) and the historians who
follow him, including the author of the account in *Chron. Maj.*
(I. 255), give Thanet as Augustine's landing-place. Hughes, who
contributed a paper on 'The Landing-Place of St. Augustine' to
Mason's *The Mission of St. Augustine to England according to the
Original Documents* (Cambridge, 1897), pp. 209-234, believes that the
Roman missionaries landed at Richborough, an island in the Want-
some which separated Thanet from the mainland. Richborough is
distant from Sandwich only half a mile, as the crow flies. The poet,
therefore, was more correct than he perhaps knew, when he wrote
'Sandewiche' instead of 'Thanet.' In all probability, however, his
employment of one name instead of the other is to be ascribed, not so
much to a detailed knowledge of the Kentish coast, as to a desire
to preserve the proper alliteration of the line. Because of its inclu-
sion among the Cinque Ports, Sandwich was one of the chief ports
for the continent. In *Morte Arthure* (634-5) King Arthur's fleet
assembles at Sandwich:

Wythin sexten dayes hys fleet whas assemblede
At Sandwyche on þe see: saile when hym lykes.

14. communnates. 'Communities.' Several differing views as to
the precise meaning of the term *communitas* prevail; cf. Hudson,
Archaeological Journal 46, No. 184, pp. 318-9, and Mrs. J. R. Green,
Town Life in the Fifteenth Century 2. 368-9. The writer last named,
however, admits the probability of the word being used 'in a popular
sense, and sometimes with an air of obloquy or contempt, to describe
the general mass of citizens who had the right of meeting in common
assembly, as distinguished from the official class.' It is in this
popular sense that the word is here used. London first obtained legal
recognition as a commune in 1191 (cf. Stubbs, *Constitutional History
of England*, 6th ed. I. 455).

15. temyd. 'Belonged.' Cf. *Pat.* 316: 'Efte to trede on þy temple & teme to þy seluen,' and *Pur.* 9: 'Thay teen unto his temmple and temen to hymselven.'

18. chevely. 'Primarily, as a chief preliminary,' as G. paraphrases. Neither Morris (*Sir Gawayne and The Green Knight,* EETS. 4) nor Tolkien-Gordon (*Sir Gawain and the Green Knight* (Oxford, 1925)) have noted the occurrence of this meaning in *Gaw.* 883, 978, 1876.

chargit hom better. 'He filled them to better purpose,' i. e. with the Christian altar, the crucifix, and the images of the saints. It is possible, as G. suggests, that the poet may have here paraphrased a clause to be found in Geoffrey of Monmouth's account of the first conversion of Britain to Christianity (*Hist. Regum Brit.* 5. 1) : 'in meliorem usum vertens, ecclesiis fidelium permanere concessit.'

19. See section on *Sources* V (a).

20. See section on *Sources* V (b).

Mahon. This name, derived from OF. *Mahun,* a shortened form of *Mahomet,* was applied generally by mediæval Christians to denote any false god, under the notion that the false prophet was worshipped by his followers. Cf. *Dest. of Troy* 4311-2:

> The false goddes in fere fell to þe ground;
> Bothe Mawhownus & maumettes myrtild in peces.

Further evidence of the worship of Mahon in Britain is given in the *Chronicle* of Robert Mannyng of Brunne (Rolls Ser.) 5755-9:

> In hys tyme were temples olde,
> Eyght & twenty flamins men tolde,—
> Þe Latyn calleþ temple ˙'flamins,'—
> Somme of Mahoun, & somme of Appoll(i)ns,
> Somme of Dyane, somme & of Berit.

Chron. Maj. (3. 55) tells us that the papal legate, after the capture of Damietta by the Crusaders in 1219, 'de maxima mahomeria civitatis fecit ecclesiam in honorem Beatæ Virginis Mariæ et omnium Apostolorum, ad gloriam et exaltationem fidei Christianæ et Sanctæ Trinitatis.'

21. See section on *Sources* V (c).

22. See section on *Sources* V (d).

23. G. suggests the omission of *hom* from the text, construing the clause introduced by *þat* (24) as the direct object of the two verbs, *dedifiet* and *dyght.* If the clause in 24 be regarded as the direct object of both verbs, *hom* would be a redundant pronoun. But the poet's meaning is made clear, if, as my colleague, Professor Gerould, suggests, a comma be placed after *dedifiet.* In the line thus punctuated, *hom* is to be construed as the direct object of *dedifiet, alle* as the direct object of *dyght*, and the textual reading is preserved. Though it is possible to regard *alle* as an adverb meaning 'entirely, wholly,' I have construed it as an adjective, and the antecedent of *þat* in the following line.

24. sett of Sathanas. 'Established by (or for) Satan.' Cf. *Wars of Alex.* (Ashmole MS.) 1648-9:

> Þan gas he furth with his gingis to godis awen temple,
> Þat of sir Salamon þe sage sett was & foundid,

and *Pur.* 1449: 'Now is sette for to serve Satanas þe blake.' G. unnecessarily suggests *sete*, 'seat, see.'

25. New Troie. The alliterative poets were fond of referring to the legendary establishment of a British kingdom by Brutus, the Trojan exile. Cf. *Gaw.* 1-19; *Winner and Waster* 1-2. *Chron. Maj.* (1. 22) gives the following account of the founding of Troynovant:

> Affectavit Brutus civitatem ædificare. Affectum itaque suum exequens, circuivit totius patriæ situm, donec ad Themensem fluvium perveniens. . . . Condidit itaque civitatem ibidem, eamque Trojam novam vocavit.

For an account of the legendary establishment of the British kingdom by the Trojans, see G. Gordon, 'The Trojans in Britain': *Essays and Studies by Members of the Engl. Assoc.* 9. 9-30.

27-30. The 'maghty devel' referred to in these lines is probably to be identified with the Saxon god, Woden. Cf. the account of the Saxon divinities given by Hengist to Vortigern (*Chron. Maj.* 1. 189):

> Cumque tandem in præsentia regis essent constituti, quæsivit ab eis, quam fidem, quamque religionem patres eorum coluissent. Cui Hengistus, 'Deos patrios, scilicet, Saturnum, Jovem, atque cæteros qui mundum gubernant colimus, maxime autem Mercurium, quem lingua nostra Woden appellamus.'

28. title. G., regarding *title* as in the dative case, paraphrases: '"and his name was given to the title of the temple," i. e. bestowed as designation.'

30. solempnest of his sacrifices. Cf. *Pur.* 1447: 'In þe solempne sacrefyce þat goud savor hade,' and *Dest. of Troy* 2001-2:

> With knelyng & crie to þere kynd halowes,
> And with solempne sacrifice to seke þai awowet.

31. Triapolitanes. The form of the word is difficult of explanation, though it seems almost certainly to be derived from the Latin.

It is not to be found in *Promptorium Parvulorum*, the *Glossarium* of Du Cange, the *Lexicon* of Maigne D'Arnis, or the NED. G. believes it to be an erroneous formation for *tripolitans* in the sense of a trinity of metropolitan cities. This explanation of the meaning of the word is strengthened by the presence of *thrid* in the same line. Further evidence of the correctness of this suggestion, as far as the meaning of the term is concerned, is afforded by the following quotation from the fourteenth century *Eulogium Historiarum* (Rolls Ser.) 2. 41:

> Tripolitanam provinciam Græci ita nominant. Duplex est Tripolitana, una in Phœnice. . . . Alia est in Africa inter Pentapolim et Byzantium sita, a tribus magnis urbibus sic dicta.

It should be noted, however, that the occurrence of *Tripolitana* in the quotation above makes it possible that the word may be derived, not from *tripolitans,* as G. supposes, but from the adjective *tripolitanus.* The present form may be the result of misspelling on the part of author or scribe, or of faulty copying on the part of the scribe. Geoffrey of Monmouth's account of the Christianizing of Britain (*Hist. Regum Brit.* 4. 19), much more detailed than the accounts given by *Chron. Maj.* and *Flor. Hist.*, is quite evidently the source of the poet's statements about the three pagan temples:

> Ubi erant Flamines, Episcopos: ubi erant Archiflamines, Archiepiscopos posuerunt. Sedes autem Archiflaminum in tribus nobilioribus civitatibus fuerant, Londoniis videlicet, atque Eboraci, et in urbe Legionum, quam super Oscam fluvium in Glamorgantia veteres muri et ædificia sitam fuisse testantur.

33. art. G. paraphrases as 'discipline,' and takes the word to refer to the ecclesiastical usage of Rome as opposed to that of the Celtic Church. But as the poet has already told us that the Roman Catholic worship had been firmly established by Augustine in the southeastern portion of England (13), he would probably not think it necessary to assure us that Erkenwald adhered to that form of worship. It is more probable that the word is derived from Gaelic *aird, àrd* (Mod. Scottish *airt*), 'a point or quarter of the compass.' Cf. *Curs. Mund.* 2267-8:

> Þere were alle þe speches part
> Of dyuerse londes to dyuerse art.

EDD. (s. v. *art,* sb., 2) gives the wider meaning of 'locality, district' as a usage of the northern and western counties and Yorkshire. This translation of *art* is confirmed by the instructions as to the ecclesiastical organization of the English Church given by Pope Gregory the Great to Augustine (Bede, *Eccl. Hist.* I. 29) :

Et quia nova Anglorum ecclesia ad omnipotentis Dei gratiam, eodem Domino largiente et te laborante, perducta est, usum tibi pallii in ea ad sola missarum solennia agenda concedimus; ita ut per loca singula duodecim episcopos ordines, qui tuæ subjaceant ditioni, quatenus Londoniensis civitatis episcopus semper in posterum a synodo propria debeat consecrari, atque honoris pallium ab hac sancta et apostolica, cui, Deo auctore, deservio, sede percipiat. Ad Eboracam vero civitatem te volumus episcopum mittere, quem ipse judicaveris ordinare, ita duntaxat ut, si eadem civitas cum finitimis locis verbum Dei receperit, ipse quoque duodecim episcopos ordinet, et metropolitani honore perfruatur; quia ei quoque, si vita comes fuerit, pallium tribuere, Domino favente, disponimus, quem tamen tuæ fraternitatis volumus dispositioni subjacere; post obitum vero tuum ita episcopis, quos ordinaverit, præsit, ut Londoniensis episcopi nullo modo ditioni subjaceat.

Thus Erkenwald was one of the twelve bishops of the southern province (*Augustynes art*), who were to be ordained, according to the instructions of Pope Gregory, by the Archbishop of Canterbury.

34. love. The third letter of this word as it appears in MS. may be either *n* or *u* (= *v*). But as it is unlikely that the poet would describe the metropolis by the adjective *lone*, 'deserted, uninhabited,' *love* is the preferable reading. G. suggests two explanations of the present form: (1) the correct reading may be *loved*, 'famed, praised'; (2) the poet may have written *o* instead of *e* as the second letter of the word, in which case the form is identical in meaning with *leve* (OE. *lēof*), 'dear.' This suggestion is supported by the phrase 'leeve London,' quoted in EDD. from Richardson's *Borderer's Table-Book* (1846). The writing of *o* for *e*, whether purposive or by error, is found in *ʒorde* (88), and probably in *glow* (171); for the occurrence of forms with *o* where one might expect *e* in the works of the *Pearl*-poet, see Emerson, *Publ. Mod. Lang. Assoc.* 37. 56. Holthausen (*Angl. Beibl.* 34, 17) believes that this form is the result of the shifting of the accent of the OE. diphthong from the first to the second member, and cites Mod. Engl. *show, sow, four,* and *choose* as examples of that shifting. The last explanation is more satisfactory than any other, but Holthausen has failed to make it clear that the linguistic phenomenon that he has noted is to be attributed in this case solely to dialectal peculiarity. The first vowel of the word represents the West Midland development of OE. *ēo,* which in East

Midland and Northern became *e;* see Luick, *Hist. Gram.* § 357
(notes 1, 2) :

> Im westlichen Mittelland und im Süden (ausser Kent) wurde
> dagegen der *ö*-Laut, wenn auch vielleicht mit schwächerer
> Rundung, länger bewahrt. In der Schreibung wurde hier *eo*
> weitergeführt, dann unter Einfluss anglonormannischer Schreib-
> gewohnheiten mehr und mehr durch *o* und *ue*, zum Teil auch
> durch *u* ersetzt. So . . . *lōf, lūef, lūf* 'lieb.'

35. Cf. *Wars of Alex.* (Ashmole MS.) 548 : 'And syttand so in
hire sege was softly delyuerd.'

37. Cf. Mandeville, *Voiage and Travaile* (Cotton MS., ed. Halliwell, p. 95) : 'Jerusalem hathe often tyme ben destroyed, and the
Walles abated and beten doun and tombled in to the Vale.' For
evidence of the *Pearl*-poet's acquaintance with Mandeville's *Travels*,
see Menner, *Pur.*, p. xli.

38. Cf. *Dest. of Troy* 284: 'Mony noble for þe nonest to þe
note yode.'

New Werke. The rebuilding of that part of the old Norman
minster which was called 'New Work' was begun in 1251 (Stow,
Survey, ed. Thoms (1876), p. 122). At the time at which the
poet wrote, the tomb of St. Erkenwald was situated in the 'New
Work' (Dugdale, *History of St. Paul's Cathedral* (1658), p. 28;
Chronicles of the Reigns of Edward I and Edward II (Rolls Ser.),
i. 276, 311). As G. (p. xxvii) says, 'the poet is obviously transferring to the time of Erkenwald the structural additions belonging
to the middle of the thirteenth century.'

42. G. paraphrases : 'So that the foundation in the first place
should hold the foot.'

43. m(u)kkyde. MS. *makkyde.* G.'s emendation to *m(u)kkyde*,
from ON. *moka*, 'remove dirt,' is almost certainly correct.

45. Cf. *Dest. of Troy* 11,179: 'As was due to the dede, to delue in
þe erthe.'

49. Thre sperle(s) of þe spelunke þat sparde hit olofte. MS.
thre sperle (or *spert*(?)) *of þe spelunke þat spradde hit o lofte.*
As G. notes, this is the only occasion where single final *l* is crossed
by a horizontal stroke, as if it were final *ll*. I adopt the very
reasonable and ingenious reading of Craigie, who cites this line in his
definition of *sperel* (NED. s. v. *sperel*) : *Thre sperlis of þe
spelunke þat sparde hit o lofte*, 'three bars (or bolts) of the tomb
that sparred it on top.' *Prompt. Parv.* (EETS. *Ext. Ser.* 102)
glosses *sperel* as 'Sperel, or closel in schettynge : *ffirmaculum*'
(column 428), and gives an example of its use in the phrase

'Ondoynge, or onpynnynge schettis or sperellys' (col. 315). G. reads *The spe(k)e of þe spelunke þat spradde hit o-lofte.* This reading he would support by *Piers Plow.* B. 15. 269-70:

> Monkes and mendynauntz, men bi hem-selue,
> In spekes and in spelonkes selden speken togideres.

But as *speke* occurs nowhere else in English as a Latinism with the meaning 'cave' (Skeat), its insertion does not clarify the meaning of the line. G.'s definition of the word in his glossary as a 'canopied tomb' is supported by no evidence, except that which the imagination is allowed to create from the context. Scottish *spaike, spake,* a dialectal variant of English *spoke* (EDD. s. v. *spoke,* sb.[1], 2), has, however, the specialized meaning, 'a wooden bar used for carrying a coffin to the grave.' The reading of *sparde,* 'locked, shut,' for *spradde* is suggested in the margin opposite l. 66 of *La Belle Dame sans Mercy* (EETS. 15.54). This would confirm Craigie's emendation of *spradde* to *sparde.*

spelunke. *Spelunca* is glossed as *sepulchrum* by Du Cange (*Glossarium,* s. v. *spelunca,* and accompanying citation). The word is found in the *Lexicon* of Maigne D'Arnis as *spelunga,* and is there also glossed 'sepulcrum, *tombeau.*' NED. (s. v. *spelunk*) fails to note this specialized secondary meaning that arose from ecclesiastical Latin, and defines the word as 'cave or cavern; a grotto,' all of them primary meanings, citing this line in support of those definitions. The word occurs again at 217, where it is applied not only to the tomb itself, but to all the space around it enclosed by the iron grating mentioned in 140.

52. roynyshe. The word has puzzled all commentators. NED. glosses it as derived from *roin,* 'scab, scurf,' but this meaning would violate the sense of the passage, since we are told that the letters on the tomb, instead of being overgrown with scurf or obscured by mold, were clearly outlined and sharply cut. Knigge (p. 79) suggests the possibility that the word may be connected with ON. *hrynja,* though he remarks that the combination *oy* is indicative rather of Romance origin. In other alliterative poems the word occurs sometimes as *runisch* (*Gaw.* 304, 432, 457; *Pur.* 1545; *Pat.* 191), sometimes as *renischche* (*Pur.* 96, 1724; *Wars of Alex.* 2943). Tolkien-Gordon (*Sir Gawain*), in a note on *Gaw.* 457, believe that the alternation of forms having *u* with those having *e* 'points to earlier *ēo,*' and gloss the word as 'rough, fierce, horrible' (cf. ON. *hrjónn,* OE. *hrēoh, hrēow*). Binz (*Literaturblatt.* 42. 378) is of the opinion that the form is to be connected with OE. *rūn,* 'secret, rune, mystery.' I believe the word to be derived from OE. *rȳne,* 'mystery, mysterious saying.' OE. ȳ appears as *ü* (written *u, ui*, rarely *uy*) in Middle English in the West Midlands, as *ē* in parts of Essex, Middlesex, Sussex, and Suffolk; see Wright, *Elementary Middle English Grammar* (Oxford, 1923) § 57. The forms having *u*, as one would expect, are more numerous in the alliterative poems of the Northern and West Midland dialectal localities than those having *e;* the *e*-spellings, unless they be mere scribal errors, may be forms from the dialectal regions mentioned above. Since the *ü* which stands for OE. *ō* was also written *u, ui*, as well as *oi* in the fifteenth century, particularly in Scotland and the Northern dialectal areas, it is possible that the scribe became confused, and mistook the *ui* that developed from ME. *ü* (< OE. ȳ) for the *ui, oi* (= *oy*) that developed from ME. *ō* (< OE. *ō*), and so wrote *roynyshe* for *ruinyshe* or *runyshe;* see Luick, *Hist. Gram.* § 406; Wright, *Elem. Middle Eng. Grammar* §§ 55, 57. The meaning 'mysterious' fits exactly into the impression that the poet was endeavoring to convey, of a tomb whose origin and content are obscured, rather than revealed, by the hieroglyphics carved on its border. Whenever the word occurs in the works of the *Gawain*-poet, its meaning seems to favor 'strange, mysterious, unearthly' (I should gloss *runyschly* in *Pat.* 191 as 'uncouthly'), rather than 'fierce.'

52-6. The passage presents difficulties of interpretation. As punctuated by G., with no mark after *mouthe* (54) and a semicolon after *shulde* (54), what I take to be the true meaning of the lines is obscured. Thus punctuated, the lines must be read as follows: 'But mysterious were all the sentences (*resones*) that there stood in row. Full exact were the figures, many observed them there, but all were nonplused to express it(?) and its meaning (*quat hit mene shulde*); many clerks . . . busied themselves there to no avail, that they might translate them (*hom*),' i. e. the 'roynyshe resones.' My colleague, Professor Gerould, suggests that the clause, 'and quat hit mene shulde,' ought to be taken with what follows rather than with what precedes, and that a more correct meaning of the passage can be secured by the insertion of a colon after *mouthe*, and of a comma after *shulde*. The passage would then read as follows: 'But strange were all the sentences (*resones*) that there stood in row. Full exact were the figures, many observed them there; but all were nonplused to express it(?): and its meaning (*quat hit mene shulde*) many clerks . . . busied themselves (over) there to no avail, that they might translate them (*hom*),' i. e. the 'roynyshe resones.' The presence of *hit* in 54 and of *hom* in 56 makes an absolutely clear interpretation a very difficult matter. As the passage stands, the antecedent of *hom* would appear to be *resones* (52).

55. Mony clerke(s). MS. *mony clerke*. The plural *crownes* would indicate that the scribe had forgotten to make *clerke* plural; though the combination of adjective and singular noun may have been regarded as plural according to sense.

56. aboute noȝt. 'Fruitlessly, without result, to no avail.'

62. Cf. *Dest. of Troy* 9233: 'He made hym redy full rad, ron to the toun,' and *Pur.* 797: 'He ros up ful radly and ran hem to mete.'

64. walon. The etymology of the word is difficult to determine. Four explanations are possible. (1) NED. (s. v. *wale*, vb.[1]) gives the word as one formed on the substantive *wale*, 'choice' (adopted from ON. *val*, 'choice'); besides the meanings 'choose, select, make choice,' it lists the meaning 'seek,' which it supports by citing *Gaw.* 398: ' "Where schulde I wale þe," quoþ Gauan, "where is þy place?" ' (2) G. glosses as 'betook themselves, chose their way,' and believes that the form stands for *walen*, the strong past participle of *wale*, 'choose,' which he takes as representing ON. *valinn*, a strong past participle, coexisting with *valiðr* and *valdr*, of *velja*, 'choose.' (3) EDD. (s. v. *wale*, sb.[1] and vb.[1]) gives *wale* as a verb, generally used with the adverbs 'away' and 'on,' to be found in the dialect of Yorkshire, meaning 'hurry,' and possibly to be connected with OE. *walu*, 'weal, mark of blow.' It is possible that we should read *wal on*, and paraphrase, 'as if all the world were hurried on thither within an instant.' (4) It is possible that the word may be connected with OE. *weallian*, 'go on pilgrimage'; cf. *Digby Mysteries (Mary Magdalene)*, ed. Furnivall, New Shakspere Society (London, 1882), 1848-9:

> With me xall ȝe wall to have more eloquens,
> & goo vesyte þe stacyons by and by.

While the weight of scholarly opinion would seem to favor derivation of the word from ON. *val*, perhaps ON. *velja*, evidence sufficiently strong to disprove the other two possible explanations is lacking.

66. sextene. 'Sacristan or custodian of the cathedral'; cf. Walcott, *Cathedralia*, p. 57: 'The custos . . . had the charge of the cathedral and all that it contained, but at length became the superintendent of deputies discharging his personal duties.' Whether the 'sextene' here mentioned is the principal functionary himself or one of his deputies, I have been unable to find out. The duties of the sacristan or treasurer are to be found enumerated in Dugdale's *History of St. Paul's*, p. 242 (Appendix): 'Thesaurarius, Capituli minister, totius Ecclesiæ thesauri custos est; ut sunt Reliquiæ, Libri, Vasa, Vestimenta, etc. . . . Hæc omnia ejus fidei & custodiæ commissa & tradita.' Charged with these duties, the sacristan would naturally be concerned lest the assemblage of such a crowd in the cathedral lead to destruction of property and other disorder.

68. lome. 'Chest, coffin' (OE. *gelōma*). For other meanings of the word, see *Pat.* 160; *Pur.* 314, 412, 443, 495.

69. Cf. *Wm. of Palerne* 2242: 'Þat werkmen forto worche ne wonne þidere sone.'

74. to knowe. MS. *to to knowe.* G. takes the second *to* of the MS. reading as a prepositional prefix to the verb which he regards as the Middle English representative of OE. *tōcnāwan,* 'discern, understand.' But since *tocnawe* is not to be found in any glossary or dictionary of Middle English, and is unrecorded in NED., it is best to treat the double occurrence of the preposition before *knowe* as a case of dittography.

75. glode. G. paraphrases as 'bright inside,' and a study of the uses of this word that is peculiar to the alliterative poems confirms his rendition. The form is probably to be connected with ON. *glaðr,* 'shining, bright' (of the sky). With *glaðr,* Mod. Engl. *glade,* would seem to be connected; cf. Swed. dialectal *glänna,* (1) 'sunny spot,' (2) 'open place in a wood' (s. v. NED. *glade,* sb.²). With Mod. Engl. *glade* compare *gladden* (s. v. NED. *gladen*), which Skeat takes to be a Northern dialectal word, and explains as (1) 'a glade' (EDS. Gloss. 1), or (2) 'a void place free from encumbrances' (EDS. Gloss. 17); as an example of the second meaning, see *Wars of Alex.* 131: 'a gladen he waytis,' i. e. he watches out for a free pathway (one unobserved by onlookers). NED. (s. v. *glade,* sb.²) suggests that *glade* and *glode* may represent respectively Northern and Midland forms of an OE. **glāda,* wk. masculine. G. (*Pearl* (1921), 79 n.). believes *glode* to be a provincial form of *glade.* Emerson (*Jour. Engl. and Germ. Phil.* 21. 405) suggests that those cases in the works of the *Pearl*-poet where this form occurs are to be explained by *a-o* confusion on the part of the scribe of the manuscript. But the occurrence of *glode* in the present poem and in the *Wars* reduces the value of that suggestion. Cf. *Gaw.* 2181, 2266; *Wars of Alex.* (Ashmole MS.) 1334. The idea that the poet seeks to convey is that the gilding of the interior of the tomb was untarnished by age.

78. Cf. *Pearl* 165: 'As glysnande golde þat man con schere.'

80. Cf. *Gaw.* 2395: 'And I gif þe, sir, þe gurdel þat is golde-hemmed.'

81. The presence of miniver upon the cape distinguished the robe or cloak of the justice from that of the sergeant-at-law. Fairholt (*Costume in England* 1. 202) quotes the following excerpt from Fortescue's *De Laudibus Legum Angliæ* concerning the garb of a justice:

He shall henceforward from time to time change his habit in some points; for being a sergeant-at-the-law, he is clothed in a long priest-like robe, with a furred cape about his shoulders, and thereupon a hood with two labels (such as doctors of the law wear in certain universities with their coif); but being made a justice, instead of his hood he must wear a cloak closed upon his right shoulder, all the other ornaments of a sergeant still remaining, saving that his vesture shall not be parti-coloured as a sergeant's may, and his cape furred with minever, whereas the sergeant's cape is ever furred with white lamb-skin.

83. coyfe. A close hood for the head worn by justices and sergeants-at-law (cf. Fairholt, *Costume in England* 1. 200-1, 270; 2. 125; Pulling, *The Order of the Coif* (London, 1884), pp. 13-23). Cf. *Rich. Redeless* 3. 320: 'They cared ffor no coyffes that men of court vsyn.'

84. Cf. *Wars of Alex.* (Ashmole MS.) 198: 'Quen he was semely vp set with septour in hand.'

87. Cf. *Death and Life* 65: 'Shee was brighter of her blee then was the bright sonn,' and *Wars of Alex.* (Ashmole MS.) 466: 'Þus bayst he þe briȝt qwene þat all hire ble changid.'

88. ȝorde. Holthausen (*Angl. Beibl.* 34. 17) remarks '*ȝorde* steht doch wohl für *ȝerde,* da hier das *o* nicht zu erklären ist.' To regard this form as a scribal error would be wrong, for it is well authenticated by Mirk's *Festial* (*EETS. Ext. Ser.* 96, pp. 179, 244, 269, 271, 280, 297). It is probably to be explained as follows: OE. *gēard* by shifting of diphthongal stress would develop a by-form *geárd,* which would regulaily be lengthened to *geārd,* and this last form would give in ME. *ȝord.*

I am unable to find any reference to the presence of clothiers' shops in St. Paul's churchyard in mediæval times.

92. Cf. *Pat.* 186: 'Slypped vpon a sloumbe-slepe, & sloberande he routes,' and *Gaw.* 244: 'As al were slypped vpon slepe so slaked hor loteȝ.'

in sounde. 'In soundness, in health.' The expression occurs also in *Gaw.* 2489: 'And þus he commes to þe court, knyȝt al in sounde.'

93. For the expression *spyr on,* cf. 'ask on' for 'ask of' (EDD. s. v. *ask,* vb.¹).

95. lere. 'Face' (OE. *hlēor,* 'face'; ON. *hlȳr,* 'cheek'), and not 'flesh' (OE. *lira,* 'flesh, flank, loin'), as G. glosses. The poet has just called our attention to the ruddy complexion and red lips of the corpse. As in the majority of instances in this poem East Midland *e,* and not the West Midland *o,* appears as the representative of OE. *ĕo.* *Lire* (149) is probably a derivative of OE. *lira.*

98. Cf. *Pur.* 1201: 'Þenne þe kyng of þe kyth a counsayl hym takes,' and *Wars of Alex.* (Ashmole MS.) 3188: 'Sone as þe kyng of þat kith of his come herys.'

100. **couthe.** G. thinks that we might more reasonably expect 'were' than *is* in 99, and paraphrases the two lines thus: 'it were a great wonder unless some person had stated that he had seen him, i. e. if there were no written statement to that effect in chronicles or the like.' Such a translation is based on the belief, expressed in a note on this word, that it stands not for the past tense of *can*, 'be able,' but for *gan*, 'did,' past tense of *ginnan*. With this view Holthausen (*Angl. Beibl.* 34. 17) agrees. But the way in which the phrase *couthe say* is echoed by *nourne couthe* (101), plainly equivalent to 'could not say,' seems to me to militate against G.'s suggestion. The exact meaning of the two lines is obscured by the confusion of tenses (and possible confusion of moods) arising from the presence of *is* in 99 and of *couthe* in 100, but the obscurity is not to be removed by the adoption of the reading 'did' for 'could.' See Funke's article, 'Die Fügung *ginnen* mit dem Infinitiv im Mittelenglischen' (*Engl. Stud.* 56. 22-5) for examples of the use of *con* for *gan* in the alliterative poems.

101-4. 'For none could declare either by inscription, sign, or by traditional legend that was ever recounted in town, or written down in book, which ever recalled such a man at all.' Þat (104) modifies *title, token,* and *tale.*

101. **nourne.** See also 152, 195. This word, peculiar to the *Gawain*-poet, occurs five times in *Gaw.* (1661, 1669, 1771, 1823, 2443), and thrice in *Pur.* (65, 669, 803). Its origin is unknown; though cf. Swed. dialectal *norna, nyrna,* 'to inform (secretly).'

couthe. Here plainly 'could.'

102. G. paraphrases, 'Either by inscription, sign or record, or by story, tradition.'

103. **burghe.** The author has brought *burghe* into antithesis with *boke;* the contrast is between oral tradition and written record. G., believing that the scribe wrote *burghe* by mistake for *brut* (M. Welsh *brut,* 'chronicle'), so emends, supporting the change by citing *Parl. of the Three Ages* 407 (see below). He paraphrases the expression *brevyt in b(rut)* as 'recorded in the annals or chronicles of the land of Britain.' ON. *brēfa,* however, meant not only 'commit to writing,' but 'tell, recount' as well (see Emerson, *Jour. Engl. and Germ. Phil.* 21. 371). Cf. *Gaw.* 2521: 'As hit is breued in þe best boke of romaunce'; *Pur.* 197: 'Bot never ȝet in no boke breved I herde'; *Parl. of the Three Ages* 407: 'When the Bruyte in his booke Bretayne it callede'; 424: 'In a booke of the Bible that breues of kynges.'

105. Cf. *Wars of Alex.* (Ashmole MS.) 1458: 'And bodword to
þe bischop broȝt of his come,' and *Gol. and Gaw.* 171: 'And broght
to the bauld king boidword of blis.'

106. **bolde.** 'Great, mighty'; cf. the following quotation from
the *Ludus Coventriæ* (ed. Halliwell (Shakespeare Soc.), p. 3): 'He
sent to Noe an angel bolde.' Holthausen (*Angl. Beibl.* 34. 17)
equates *bolde wonder* with *derfe wonder* (99). G., doubting the
correctness of this, word, suggests that the poet may have written
beu for *beau,* 'fair.'

107. **primate.** Here quite plainly used for the Bishop of London,
and not for the Archbishop of Canterbury.

108. **In Esex.** The visit here alluded to was probably made to
the nunnery of Barking in Essex, over which St. Erkenwald had
placed his sister Ethelburga as abbess. Cf. Bede, *Eccl. Hist.* 4. 6:

> Hic sane priusquam episcopus factus esset duo præclara
> monasteria, unum sibi, alterum sorori suæ Ethelbergæ, construx-
> erat, quod utrumque regularibus disciplinis optime instituerat.
> Sibi quidem in regione Suthergeona, juxta fluvium Tamensem,
> in loco qui vocatur 'Cerotesei,' id est 'Ceroti Insula'; sorori
> autem in Orientali Saxonum provincia, in loco qui nuncupatur
> 'In Berecingum,' in quo ipsa Deo devotarum mater ac nutrix
> posset existere feminarum.

109. Cf. *Pur.* 1623: 'Hit is tolde me bi tulkes þat þou trwe were.'

110. The line may be construed in either one of two ways.
(1) It may be regarded as a phrase dependent on *tolden* (109), in
which case *crakit* would have to be parsed as a past participle modify-
ing *cri.* The meaning of 109-110 would then be: 'Men told him the
story together with the public disturbance, and (told him of) such a
report uttered continually.' If 110 be thus paraphrased, *crakit* would
have the meaning 'uttered.' (2) It may be regarded as a dependent
clause whose main clause is 111, *crakit* being parsed as the finite verb
whose subject is *cri.* The meaning of 110-111 would then be: 'And
such a report about a corpse resounded so continually, that the bishop
sent to put a stop to it.' If 110 be thus paraphrased, *crakit* would
have the meaning 'resound'; cf. *Ywaine and Gaw.* 370 (*Ancient
Engleish Metrical Romanceës*, ed. Ritson, London, 1802, Vol. I, p. 1):
'And the thoner fast gan crak.' To the present editor it seems that
the use of the phrase *and suche,* indicative as it is not only of a shift
in the structure of the sentence, but of a slight change in the meaning
as well, would render the second of the two readings preferable.

114. **meere.** Holthausen (*Angl. Beibl.* 34, 18) says 'fasse ich
nicht als "mare" sondern als "Grenze," ae. *mære.*' The sugges-

tion is worthy of consideration, particularly so because the preceding line informs us that the limit or termination of the bishop's ride is St. Paul's cathedral. Yet the poet makes the explicit statement that the bishop arrived in town on horseback (112).

115. palais. Simpson (*Chapters in the History of Old St. Paul's*, p. 64) gives the following account of the location of the palace of the Bishop of London: 'On the Northern side of the Nave, at its Western end, stands the Bishop of London's Palace. (The name of London House Yard still helps to preserve the memory of it.) A private door leads from the Palace into the Nave of the Cathedral, so that the Bishop can pass directly into the grand Church.'

The expression 'pas into (up to, within, etc.) þe palais' occurs frequently in *Wars of Alex.* and *Dest. of Troy.*

116. And devoydit fro þe dede. 'Kept away from the dead (body),' i. e. after entering his palace, he did not go to the church to see the tomb and its contents. G's emendation of *dede* to *d(outh)e,* 'company' (OE. *duguþ*), cannot be justified.

117. Þe derke nyȝt overdrofe. Cf. *Dest. of Troy* 4664: 'The derke ouerdrogh, & the dym voidet,' and *Wars of Alex.* (Ashmole MS.) 1505: 'Sone þe derke ouire-drafe & þe day springis.' The expression is common in the alliterative poems of the school, particularly so in the *Dest. of Troy.*

121. avis(i)on. NED. (s. v. *avision*) gives two meanings for the word: (1) 'dream, vision,' (2) 'warning or monition (given in a dream).' St. Augustine (*Liber de Spiritu et Anima* (Migne, *Patr. Lat.* 40. 797)) distinguishes three *genera* of *visio—corporale, intellectuale,* and *spirituale:*

> In intellectuali visione nunquam fallitur anima: aut enim intelligit, et verum est; aut si verum non est, non intelligit. In visione autem corporali sæpe fallitur anima, cum in ipsis corporibus fieri putat, quod fit in corporis sensibus. . . . In visione etiam spirituali anima fallitur et illuditur, quoniam ea quæ videt, aliquando vera, aliquando falsa, aliquando perturbata, aliquando tranquilla sunt. Ipsa autem vera aliquando futuris omnino similia; vel aperte dicta, aliquando obscuris significationibus vel quasi figuratis locutionibus prænuntiata. In ecstasi vero quando ab omnibus corporis sensibus alienatur et avertitur anima, amplius quam in somno solet, sed minus quam in morte, non fallitur. Sed ipsa mente divinitus adjuta, vel aliquo ipsa visa exponente, sicut in Apocalypsi Joanni exponebatur magna revelatio est.

In his *Liber de Cognitione Veræ Vitæ* (Migne, *Patr. Lat.* 40. 1028), he further defines *visio spiritualis:*

Secunda visio spiritualis est, qua non res, sed imagines rebus similes spiritualiter videmus, sicut in somniis solemus, et sicut Joannem in Apocalypsi, et Prophetas multa vidisse novimus.

The revelation by *avis(i)on* for which St. Erkenwald prayed, must have been imparted in *ecstasi*, a state of the *visio spiritualis* in which the inabilities and imperfections natural to the mind are overcome by divine aid. Study of 117, 118, 119, 127 will show that before dawn the *ansuare* was granted, and that it came after a recital of the canonical prayers that lasted almost (but not quite) all night.

123. Thurghe his deere debonerte. The personal pronoun *his* I take to refer to the bishop. 122-3 are to be paraphrased thus: ' "Though I be unworthy," he said, weeping because of his noted meekness, "vouchsafe it, O Lord." ' G's emendation of *his* to (*þi*), in order to make the phrase refer to *Lorde,* is too bold.

129. heghe masse. At the time at which our author wrote, high mass was celebrated at the Cathedral according to the *Usus Sancti Pauli.* No documents exist which give this use, though there are extant two offices, one of St. Erkenwald, and the other of the Commemoration of SS. Peter and Paul, and a short series of detached collects which may be relics of it (see W. Sparrow Simpson, *Documents Illustrating the History of St. Paul's Cathedral* (Camden Soc. New Ser. 26), pp. xxi-xxvii). Canon Simpson believes that these offices were composed by the clergy of St. Paul's in obedience to the *Monitio* issued by Bishop Braybroke in 1386 (Ibid. pp. xxiv-xxvii) ; see section on *Date.* Dugdale (quoted in *Documents Illustrating the History of St. Paul's Cathedral,* p. xxvi) tells us that in 1414 Bishop Clifford ordained that from December the first of that year 'the solemn celebration of Divine service, which before that time had been according to a peculiar form anciently used and called *Usus Sancti Pauli,* should thenceforth be conformable to that of the Church of Salisbury for all canonical hours both night and day.'

130. Cf. *Morte Arthure* 4335: 'Pontyficalles and prelates in precyouse wedys.' Cf. also Dugdale, *History of St. Paul's,* p. 23: 'divers Bishops and Abbots *in Pontificalibus.*'

131. Manerly with his ministres. Rock (*The Church of Our Fathers* 4. 214) informs us that when a bishop prepared to sing high mass according to the rite of Sarum, 'he had never less than three deacons and three subdeacons, except upon Good Friday, when he had but one each of those ministers.'

132. Spiritus Domini. The *Sarum Missal* (ed. Legg, pp. 385, 401) gives two masses, each having the Officium 'Spiritus domini repleuit orbem terrarum alleluia et hoc quod continet omnia scienciam habet uocis alleluia alleluia alleluia.' The first of these is entitled

Missa de sancto spiritu; the second *Missa ad inuocandam graciam spiritus sancti.* The first is also part of the order of service for Whitsunday, the second a votive mass with the same *Officium,* but with a different *Oratio, Secretum,* and *Postcommunio.* Since both these masses appear also in *Missale Romanum* (ed. Lippe 1. 451-3; 2. 277) with few changes, the *Missal of St. Paul's*(?) would hardly show a very different order of service. The phrase *for his spede, on sutile wise,* and the *Oratio* of that mass: 'Deus cui omne cor patet et omnis uoluntas loquitur et quem nullum latet secretum,' etc., make it almost certain that the mass said by the bishop was the *Missa ad inuocandam graciam spiritus sancti.*

133. With queme questis of þe quere. A fine figure. *Quest* is the word used to describe the cry of hounds who are hunting for, or have found the scent, or who have sighted the game. The different voices of the choir suggest the different tongues of a pack of hounds. Cf. *Gaw.* 1150, 1421.

135. St. Paul's was the cathedral church of the metropolis.

136. later ende. 'Concluding portion.' Cf. *Chron. Vilodunense* 2219 (ed. Horstmann) : 'In þe laterhende of þe office.'

138. playn. 'Level (floor or pavement).' See NED., s. v. *plain,* adj.[1]; the use of the adjective as a noun is a stylistic characteristic of the *Gawain*-poet. Dugdale *(Hist. of St. Paul's,* p. 15) tells us that 'in *Anno* MCCCXII (6 E. 2) was the *Pavement* of the *New Work* made of good and firm Marble, which cost V[d] the foot.'

140. cloyster. 'Enclosed space.' Dugdale *(Hist. of St. Paul's)* gives a picture of the altar of St. Erkenwald (facing p. 113), which shows an iron grating surrounding it. The legend of the picture reads, 'Clausura circa Altare S. Erkenwaldi, sub feretro ejusdem.' He further tells us that the 'Iron Grate' about the tomb extended five feet ten inches in height, weighed 3438 pounds, and had 'Locks, Keys, Closures, and Openings' (p. 21).

141. The moment was a tense one. The calm and determined Christian priest was going to deal with unknown forces of the spiritual world, and the populace awaited the outcome with deep anxiety.

144. devysit. 'Recounted, described,' rather than 'arranged,' as G. glosses. The dean gave a complete account of the finding of the tomb as a preliminary step (*on fyrst*).

145. Cf. *Wars of Alex.* (Ashmole MS.) 1089: 'Toward a miȝti montayne him myntis with his fynger.'

151. Cf. *Wars of Alex.* (Ashmole MS.) 1094: 'So sall þi name fra now furth be mynned in mynde.'

154. Þat . . . his = *whose,* see Kellner, *Hist. Outlines of Engl. Syntax.,* p. 66.

155. librarie. Dugdale (*Hist. of St. Paul's*, p. 8) mentions the cathedral library as existent in Henry I's time. At the time at which the poet wrote we do not know the extent of its collections or its location. The detailed descriptions given by Dugdale of its location apply to the library erected by Walter Shiryngton, Chancellor of the Duchy of Lancaster under Henry VI (1421-71).

161. providens. NED. (s. v. *providence*, sb., 3) glosses the word as 'The foreknowing and beneficent care and government of God (or of nature, etc.); divine direction, control, or guidance,' and cites this line as an example of its definition. Cf. *Winner and Waster* 296: 'It es plesynge to the Prynce þat paradyse wroghte'; *Death and Life* 13: 'If thou haue pleased the Prince that paradice weldeth'; *Pur.* 195: 'Þat þat ilk proper Prynce þat paradys weldez.' Cf. also *Scottish Field* 87, 203.

163. and his mynde passyde. 'His mental powers overcome.'

165. hym. The pronoun refers to God.

167-8. 'Where the creature's power swerves away from wisdom, the Creator's strengthening must needs take the cure.' It is difficult to say whether *byhoves* is used as a quasi-impersonal verb, with the thing incumbent expressed by an infinitive, and with personal object, or as a personal verb. For, as NED. (s. v. *behove, behoove*, v., 5) notes, the quasi-impersonal use of this verb was at times lost because of the confusion between the nominative and accusative cases, and the verb acquired a personal use, meaning 'to be under obligation (to do); must needs, ought, have.' This usage is given as 'of northern origin, and since 1500 only Scotch.' Cf. examples of this use given in NED. Since the word-order of 168—noun (without prep.) + *byhoves* + infinitive—more closely resembles that of the several examples that illustrate the personal use of the verb, I have paraphrased it as having that use. There is no evidence to support G.'s suggestion that *byhoves* 'was probably originally the Northern form "bus."'

168. Cf. *Morte Arthure* 2196: 'And caughte his Creatoure, þat comfurthes vs all(e).'

169. so. 'In this way' (G.).

171. glow. Despite the gloss on the margin of the MS. (see note), the word is probably not *glow*, 'gaze, stare' (NED., *glow*, v.²), but a West Midland development of ME. *glew*, 'call on,' which NED. lists as formed on *gleow, glew* (OE. *glēo*, sb.); though derivation from OE. *gleowian*, 'play on an instrument, sing,' is also possible. OE. *ēo* became *o* in West Midland localities; see Luick, *Hist. Gram.* § 357. Cf. *Pat.* 164: 'Bot vchon glewed on his god þat gayned hym beste.'

172. **Þat careles is of counselle.** 'Generous of counsel.' Cf.
Pearl 605: 'For þe gentyl Cheuentayn is no chyche.'

173. **(Anande) þat.** 'Anent that.' The words refer to God's
power to send comfort (172).

175. **upon longe.** 'At length, finally.' Menner notes on *Pur.*
1193 that NED. does not record *up(on) long* in a temporal sense.
The present instance and that in *Pur.* are the only cases of the occurrence of the phrase with its present meaning.

176. **And fayne ȝour talent to fulfille.** 'Well pleased to fulfill
your desire.' *Prompt. Parv.* (EETS. Ext. Ser. 102. 715) defines
talent as 'desire.'

181. Cf. *Gaw.* 852: 'And þere were boun at his bode burneȝ
innoȝe,' and *Wars of Alex.* (Ashmole MS.) 2805:

'And I am boun at ȝour bode & buxsom was euire.'

190. **brayed.** 'Stirred.' NED. (s. v. *braid*, v.¹, 1) derives the
word from OE. *breȝdan,* gives *brayed* as a pret. tense in ME., and
glosses as 'make a sudden movement with (the hand, foot, etc.).'
G. emends to *bray(þ)ed,* believing the word derived from ON. *bragða.*
Both derivation and emendation are unnecessary.

192. The awkward structure of this line is noticeable. *Lant* is
separated from its direct object, *lyfe,* by an intervening word. It is
possible that the original word-order may have been altered by a
transcriber, for the poet is ordinarily very careful to preserve a
proper grammatical relationship between the words of a given line.
If *lant* be transposed so that it follows, instead of preceding, *goste,*
the obvious meaning of the line is preserved, and the syntactical
order clarified. But any change in the word-order would affect the
rhythm of the line. Since it is possible that the poet wrote out the
line as it stands, and deliberately sacrificed grammatical structure to
the demands of metre, I do not feel justified in changing or emending
it. Certainly G.'s emendation to

Þurghe s(um) lyf(ly) goste, lant of hym þat al redes,

and that of Holthausen (*Angl. Beibl.* 34. 17) to

Þurghe s(um) lyf(es) goste, lant of hym þat al redes

are too bold.

At first sight it is somewhat puzzling to find the dead body endowed
with life, while the soul, as would appear from 334-6, is condemned
to hell. The necessity of dramatic suspense requires the poet to give
to his readers the impression that the soul which once held possession
of the dead body was in hell up to the time of its miraculous deliverance. Actually, however, the judge's soul reëntered its former habi-
tation after the corpse had been adjured to speak. The status of the
soul separated from its body, its condition, powers, attributes, and

the possibility of its leaving its place, are discussed at great length in the *Summa Theologica* of St. Thomas Aquinas (Pars 3 (Supp.), Quæst. 69, Artl. 3, 7; Quæst. 70, Artl. 1, 2, 3; Quæst. 71, Art. 5). In his discussion of how it were possible for the soul of the pagan Emperor Trajan to be released from hell through the prayers of St. Gregory, St. Thomas says that it is probable that the soul of Trajan entered his body as soon as the prayers of St. Gregory had recalled that body to life, and that it was possible for it to do so, because it had never been finally and irrevocably damned, but only for a season. Cf. *Summa Theolog.*, Pars 3 (Supp.), Quæst. 71, Art. 5:

> Dicendum, quod de facto Trajani hoc modo potest probabiliter æstimari, quod precibus B. Gregorii ad vitam fuerit revocatus, et ita gratiam consecutus sit, per quam remissionem peccatorum habuit, et per consequens immunitatem a pœna: sicut etiam apparet in omnibus illis qui fuerunt miraculose a mortuis suscitati, quorum plures constat idololatras et damnatos fuisse. De omnibus talibus enim similiter dici oportet, quod non erant in inferno finaliter deputati, sed secundum præsentem propriorum meritorum justitiam: secundum autem superiores causas, quibus prævidebantur ad vitam revocandi, erat aliter de eis disponendum.

195. Cf. *Wars of Alex.* (Ashmole MS.) 619: 'And so him neuyned was þe name of his next frendis.'

199. Cf. *Parl. of the Three Ages* 605: 'Bothe with kynges and knyghtis and kaysers ther-inn'; *Winner and Waster* 327: 'Ne es nothir kaysser, ne kynge, ne knyghte þat the folowes.'

201. mayster-mon. 'Chief man, executive officer'; cf. note to *Dest. of Troy* 1.

203. Cf. *Pur.* 167: 'For aproch þou to þat Prynce of parage noble.'

205. lewid. The meaning of the word in this line may be an extension of the ordinary meaning of 'unlettered, untaught.' A *lewid date* might mean an 'unlettered date,' i. e. one difficult to represent to the ordinary man by figures or symbols. The word may also have the general and stereotyped meaning of 'bad'; cf. *Piers Plow.* A. 1. 163: 'As lewed as a laumpe that no liht is inne.' If used in this sense, one might paraphrase the word as 'unsatisfactory, difficult.' G., believing that the scribe meant to write *lappid*, but that he misread *þþ* as *w* and changed *a* to *e*, emends to *l(app)id*. Since the Wycliffite version of Matt. 27. 59 translates *involvit* by *lappide*, G. glosses as 'enveloped.' Cf. *law*, 'pile up, load' (*lewid*= freighted with years(?)), and *lew*, 'protect from the wind, shelter' (*lewid* =

obscure(?)); EDD. gives the first verb (s. v. *law*, v.², deriv. OE. *hlāw*, 'mound') as current in north Devonshire, and the second (s. v. *lew*, v.¹, deriv. OE. *hlēo*, 'shelter') as current in Kent, Somerset, and Devonshire.

206. Hit (is) to meche. I adopt Horstmann's reading (*Altengl. Leg.*). G.'s emendation of *meche* to *m(ut)he* seems to obscure both syntax and meaning.

208. (aght). MS. *fife.* Schumacher (*Bonner Stud. zur Engl. Phil.* 11. 87-8) noting that this line was imperfect in its alliteration, remarks: 'Die Zahlwörter werden in mittelenglischen Texten meist sehr willkürlich behandelt; es ist vielleicht "eighte" st. *fife* zu lesen.' G. suggests *aght* for *eighte;* his spelling is preferable, because the scribe has written *aght* in 210.

210. (Þre hundred). MS. *a pousande.* The MS. reading is certainly wrong. Since Belinus and Brennius waged war with the Romans (*Chron. Maj.* 1. 59), they must have lived after the date of the founding of Rome, 753 B. C., one well known to mediæval historians and chronologists. 1054 B. C., therefore, cannot stand as the date at which King Belin reigned. G., conjecturing that the word *pousande* is a misreading of the symbol iijc, suggests in its place *pre hundred*. The date of the judge's incumbency would then be 354 B. C.

207-12. The mediæval system of chronology seems to have been based to a considerable extent upon two works by Bede, the *De Temporibus Liber* and the *De Temporum Ratione* (*Works,* ed. Giles (London, 1843), 6. 123-342), from which shorter and more convenient compilations were made by succeeding chroniclers and historians, though the dates given by Bede were accepted as correct almost without exception. In the solution of the chronological points brought up by these lines, I have collated with the two works of Bede the *Chroniculi S. Pauli London ad Annum 1399,* reprinted in *Documents Illustrating the Hist. of St. Paul's Cathedral* (Camden Soc., New Ser. 26), pp. 58-60, 222-8. When necessary, I have consulted the Vulgate version of the Old Testament, for it is possible that the poet may have used it in his work of computation, if not by actual reference, at least indirectly. The fact that both Bede and the *Chroniculi* are necessary for a correct solution of the chronological difficulties of the poem, seems to me to make it almost certain that the poet derived his figures from some manuscript containing matter derived, directly or indirectly, from both. The first historic event, the founding of Troynovant, is said by *Chron. Maj.* (1. 22) to have taken place while Eli was high priest of Jewry, and the Ark of the Covenant was captured by the Philistines. According

to Bede, there are six great cycles of the world's history. The first
year of the sixth cycle is the first year Anno Domini. The fifth
cycle, from the beginning of the Babylonian Captivity to the birth
of our Lord, has 589 years; the fourth, from the accession of David
to the Babylonian Captivity, 473 years according to the Hebrew text,
485 years according to the Septuagint. Saul reigned over the Jews
for 20 years, and Samuel was their prophet for 12 (Samuel and Saul
together 32 years; cf. *De Temporibus,* p. 134). I Samuel 7. 2 says
that 20 years intervened between Eli's death and the great gathering
at Mizpah when Samuel reorganized the national worship; cf. also
the article on Samuel in *Cyclopædia of Biblical, Theological, and
Ecclesiastical Literature* 9. 318. The addition of these figures
amounts to 1126 (1114 according to the Hebrew text), which should
be the date of the founding of Troynovant. According to the
emended text, 782 years after the founding of Troynovant equates
with 354 B. C. 782 subtracted from 1126 quite evidently does not
leave a remainder of 354. Now the *Chroniculi* gives the same number
of years in the fourth cycle as does Bede (according to the Hebrew
text), but gives two different readings in the case of the fifth cycle.
Here the *Chroniculi* (p. 223) reads: 'Quinta ætas a transmigracione
Babilonis usque ad Christum continet quinque centenos octoginta
quinque annos; secundum alios, quinque centenos nonaginta novem
annos.' If 599 be substituted for 589 as the number of years in the
fifth cycle, the other figures remaining the same (those of the Septuagint as given by Bede), the resulting sum will be 1136; and 782
subtracted from that will give 354 as a remainder. The poet then
regarded 1136 B. C. as the date of the building of London.

211. (o)n heire of an oye(r). MS. *an heire of anoye.* 'This
statement,' as G. remarks, 'seems to have been a source of much
trouble to all those who have attempted to deal with the line.'
Neilson suggests that *oye* (Gael. *ogha*), 'grandson,' may be meant,
though he queries that explanation. Horstmann's paraphrase, 'ein
gefürchteter Herr' (OE. *hearra, herra,* 'lord, master'), is better, but
misrepresents the poet's meaning, since it might lead the reader to
suppose the judge cruel and tyrannical. Better still is the paraphrase, 'child of wrath,' i. e. one not an heir of everlasting life, an
infidel (cf. Ephesians 2. 3, 'filii iræ'). But, as G. notes, the judge
has already referred to his paganism in 203-4, and the present reading
is paralleled by 216. There is, then, no reason why G.'s brilliant
emendation, *(o)n eire of an oye(r),* 'on circuit of an oyer,' should
not be accepted, though I prefer to follow the MS., and read *heire*
instead of *eire;* cf. *heyre* given by NED. (s. v. *eyre, 2*) as an Anglo-
French spelling to be found in Britton (1292). According to the

line as thus emended, the judge was a justice of the Iter, *justitiarius itinerans.* Subsequent statements do not invalidate this interpretation. The statement in 201-3 that he was a royal officer would, of course, be true, for the justices of the Iter were Crown judges (see quotation from Bracton below). The statements in 202 and in 227 might lead one to infer that the judge was Justiciar, or royal deputy, with control of all administrative, financial, and judicial functions of the government in London during the absence of the king (cf. Stubbs, *Constitutional Hist. of England* (Oxford, 1880) 1. 392-8; Sharpe, *London and the Kingdom* 1. 43). At an early date London was granted its own Justiciar, who must not be confused with the Justiciar of England, though the office lapsed at the accession of Henry II. But whether or not the judge held the justiciarship of London, he was at all events chief legal officer of the city of London and royal deputy. The following quotation from Bracton (*De Legibus Angliæ* (Rolls Ser.) 2. 160) will show that the jurisdiction of the justice in the poem was very wide since he was one of those judges who sat 'ad omnia placita':

> Habet etiam justitiarios itinerantes de comitatu in comitatum, quandoque ad omnia placita, quandoque ad quædam specialia, sicut assisas novæ disseysinæ & mortis antecessoris capiendas, & ad gaolas deliberandas, quandoque ad unicam vel duas & non plures: in iis casibus omnibus erunt curiæ ipsius domini regis.

213-5. For an account of the strife between Belinus and his brother Brennius, and of its termination through the good offices of their mother, see *Chron. Maj.* 1. 57-8. The poet or scribe probably wrote *Berynge* (213) for *Brennius,* either through carelessness or inability to read the manuscript correctly.

216. Cf. *Sege of Jerusalem* 80: 'Þat is iustise & iuge of jewen lawe.'

219. Cf. *Gaw.* 2293: 'Bot stode stylle as þe ston, oþer a stubbe auþer'; *Pur.* 1523: 'Þat were of stokkes and stones, stille evermore.'

227. deputate. Cf. *Court of Venus* (Scottish Text Soc. 3) 3. 181: 'Rhamnusia, quhill was Iuge deputate.'

duke. The title was often used in a general sense by the alliterative poets for 'leader, chief, king' (Lat. *dux*). Cf. *Sege of Jerusalem* 924: '& þo deyed þe duke & þe diademe lefte,' where the reference is to the Emperor Galba.

229. gentil. I follow G., and gloss as 'noble,' but cf. the meaning in 216.

231. felonse. MS. *felonse* or *felouse.* NED. (s. v. *felon,* adj.) gives the form *felo(u)ns* as occurring in the fourteenth and fifteenth

centuries, and offers as possible the explanation that it may be due to
-*s* of the nominative case of OF. Cf. a similar case in *Dest. of Troy*
6063, where the editors read *felous,* and suggest the other reading in
the note to that line.

fals. It is possible that the word may not here have its ordinary
meaning of 'treacherous,' but the meaning that it now has in the
northern and midland counties of 'clever, shrewd'; cf. EDD. (s. v.
false, adj.). If used in that sense, the judge would have us understand that the folk of Troynovant were artful in evading the law.

232. Cf. *Dest. of Troy* 5778: 'Mony harmys þai hent er hor helpe
come.'

241. The judge had lived a perfect life, so far as a pagan can
do so.

heghe gate. Neilson (*Huchown of the Awle Ryale,* p. 107)
believes the phrase a rendition of *via regia,* 'the king's highway,' and
quotes the following illustration of the term from the late thirteenth
century *Fleta seu Commentarius Juris Anglicani,* London, 1685,
pp. 45-6:

> & quod a recta via non se divertet donec regnum exierit. Et
> tunc interdicatur ei ne viam regiam exeat donec transitum
> invenerit.

Cf. *Pearl* 395.

243-4. 'Though it had been my father's murderer, I gave him no
wrong decisions, nor false favor to my father, though it fell to him
to be hanged.'

246. Cf. *Pearl* 642: 'To dyʒe in doel, out of delyt'; *Pur.* 1329:
'Bot al drawes to dyʒe wyth doel up(o)n ende.'

248. to bounty. 'For a reward' (G.).

249. curtest. A correct form of *curtesest,* 'most noble,' as
G. notes.

couthe. Here plainly 'did,' and not 'could.' Cf. note on 100.

252. me. G.'s emendation of *me* to (*þer*) is unnecessary; the
meaning is plain as the line stands.

254. Cf. *Wars of Alex.* (Ashmole MS.) 2280: 'Þou sall be
crouned, or I caire for kiddest of þe gamen.'

255. The poet would seem here to be endeavoring to establish a
test case as to whether a righteous infidel can be saved. St. Thomas
Aquinas (*Summa Theolog.,* Pars 2, Quæst. 58, Art. 12) says of legal
justice: 'Manifestum est quod ipsa est præclarior inter virtutes
morales, inquantum bonum commune præeminet bono singulari unius
personæ.' The judge is then characterized as one who, though a
pagan, is endowed, as far as any human being may be, with the fore-
most of the moral virtues.

257. **baythes.** 'Ask' (ON. *beiða*, 'ask'). NED. (s.v. *baithe*,
v.) gives no instances of the survival of the ON. meaning in ME.
260. Cf. *Pur.* 144: 'In on so ratted a robe and rent at þe sydez.'
261. Cf. *Wars of Alex.* (Ashmole MS.) 3319: 'Þan was his body
enbawmed &, as he bede, grauen.'
262. **thar.** 'May.'
ryve. It is impossible to tell whether the third letter of the word
as it stands in the MS. is *n* or *u*(= *v*). *Ryve*, 'tear, is supported
by the following quotation from Hampole's *Prick of Conscience* 888:
'Wormes sal ryve hym in sondre.' G. reads *ryne*, 'touch.' Cf. a
similar instance in *Gaw.* 2290, where Tolkien-Gordon read *ryueʒ*.
268. Cf. *Pearl* 285: '& loue my Lorde & al his laweʒ'; *Pur.* 1066:
'And lelly lovy þy Lorde, and his leef worþe.' Cf. also *Wars of
Alex.* (Ashmole MS.) 880.
269. Cf. the quotation from St. Thomas Aquinas under 255.
270. Cf. *Pur.* 613: 'Ʒif ever þy mon upon molde merit disserved.'
275. **as he has riʒt servyd.** G. renders, 'as he has rightly
deserved.' This paraphrase seem to me more in keeping with all the
poet's thought on the problem of grace and merit; cf. *Pearl* 595.
Yet the phrase may also be taken to mean 'as he has served (been
faithful to, been obedient to) Justice.'
276. 'Might hardly omit to give thee some portion of his grace.'
277-8. The reference is almost certainly to Psalm 23. 3-4
(Vulgate) : 'Quis ascendet in montem Domini? Aut quis stabit in
loco sancto ejus? Innocens manibus et mundo corde.' The Vulgate
phrase, 'Innocens manibus et mundo corde,' is translated in 278,
though the Latin order has been reversed in translation, since
unskathely renders 'innocens manibus,' and *skilfulle*, 'following
reason, doing right,' 'mundo corde.' The Paris Psalter (*Liber
Psalmorum*, ed. Thorpe, Oxford, 1835, p. 51) translates 'innocens
manibus' by 'þe unscæðfull byð mid his handum.' A paraphrase of
these two verses occurs in *Pearl* 674-683. There, as here, the poet
has placed the answer to the third verse of the Psalm directly in the
mouth of the Lord, whereas to the Psalmist His answer is only
implied.
278. **skelton.** NED. (s.v. *skelt*, v.) gives the word as one of
obscure origin. It is found in ME., only in the alliterative poems.
G. believes that a number of words of different origin are included
under this one word. The present form he takes to be derived from
OF. **esquelete, eschelete* (cp. *esquele*, Mod. Fr. *échelle*, 'ladder.')
Eschellett, 'small ladder,' is found, so he tells us, in sixteenth-
century English. *Skelt* he would, therefore, equate with an hypothetical OF. *esqueleter*, 'mount the steps of a ladder,' which renders

Lat. *ascendere* (Vulgate *ascendet*). To him the poet would seem to be thinking of *scala cœli,* 'the ladder unto heaven.' The suggested derivation is ingenious, but the meaning 'hasten' given by NED., or some meaning allied to that action, such as 'approach, bend one's way towards,' would fit the sense of every passage save one in which the word is found in ME., and is strengthened somewhat by the occurrence of the word *skelt* in the dialect of Herefordshire with the meaning, 'roam, wander,' which EDD. (s. v. *skelt,* v.) gives as of obscure derivation. Thus *Pur.* 1554: 'Scoleres skelten þeratte þe skyl for to fynde,' might well be rendered 'scholars hasten thereto,' instead of 'scholars cudgel their brains,' as G. paraphrases, believing the word to be derived from the weak past of ON. *skjalla,* or causal *skella,* 'clash, hammer.' This meaning is supported by 1551: 'He bede his burnes boӡ to, þat wer bok-lered.' The notion of acceleration is also implied in *Pur.* 1186, 1206 (but not in 827). The word may also be glossed as 'approach' in the two quotations from *Dest. of Troy* which follow (1089, 6042):

Skairen out skoute-wacche for skeltyng of harme
and
With skowte wacche for skathe & skeltyng of harme

The meaning of both passages is that scouts were sent out for (because of) the approach of harm, i. e. lest harm come near.

279. in sele quere ho wonnes. 'In bliss where she dwells.' These lines seem clearly to indicate the poet's belief in the inequality of heavenly rewards.

283. Cf. *Pat.* 482: 'A! þou maker of man, what maystery þe þynkeӡ.'

285. plite. In the case of this word, confusion between Anglo-French *plit* and OE. *pliht* exists. One may gloss either as 'nature,' or as 'pledge, plighting.' NED. (s. v. *plight,* sb.[1], 3) cites the word in this line as meaning, 'pledge, plighting,' though in its discussion of derivation it queries its statement that *plyt, plyte, plit, plite,* are connected with OE. *pliht,* and adds below that in the fourteenth century the loss of *h, ӡ,* or *gh* in the combination *-ight,* leaving *-īt,* led to identity of pronunciation and spelling in the case of the two words. It is, therefore, quite possible that the word may be rendered 'plight,' and that its reference may be to God's 'plight,' the Everlasting Covenant. That confusion between the two words might well take place was noted by G. in a comment on *Pearl* (1891) 1075. 'Confusion in pronunciation and spelling,' however, as Emerson (*Publ. Mod. Lang. Assoc.* 37. 75) says in a note on *Pearl* 647, 'could have taken place only after ME. *ӡt,* MnE. *ght* had completely lost the spirant *ӡ(gh).*' At this time loss of the spirant would appear to have taken place, for Knigge (p. 70) notes that in *Pearl,* in the case of this word, *-yȝt* and *-yt* rhyme with one another. Regarding the rhyme in *Pearl* 1015: *tyȝt (tyhtan* or *dihtan*(?)) : *plyt (plyht)* : *quyt (hwīt)* he remarks: '*Plyȝt* hat nun freilich schon im ae. die Nebenform *plyt* zur Seite. Aber dann bleibt noch der Reim: *tyȝt: quyt* über. Dieser zeugt wieder für die flüchtige Aussprache des *ȝ.* Später verstummte es bekanntlich ganz.' Cf. *plyȝtles,* 296.

287. faitheles. 'Without faith,' i. e. a pagan.

290. Cf. *Pearl* 646: 'Ryche blod ran on rode so roghe'; 705: 'Bot he on rode þat blody dyed.'

291. Quen þou herghedes helle-hole. The reference is to the belief, universally held in the Middle Ages, of Christ's Harrowing of Hell. Though the document upon which the tradition is based, the second or third century *Descensus Christi ad Inferos,* is apocryphal, the account of the happenings it relates is based upon several texts of the New Testament, notably I Peter 3. 19; 4. 6. At the time at which the poem was written, however, the legend had become a part of Catholic dogma, and is explicitly recognized as such by Aquinas (*Summa Theolog.,* Pars 3, Quæst. 52, Artl. 1-8). Brown (*Publ. Mod. Lang. Assoc.* 19. 126, note 2) is, therefore, wrong in classing the account of the Harrowing of Hell and the Limbus Patrum (292) as 'legendary material.' For more complete discussion of the place which the doctrine of Christ's descent into Hell occupied in Catholic belief, see W. H. Hulme, *The Harrowing of Hell and the Gospel of Nicodemus* (*EETS. Ext. Ser.* 100), pp. lx-lxx.

292. Þi loffynge. Since several explanations of the phrase, beyond the one of mere scribal error, are possible, I have not ventured to emend. G., noting a stage direction in Chester Plays 17 (Christ's Descent into Hell (*EETS. Ext. Ser.* 115. 329)): 'Et sic Ibunt glorificantes Deum, cantantes "Te Deum,"' emends *Þi* to *Þ(e),* and reads 'praising Thee.' This rendition of *glorificantes Deum* by *Þe loffynge* would be acceptable in view of similarity in the context and situation of the two passages, and of the occurrence of *lovynge* (vbl. sb.) in 349, which some might regard as a present participle, if it were not for the fact that the regular ending of the present participle in this poem is *-ande* and not *-ynge,* and that the scribe is generally careful to keep the distinction between present participle and verbal noun. Less radical, because no emendation is required, would be the reading *Þi loffynge,* 'Thy praising (ones),' or perhaps 'Thy loving (ones),' yet that rendition would still be open to the objection that *loffynge* would have to be parsed as a present participle. Better than the two preceding is the reading of Holthausen (*Angl. Beibl.* 34. 17), *lēffynge,* 'residue, remnant,' i. e. the righteous in Limbo. NED.

(s. v. *leaving*, vbl. sb., 2) cites the form with *f*-spelling as a verbal noun as early as 1340. *O* appears for *e* in another instance that cannot easily be explained (*glotte*, 297). Cf. *loving*, 'dear' (term of endearment), which EDD. (s. v. *loving*, vbl. sb. 3) gives as occurring in Devonshire; as a part. adj. meaning 'cleaving closely to,' the word is found in Yorkshire (EDD. *loving*, 2).

Limbo. The Limbus Patrum. Cf. St. Thomas Aquinas, *Summa Theolog.*, Pars 3 (Supp.), Quæst. 69, Art. 5:

> Sancti patres, in quibus minimum erat de ratione culpæ, supremum et minus tenebrosum locum habuerunt omnibus puniendis.

293. þat se may no fyrre. According to St. Thomas Aquinas (*Summa Theolog.*, Pars 3 (Supp.), Quæst. 97, Art. 4) the fire of hell is so thick, cloudy, and reeky that clear sight is impossible, though sight of a sort is possible, i. e. where it can bring torment to those who are possessed of it:

> In inferno hoc modo debet esse locus dispositus ad videndum secundum lucem et tenebras, ut nihil ibi perspicue videatur; sed solummodo sub quadam umbrositate videantur ea quæ afflictionem cordi ingerere possunt. Unde, simpliciter loquendo, locus est tenebrosus. Sed tamen ex divina dispositione est ibi aliquid luminis, quantum sufficit ad videndum illa quæ animam torquere possunt.

295-6. Cf. *Death and Life* 272-3:

> When Eue ffell to the ffruite with ffingars white
> & plucked them of the plant & poysoned them both.

296. plyȝtles. NED. (s. v. *plightless*) glosses as 'blameless,' but the context would also support the meaning 'covenantless' (see 285). The word is formed on OE. *pliht*, which means 'plight, pledge,' as well as 'blame'; furthermore it is so rare that we cannot be sure that the poet may not have used it in the sense here suggested.

297. ȝe were entouchid with his tethe, and take in þe glotte. An obscure line. G. emends *tethe* to *te(c)he*, *take* to *t(o)ke*, and *glotte* to *gl(e)tte* (OF. *glette*, 'venom, pus, corrupted matter'), and reads 'Ye were empoisoned by his sin, and imbibed the corruption.' Thus emended, the line makes sense, but three changes have been made for which the necessity does not seem warranted. The line as it stands can be rendered, 'Ye were empoisoned by his teeth, and involved in the corruption.' The words, *his tethe*, quite evidently refer to the teeth of Adam that bit into the apple (295). The poet makes the teeth which ate, instead of the act of eating, the cause of man's fall. The second half of the line is readily understandable, when one remembers that theologians of all times have taught that mankind was corrupted by Adam's first sin. While *glotte* can be explained as a possible scribal error, it would seem more reasonable to account for it on the analogy of *love* (34) and *glow* (171), as a dialectal form characteristic of the West and Northwest; see Luick, *Hist. Gram.* § 357 (notes 1, 2). A more doubtful explanation than the one just given, though it deserves mention, is that *glotte,* instead of being derived from OF. *glette,* has some connection with ON. *glotta,* which the Norweg.-Dänisch. Etymolog. Wörterbuch (s. v. *glytte*) defines as 'höhnisch lachen, so dass man die zähne zeigt'; or with Mod. N. *glott,* 'opening, rift in the clouds.' The reader should note that the first word means 'to open the mouth (in laughter) so that the *teeth* show,' and that the second word means 'aperture, orifice.' It may be that the poet had in his mind the idea of hell-mouth, and that *take in þe glotte* means 'taken into the yawning mouth of hell.'

entouchid. As G. notes, the appearance of this word, a derivative of OF. *entouchier,* in Middle English writings is limited to this line.

299. Baptism and correct belief are complementary. Neither is effective for salvation without the other. Cf. *Pur.* 164: 'Þat ever wern fulȝed in font þat fest to have.'

300. merciles. NED. (s. v. *merciless,* adj.) gives no example of the word, with this meaning of 'obtaining no mercy,' earlier than 1560.

302. lake. 'Pit.' Cf. Wycliffe, Isaiah 38. 18: 'Thei shul not abyden thi treuthe, that gon doun in to the lake.'

305. sike. 'Sorrow and sighing.' I regard *sike* as a noun; see NED. s. v. *sike,* sb.², b. The verb occurs twice in the poem (189, 323), and on both occasions is spelled with *y.*

colde. 'Gloomily, wretchedly.' It is possible, however, to gloss 'in powerless fashion'; for *colde,* in the sense that the NED. gives, of 'without power to move or influence,' see Emerson's note on *Pur.* 1231 (*Jour. Engl. and Germ. Phil.* 20. 233-4).

307. meeles. See 332 and 336.

311. Cf. *Pearl* 807: 'Al oure baleȝ to bere ful bayn.'

315-23. The conditions required for the sacrament of baptism are all fulfilled in this novel case. As enumerated by St. Thomas Aquinas they are as follows: (1) The water of baptism must fall on the body, and not on the clothing of the person to be baptized (*Summa Theolog.,* Pars 3, Quæst. 66, Artl. 1, 7); (2) The baptism must be conferred in the name of the Father, and of the Son, and of the Holy Ghost (*Summa Theolog.,* Pars 3, Quæst. 66,

Art. 5); (3) The baptism must be conferred by some liquid that preserves the species of water, if not by pure plain water (*Summa Theolog.,* Pars. 3, Quæst. 66, Art. 4). According to the present day belief of the Roman Catholic Church, baptism conferred by a tear is invalid; see *Catholic Encyclopedia: Baptism* VI. Even in the Middle Ages the trend of opinion among theologians ran counter to any other substance than *aqua pura* for the matter of baptism. The opinion of St. Thomas is, therefore, more liberal than that of many other theologians, Hugo of St. Victor (*De Sacramentis 2. 6.* 14: Migne, *Patr. Lat.* 176. 460), for instance, who makes no attempt to distinguish between the kinds of water; see also the *Summa Sententiarum* 5. 10 of the same writer (Migne, *Patr. Lat.* 176. 136). The poet of *Erkenwald,* however, must not be judged too severely by theological standards.

318. Cf. *Joseph of Arimathie* 683: 'In þe nome of þe fader Ioseph him fulwede.'

321. With þat worde þat he warpyd. A common alliterative formula; cf. *Pat.* 356; *Pur.* 152, 213.

328. lures. 'Losses' (OE. *lyre*). These are (1) deprivation of the sight of the Beatific Vision (293); (2) absence from the Marriage Supper of the Lamb (332). The more general meaning 'harm' is also possible. G. renders 'lourings, glooms, darknesses,' though querying those meanings, and suggests connection with OE. **lūrian.*

332. Cf. *Pur.* 829: 'Þenne seten þay at þe soper, wern served bylyve.'

333. weshe us. G., noting that *weshe* is evidently a pres. plural, suggests that the poet may have written *weshes of payne,* and that *us* may be due to scribal misreading.

334. Cf. *Wars of Alex.* (Ashmole MS.) 553: 'Þe liȝt lemand late laschis fra þe heuyn.'

335. sprent. Ordinarily 'leapt, sprang,' but here, as Mrs. Wright (*Engl. Stud.* 36. 222) notes upon *Gaw.* 1896, quite possibly with the more vivid sense of 'dart forward with a spring or sudden motion' (EDD. s. v. *sprent,* v.², 1).

336. Cf. *Chron. Maj.* 3. 99:

Quam suavis sit et delectabilis sanctarum refectio animarum et regnare cum Christo, ubi frigiditas nullum afficit, fames et sitis neminem affligit.

337. Cf. *Pur.* 91: 'Ful manerly wyth marchal mad for to sitte.'

340. Cf. *Death and Life* 21: 'Bringe vs into blisse, that brought vs out of ball.'

344. rottok. NED. (s. v. *rottock*) defines as 'decayed or musty thing,' and suggests that the word is formed on *rot*, v., though querying that statement. Holthausen (*Angl. Beibl.* 34. 18) is of the same opinion, and cites Mod. Engl. *bullock, hillock* as analogues. After quoting this passage, NED. next records the word as occurring in Jamieson's *Popular Ballads* (1806), where it is rendered as 'old musty corn.' EDD. (s. v. *rottack*, sb., 2), quoting from the Banff-shire Glossary (1867), has 'anything stored up for a long time, with the idea of mustiness.' Cf. *mullok*, 'heap of refuse' (*Cant. Tales: Reeve's Prologue* 19 (A. 3873)).

345. sesyd in blisse. A legal term. NED. (s. v. *seize*, v., 1 b) defines *to be seised in* as 'to be the legal possessor of.' Cf. *Pearl* 417: '& sesed in alle hys herytage.'

351. Cf. *Morte Arthure* 4014: 'Apas in processione and with the prynce metys.'

352. Cf. *Thomas off Ersseldoune*, stanza 2 (*Engl. and Scottish Popular Ballads*, Boston, 1882, ed. Child 1. 326): 'Þe wodewale beryde als a belle.'

PREFATORY NOTE TO THE GLOSSARY

The glossary aims to record, with the exception of the articles, not only every word, but in all but the commonest words, every instance of each form of a word. Where it is doubtful whether the nominative or infinitive form of a word ends in -*e,* I have indicated the possibility of its occurrence at the end of the word by including it within a parenthesis. No omission has been made unless the numbers are followed by 'etc.' When the designations of mood and tense are omitted, supply pres. ind.; when the mood only, supply ind. When the preterite forms of weak verbs are not given, they end regularly in-(*e*)*d.* To save space, many verbal and nominal forms have been condensed by means of the hyphen. This division is merely a mechanical device, and does not mark the morphological ending. The dash always represents the form in black-face type, and never refers to the form that has immediately preceded.

Initial *ȝ* follows *y* in this glossary. I have not thought it advisable in the etymologies to attempt to define in each case the precise relationship of the Middle English word to the one from which it is derived, or to which it is related; when the relationship is indirect, the etymon is preceded by 'Cf.' No etymology is given for a word obviously derived from the one preceding or following, if the derivative is found only in Middle English. Similarly, no etymology is given for a compound if it is found only in Middle English, and the simple word(s) occur in the text. Where two forms of the Old English etymon occur, the first is the West Saxon form, the second the Mercian. The definitions in some cases are contextual, since alliterative verse at times requires a considerable extension of the original meaning of a word. The following abbreviations are used:

AN.	Anglo-Norman.
Fris.	Frisian.
Gael.	Gaelic.
Lat.	Latin.
LOE.	Late Old English.
MHG.	Middle High German.
MLG.	Middle Low German.
NF.	Norman French.
OF.	Old French.
OHG.	Old High German.
OM.	Mercian dialect of Old English.
ON.	Old Norse (Icelandic).
OS.	Old Saxon.
Swed.	Swedish.

GLOSSARY

A.

a, indef. art., 3, 27, 38, 39, etc. OE. ān.

abate, v. tr., *demolish, destroy:* pp. abatyd, 37. OF. abatre.

abbay, n., *abbey,* 108. OF. abaïe.

aboute, adv., *on every side,* 48: prep., *concerning,* 56, 110. OE. ābūtan.

abyme, n., *abyss,* 334. OF. abi(s)me.

acounte, n., *reckoning,* 209. OF. acunt.

Adam, prop. n., 295. Lat. Adam.

adoun, adv., *down,* 322. OE. ādūne<of dūne.

after, adv., *behind, afterward,* 112, 116, 141. OE. æfter.

after, conj., 207.

after, prep., 126, 304, 307; *by,* 195. OE. æfter.

afterwarde, adv., 127. OE. æfterwearde.

age, n., 150. OF. age.

aghe, n., *awe, fear,* 234. ON. agi.

aghe, v., *own, possess:* pret. 2 sg. aghtes, 224; 3 sg. aght, 27. OE. āgan.

aght, adj., *eight,* 208, 210. OE. eahta, æhta.

aghtene, adj., *eighteen,* 208. OE. eahtatēne.

al, adj., *all,* 14, 23, 32, 96, 351, etc.; *the whole,* 64, 106, 119, 137, etc.; as pron. *everybody,* 54, 171, 219; *everything,* 192: sg. al, 96, 106, 119, 192, etc., alle, 10, 137, 246; pl. alle, 14, 32, 166, 247, etc.; gen. pl. in cpds. alder- (q. v.).

OE. eall, all. See also allekynnes.

al, adv., *completely, wholly,* 75, 78, 144; *greatly, very much,* 122, 226: alle, 48, 300. OE. eall, all.

alder, n., *ancestor,* 295. OE. (e)aldor.

aldergrattest, superl. adj., *greatest of all,* 337: aldergrattyst, 5. OE. ealra + grīetest.

allas, int., *alas,* 288. OF. (h)alas.

alle-kynnes, adj., *of every kind,* 63. Originally gen. alles cynnes. OE. all + cynn.

alowe, v. tr., *commend, praise:* pres. 3 sg. alowes, 267. OF. alouer.

als, see **as**.

also, adv., *also,* 327, 339. OE. eall + swā.

altogeder, adv., *wholly,* 228. OE. eall + tōgædre.

amounte, v. intr., *reach to,* 284. OF. amonter, AN. amunter.

(anande), *concerning,* 173. OE. on efn + -d.

and, conj., 2, 3, 9, 10, etc.; in adversative sense often = *but,* 72, 118, 155, 224, 269, etc.: ande, 59, 112. OE. and.

ansuare, n., *answer,* 127. OE. andswaru.

ansuare, v. intr., *answer:* imper. 2 sg. 184. OE. andswarian.

any, adj., 85, 206, 284. OE. ænig.

Appolyn, prop. n., *Apollo,* 19.

appulle, n., *apple,* 295. OE. æppel.

araye, v. tr., *attire, dress:* pp. araide, 77; arayed, 271. AN. arayer.

are, adv., *before,* 36. ON. ãr.

art, n., *district,* 33. Cf. Gael. aird, àrd.

as, adv., *like, as,* 91, 343; correl. with 'as' or 'als,' 88, 92, 139, 219, 316: als, 85, 87, 89, 242. OE. eall + swã.

as, conj., *as, just as,* 4, 36, 44; *since,* 135; *according as,* 275, 277; *while,* 43, 45; *as if, as though,* 64, 92; þere as, 167. OE. eall + swã.

aske, v. tr., *ask:* pres. subj. 1 pl., 171; pret. ind. 3 sg. askyd, 96. OE. ãscian.

aspie, v. tr., *catch sight of, espy:* pret. 3 sg. aspied, 65. OF. espier.

assent, n., *assent,* 66. OF. assent.

at, prep., 1, 34, 257, 332; *from,* 170; in phrases, at ones, 352. OE. æt.

atyre, v. tr., *attire, robe,* 130: pp. atyride, 130. OF. atirer.

Augustyn(e), n., *Augustine:* gen. sg. Augustynes, 33; Austyn, 12. Lat. Augustinus.

autere, n., *altar,* 137. OF. auter.

avay, v. tr., *instruct, teach:* inf. 174. OF. avei-, from avier.

avise, v. tr., *observe, view:* pret. 3 pl. avisyde, 53. OF. aviser.

avis(i)on, n., *vision,* 121. OF. avision.

ay, adv., *ever,* 278, 287, 301. ON. ei.

ay-lastande, pres. part., *everlasting,* 347. ON. ei + OE. læstende.

B.

bale, n., *torment, woe,* 257, 340. OE. bealu.

balefully, adv., *painfully, sadly,* 311. Cf. OE. bealufull.

bapteme, n., *baptism,* 330. OF. bapte(s)me.

baron(e), n., *baron:* pl. -s, 142. OF. baron.

bashe, v. tr., *surprise:* 3 sg. bashis, 261. Cf. AN. abaïss-; OF. esbaïss-; lengthened stem of OF. esbaïr.

baythe, v. tr., *ask* (?): 3 sg. -s, 257. Cf. ON. beiða, ask, beg.

be, v. intr.: inf., 94, 97, 180, 244; 2 sg. art, 185, 188; 3 sg. is, 19, 25, 33, 44; 1 pl. are, 302; 2 pl. are, 298; 3 pl. are, 164, 283; arne, 304; pret. was: 1 sg. 201; 2 sg. 186, 222; 3 sg. was, 3, 6, 12, 19; wos, 11, 31, 73, 78, 288: used as plural, 50, 350; 2 pl. were, 297; 3 pl. 32, 52, 53, 85; pret. subj. 1 sg. were, 197; 3 sg. were, 64, 72, 92, 158; imper. 2 sg. be, 181, 325, 327; 3 sg. be, 324, 326; pp. bene, 26, 88, 243; ben, 98; nas (= ne was), 285. OE. bēon.

bede, v. tr., *give, offer* (often by confusion with bidde, q. v.): pret. 1 sg. bede, 243; pp. boden, 214. OE. bēodan.

bedel, n., *beadle:* pl. -s, 59, 111. OF. bedel.

before, conj., 209. OE. beforan.

before, prep., *before,* 143. OE. beforan.

begynne, v. tr., *begin;* 3 sg. begynnes, 131. OE. beginnan.

behalve, n., *in the name of,* 181. OE. be + healfe (dat. case).

belle, n., *bell:* pl. -s, 352. OE. belle.

Belyn, prop. n., *Belin,* 213.

beme, n., *rood-tree, cross,* 182. OE.
bēam.

benche, n., *judge's seat,* 250. OE.
benc.

bende, v. tr., *bind, stretch:* pp.
bende, 182. OE. bendan.

bere, v. tr., *direct,* 311; *bring forth,
produce,* 326: pret. 3 sg. 311,
326. OE. beran.

bery, v. tr., *beat, resound:* pret. 3
pl. beryd, 352. ON. berja.

Berynge, prop. n., 213.

besie, v. intr., *be busy, occupy oneself:* pret. 3 pl. besiet, 56. OE.
bisgian.

best, see gode.

besyde, prep., *by the side of,* 142.
OE. be + sīdan.

bete, v. tr., *beat:* pret. 3 pl. bete,
9; pp. beten, 37. OE. bēaten.

bidde, v. tr., *bid, command, pray*
(often confused with bede,
q. v.) : 1 sg. bydde, 181; 3 sg.
biddes, 221; pret. 3 pl. bede, 67.
OE. biddan.

bigge¹, v. tr., *build:* pp. buggid, 207;
buggyd, 37. ON. byggia.

bigge², v. tr., *buy:* pret. 2 sg.
boghtes, 289. OE. bycgan.

bigripe, v. tr., *encircle tightly:*
pret. 3 sg. bigripide, 80. OE.
begrīpan.

biknowe, v. tr., *confess:* imp. 221.
OE. becnāwan.

bileve, n., *trust in God,* 173, 299.
OE. bi + lēafa (Northumb.).

bir, v. impers., *be proper:* pret.
burde, 260. OE. (ge) byrian.

biseche, v. tr., *beg, entreat:* inf.
120. OE. bi + sēcean.

bita, bitaa, v. tr., *assign:* pp. bitan,
28. OE. bi + LOE. tacan.

bitwene, adv., *between,* 196. OE.
betwēonum.

bitwene, prep., *between,* 214. OE.
betwēonum.

blakke, adj., *ash-coloured, dark,*
343. OE. blāc.

blee, n., *colour,* 87, 343. OE. blēo.

blessid, part. adj., 340: blessyd,
3; blissid, 326. OE. blētsian.

blis, n., *bliss,* 340: blisse, 345. OE.
blīðs.

blisful, adj., *blissful,* 326: blisfulle,
76.

blo, adj., *dark,* 290. ON. blār.

blode, n., *blood,* 182, 290. OE.
blōd.

blonke, n., *horse,* 112. OE. blonca.

blynne, v. tr., *stop, put a stop to,*
111. OE. blinnan.

blysnande, pres. part., *gleaming,
lustrous, shining,* 87. Based on
Gmc. *blus (cf. OE. āblysian).

bode, n., *command, order,* 181, 193.
OE. bod.

bodeworde, n., *announcement, mes-
sage,* 105. OE. bod + word.

body, n., *body, corpse,* 76, 94, 106,
190. OE. bodig.

boghe, v. intr., *betake oneself, go,*
59; *bow, be obedient,* 194: inf.
194; pret. 3 pl. boghit, 59. OE.
būgan.

bok(e), n., *book,* 103. OE. bōc.

bolde, adj., *bold, daring, brave,* 213;
big, mighty, 106. OE. beald,
bāld.

bone, n¹., *murderer,* 243. OE. bana.

bone, n²., *prayer, petition,* 194. ON.
bōn.

bone, n³., *bone:* pl. -s, 346. OE.
bān.

bone, adj., *obedient, prepared,* 181.
ON. būinn.

bonk(e), n., *bank, hill:* pl. -es, 32.
ON. bakki.

bordure, n., *border, edging*, 51, 82:
pl. -s, 82. OF. bordure.

bot, adv., *only*, 32. OE. būtan.

bot, conj., 52, 54, 73, 100, etc.; con-
junctive use after an expression
like, 'it might not be,' 97. OE.
būtan.

bote, n., *help, relief, remedy*, 170,
327. OE. bōt.

bothe, adj., *both*, 194. ON. bāþir.

bothum, n., *bottom*, 76. OE. botm.

bounty, n., *excellence, worth, reward*, 248. AN. bunte, OF.
bonté.

bourne, n., *brook, stream*, 330. OE.
burna.

brawnche, n., *branch, offshoot*, 276.
OF. branche.

brayde, v. intr., *stir, move:* pret. 3
sg. brayed, 190. OE. bregdan.

Bretayne, prop. n., *Britain:* gen.
sg. Bretaynes, 32. OF. Bre-
taigne.

Breton, prop. n., *Briton*, 213: pl.
-s, 9. OF. Breton.

breve, v. tr., *recount, tell:* pp.
brevyt, 103. ON. brēfa.

brode, adj., *broad, wide*, 55. OE.
brād.

brothire, n., *brother*, 213. OE.
brōðor.

Brutus, prop. n., *Brutus*, 207. Lat.
Brutus.

bryȝt, adj., *bright*, 51, 87, 190, 330.
OE. beorht, berht, breht.

brynge, v. tr., *bring*, 105, 340; with
prep. into, *drive out, expel*, 9;
translate, 56: inf. brynge, 56;
pret. 3 pl. broȝt, 9; pp. broȝt,
340; broght, 105. OE. bringan.

burgeys, n., *burgess:* pl., 59. OF.
burgeis.

burghe, n., *city*, 3, 103, 207, 352.
OE. burh.

burie, v. tr., *bury:* pret. 3 pl. buriet,
248; pp. buried, 94; buriede,
106. OE. byrgan.

burynes, n., *tomb*, 142, 190. OE.
byrignes.

busk, v. refl., *betake oneself:* pret.
3 sg. buskyd, 112. ON. būa-sk,
prepare oneself.

busmare, n., *reproach, insult*, 214.
OE. bismer.

by, adv., *by*, 72. OE. be, bī.

by, prep., *by, along*, 71, 90 (2
times); expressing agent, 111;
cause, 235; means, 102 (2 times),
121; in accordance with, 66, 209;
throughout, 32; in phrases, by
kynde, 157; adjurative, by
Goddes leve, 316; as conj., by
the time that, 113: bi, 90 (2
times). OE. be, bī.

byhove, v. impers., *it behoves:* 3
sg. byhoves, 168. OE. bi-, behō-
fian.

byschop, n., *bishop*, 3, 105, 129, 142,
159: bischop, 33, 111; bisshop,
193, 221, 265, 273; bysshop, 311,
327, 339. OE. bisceop.

byside, adv., *aside*, 67. OE. be +
sīdan.

bytyme, adv., *in good time, at an
early hour*, 112. ME. phrase by
tyme. <OE. bi + tīman.

C.

cache, v. tr., *lay hold on*, 71; *receive, contract*, 148: pret. 3 pl.
kaghten, 71; pp. caȝt, 148.
ONF. cachier.

Glossary

Glossary   **57**

calle, v. tr., *designate, name;* pret. 3 sg. callid, 16. ON. kalla.

camelyn, n., *a kind of stuff made (or supposed to be made) of camel's hair,* 82. OF. camelin.

careles, adj., *free, generous,* 172. OE. carlēas.

carpe, v. tr., *speak, utter:* inf. carpe, 317. ON. karpa.

cast, v. tr., *cast, throw, put:* inf. cast, 317; pp. kest, 83. ON. kasta.

cause, n., *cause, reason,* 221; *lawsuit,* 202; pl. -s, 202. OF. cause.

cayser, n., *emperor,* 199. ON. keisari, Lat. Cæsar.

cenacle, n., *supping room,* 336. OF. cēnacle.

cesse, v. intr., *come to an end:* pret. 3 sg. cessyd, 341; pp. cessyd, 136. OF. cesser.

charge, v. tr., *fill, furnish:* pret. 3 sg. chargit, 18. OF. chargier.

chaunge, v. tr., *change:* pret. 3 sg. chaungit, 18. OF. changer.

chere, n., *aspect, look, expression, visage,* 342. OF. ch(i)ere.

chevely, adv., *primarily,* 18. OF. chef + -ly (OE. -līce.).

child, n., *child:* gen. sg. -es, 318. OE. cild.

cite, n., *city,* 202. OF. cité.

clanse, v. tr., *cleanse, make clean:* pret. 3 sg. clansyd, 16. Cf. OE. clǣnsian.

clene, adj., *clean,* 82, 259. OE. clǣne.

clerke, n., *scholar, learned man, priest:* nom. pl. -(s), 55. OE. and OF. clerc.

cleþe, v. tr., *clothe, dress:* pret. 3 pl. cladden, 249. OE. clǣþan.

clos, n., *cathedral precinct,* 55. OF. clos.

clothe, n., *dress, raiment, vesture,* 82, 148, 263, 266; pl. *clothes. garments,* 259: pl. -s, 259. OE. clāþ.

clout, n., *rag. shred:* pl. -es, 259. OE. clūt.

cloyster, n., *enclosed space,* 140. OF. cloistre.

cluster, v. intr.: pp. clustrede, 140. OE. cluster, n.

colde, adv., *wretchedly,* 305. OE. cealde.

colour, n., *colour, complexion, hue,* 148, 263: coloure, 263. NF. colour.

come, v. intr., *come,* 63, 113, 142; followed by to, 74: inf. 74; pret. 3 sg. come, 113, 142; 3 pl. commen, 63. OE. cuman.

comforthe, n., *aid, succour, support,* 168, 172. OF. confort.

command, v. tr., *command, enjoin, order:* pret. 3 sg. comaundit, 115. OF. comander, cumander.

committe, v. tr., *appoint, commission;* pp. committid, 201. Lat. committĕre.

communnate, n., *community:* pl. -s, 14. OF. com(m)unauté.

con, v. pret. pres., *be able:* pres. 1 pl. con, 156; pret. 3 sg. couthe, 100, 101, 249. OE. cunnan.

confirm, v. tr., *confirm, establish, make firm:* pres. part. confirmynge, 124. OF. confermer.

confourm, v. tr., *conform, bring into conformity:* pret. 3 sg. confourmyd, 242. OF. conformer.

consciens, n., *conscience, moral sense,* 237. OF. conscience.

58   St. Erkenwald

convert, v. tr., *convert:* pret. 3 sg.
14. OF. convertir.
corner, n., *corner:* pl. -s, 71. AN.
corner.
coron, n., *crown,* 83, 222; *top part
of the skull, head,* 55; croun,
222; pl. crownes, 55. AN.
coroune.
corone, v. tr., *crown:* pret. 3 pl.
coronyd, 254. AN. coruner,
corouner.
corrupt, adj., *rotten, decayed,* 346.
OF. corrupt, Lat. corruptus.
cors, n., *corpse,* 110, 317: corce,
177. OF. cors.
councele, v. tr., *conceal:* imper. 2
sg. 184. OF. conceler.
counselle, n., *counsel, wisdom,* 167,
172, 266. AN. cunseil, OF.
conseil.
courte, n., *court,* 249. OF. cort.
couthely, adv., *certainly, clearly,
manifestly,* 98. OE. cūþlīce.
cover, v. tr., *cover, envelop:* pret.
3 sg. covert, 346. OF. covrir.
covetise, n., *covetousness,* 237. OF.
coveitise.
coyfe, n., *coif, cap covering top,
back, and sides of the head,* 83.
OF. coife.
crafte, n., *power, skill, wisdom,*
167; *element,* 346. OE. cræft.
crafty, n., *skilfully wrought,* 44.
OE. cræftig.
crak(e), v. intr., *resound:* pret. 3
sg. crakit, 110. OE. cracian.
creatur(e), n., *creature, human
being,* 167: gen. pl. -es, 167.
OF. creature.
Crist, n., *Christ,* 2: Criste, 209;
gen. sg. -es, 16. OE. Crist.
Cristen, n., *christian,* 124, 209. OE.

crīsten (Wright marks the *i* of
crīsten as long.)
Cristendome, prop. n., 2; Cristendame, 14. OE. crīstendōm.
cronecle, n., *chronicle,* 156: pl. -s,
44; cronicle, 156. AF. cronicle.
crosse, n., *cross,* 2. Cf. ON.
kross.
crow(e), n., *crow-bar,* pl. -es, 71.
OE. crāwe.
cry, n., *public report, rumour,* 110.
OF. cri.
cumly, adj., *beautiful, fair,* 82.
OE. cȳmlīc.
cure, n., *remedy,* 168. OF. cure.
curtes, adj., *courtly, having such
manners as befit the court* (of
law): superl. curtest, 249. AF.
curteis.

D.

dampne, v. tr., *damn, doom:* pp.
dampnyd, 302. OF. dampner.
date, n., *date,* 205. OF. date.
daunger, v. tr., *endanger, render
liable:* subj. pret. daungerde,
320. OF. dangerer.
daw(e), v. intr., *dawn:* 3 sg. -es,
306; pret. 3 sg. dawid, 127. OE.
dagian.
day, n., *day,* 236: pl. dayes, 155;
dawes, 7. OE. dæg.
day-belle, n., *day-bell,* 117. OE.
dæg + belle.
debonerte, n., *graciousness, mild-
ness,* 123. OF. debonaireté.
declyne, v. intr., *fall away, swerve
away:* pret. 3 sg. declynet, 237.
OF. decliner.
dede, n., *deed,* 169. OE. dǣd, dēd.
dede, adj., *dead,* 225, 309, 320: as
noun, 116. OE. dēad.
dedifie, v. tr., *dedicate:* inf. 6; pret.

3 sg. dedifiet, 23. Cf. OF. dēdier and OF. ēdifier.

defaute, n., *blemish, defect, flaw,* 148. OF. defaute.

deghe, v. intr., *die:* pret. 1 sg. deghed, 246. Cf. ON. deyja.

delve, v. tr., *delve,* 45; *bury* (a corpse), 99: pret. 3 pl. dalfe, 45; pp. dolven, 99. OE. delfan.

dene, n., *dean,* 144. OF. deien, dien.

deny, v. intr., *resound:* pret. 3 sg. denyed, 246. OE. dynian.

depe, adj., *deep,* 302. OE. dēop.

depe, adv., *far down,* 45, 99. OE. dēope.

deputate, adj., *deputy,* 227. Lat. dēputātus.

dere, adj., *beloved, noble, worthy,* 23, 225; *esteemed, honourable,* 29; in less precise senses, often w. meaning hardly determinable: *beloved, dear, excellent, important, precious, worthy,* 123, 144, 193: deere, 123; superl. derrest, 29. OE. dēore.

derfe, adj., *bold, dreadful,* 99. ON. djarfr.

derke, adj., *dark,* 117, 294, 306. OE. deorc.

dethe, n., *death,* 247, 294, 306. OE. dēaþ.

devel, n., *devil,* 27; *prince of devils* (Satan), 15: develle, 15. OE. dēofol.

devoyde, v. tr., *avoid, withdraw,* 116; *make void,* 348: pres. 3 sg. -s, 348; pret. 3 sg. devoydit, 116. OF. devoidier.

devyne, v. intr., *conjecture, guess:* subj. pres. 1 pl. 169. OF. deviner.

devyse, v. tr., *describe, give an account, recount, set forth in detail,*

144, 225, 309; with reflex. pron., 309: inf. 225; pret. 3 sg. devysit, 144; devisyt, 309. OF. deviser.

digne, v. tr., *vouchsafe:* imper. 2 sg. digne, 123. OF. degnier.

ditte, v. tr., *close, shut:* pret. 3 sg. ditte, 116. OE. dyttan.

dole, n., *part, portion,* 6. OE. dāl.

dome, n., *decision, judgment, sentence,* 236. OE. dōm.

domesmon, n., *deemster, judge,* 227. Early ME. dōmes + monn.

doun, adv., *down,* 6, 37, 311, doun, 320. OE. of dūne.

drawe, v. tr., *pull:* pp. drawen, 6. OE. dragan.

drede, n., *dread, fear,* 233. Cf. OE. ondrǣdan.

dreme, n., *noise, sound,* 191. OE. drēam.

drery, n., *doleful, dreary, melancholy, sad,* 191. OE. drēorig.

dresse, v. tr., *draw up, prepare:* inf. 236. OF. dresser.

droppe, v. intr., *drop, fall:* subj. pret. 2 sg. droppyd, 320. OE. dropian.

dryghtyn, n., *chief, lord,* 29. OE. dryhten.

dryve, v. tr., *'push,' utter,* 191: 3 sg. -s, 191. OE. drīfan.

duke, n., *king, leader,* 227. OF. duc.

dul, n., *grief, sorrow,* 246. OF. doel, dul.

dulfully, adv., *dolefully, mournfully, sorrowfully,* 302, 309. ME. dulful + -ly (<OE. -līce).

durre, n., *door,* 116. OE. duru.

dwell, v. intr., *dwell:* pret. 3 pl. dwellide, 10. OE. dwellan.

dwyne, v. intr., *languish, pine away,*

waste away: pres. part. dwynande, 294. OE. dwīnan.
dyȝt, v. tr., *appoint, ordain,* 23, 294;
construct, build, prepare, 45:
pret. 3 sg. dyȝt, 294; dyght, 23;
3 pl. dyȝt, 45. OE. dihtan.
dy(m)ly, adv., *dimly,* 306. Cf. OE.
dimlīc.
dyverse, adj., *evil, perverse,* 60.
OF. divers, diverse.

E.

efte, adv., *again, a second time,* 37.
OE. eft.
egge, v. tr., *give an edge, sharpen:*
pp. eggit, 40. Cf. OE. ecg.
eghe, n., *eye:* pl. eghen, 194, 311,
321, 330. OE. ēage.
eghe-lydde, n., *eyelid:* pl. -s, 178.
Cf. OE. ēage + OE. hlid.
elles, adv., *otherwise* (preceded by
or), 121. OE. elles.
enbawme, v. tr., *embalm:* pp.
enbawmyd, 261, 265. OF. en-
baumer.
enbelice, v. tr., *embellish, render
beautiful:* pp. enbelicit, 51. OF.
embellis—lengthened stem of em-
bellir.
ende, n., *end,* 136. OE. ende.
Englonde, n., *England,* 1. OE.
Engla land.
enjoyne, v. tr., *appoint:* pp. enjoynyd, 216. OF. enjoign—stem
of enjoindre.
enprise, n., *renown,* 253. OF.
emprise.
entouche, v. tr., *poison:* entouchid,
297. OF. entouchier.
er, conj., *before,* 308. OE. ǣr.
ere, n., *ear:* pl. -s, 90. OE. ēare.
ere, adv., *before,* 19, 24. OE. ǣr.
ere, prep., *before,* 118. OE. ǣr.

Erkenwolde, n., *Erkenwald,* 4, 33,
108, 118.
erthe, n., *earth, world,* 196, 198,
237; *ground,* 45. OE. eorðe.
Esex, prop. n., *Essex,* 108. OE.
Ēastseaxe.
ete, v. intr., *eat:* pret. 3 sg. ete, 295.
OE. etan.
evel, adv., *hardly, with difficulty,*
276. OE. yfele.
ever, adv., *always, at all times, in
all cases, constantly, perpetually,*
230, 256, 267, 288; *at any time,
ever,* 103, 104, 198, 255; for ever,
154, 296, 338. OE. ǣfre.
evermore, adv., *ever, for all time,*
26; *constantly, continually,* 110.
exile, v. tr., *exile:* pp. exilid, 303.
OF. exilier, learned form of
essillier.

F.

face, n., *face,* 89, 323. OF. face.
fader, n., *father,* 243, 244; of the
Lord, 318: gen. sg. fader, 243,
318. OE. fæder.
faire, adj., *fair,* 46, 317. OE.
fæger.
faithe, n., *belief, faith* (Christian
or pagan), 13, 124, 173, 204,
242; *faithfulness, fidelity, loyalty,*
252; 'good faith,' 230; faythe,
13, 204. Cf. OF. fei; perhaps
NF. feid (= feið).
faitheful, adj., *faithful,* 299.
faitheles, adj., *faithless,* 287.
falle, v. intr., *fall,* 323; *befall,* 244:
pret. 3 sg. felle, 244, 323. OE.
feallan, fallan.
fals, adj., *deceitful, deceptive, insidi-
ous, treacherous,* 231, 244. OF.
fals.

fastynge, n., *establishment, confir-mation, 173.* Cf. OE. fæstan.

favour, n., *favor,* 244. OF. favour.

fayle, v. tr., *lack,* 287; intr., *wane, grow dim,* 342: pret. 3 sg. faylid, 287; faylide, 342. OF. faillir.

fayne, adj., *well-pleased, eager,* 176. OE. fægn.

felonse, adj., *fierce, cruel,* 231. Cf. OF. felon, (adj.).

ferforthe, adv., in phrase, as fer-forthe as, with reference to degree or extent, 242. OE. feor(r) + OE. forð.

ferly, adj., *strange, wondrous,* 46; as n., *marvel, wonder,* 145. OE. færlic, ferlic.

fest, n., *feast,* 303. OF. feste.

fleshe, n., *flesh,* 89. OE. flæsc.

flore, n., *floor,* 46. OE. flōr.

folke, n., *folk, people,* 231. OE. folc.

folwe, v. tr., *baptize:* pres. 1 sg. folwe, 318. OE. fulwian.

fonte, n., *baptismal font,* 299. OE. font.

for, conj., *for,* 29, 45, 329, 345; *because,* 7, 101, 245, 256, 347; *since,* 277. OE. for.

for, prep., *on account of, because of,* 215, 237, 246, 253; *for the sake of,* 194, 233, 234 (3 times); *as,* 222, 249, 250, 251; *with a view to,* 132; for to, with inf., 40, 41, 236, 298; for þe nones, 38; for ever, 154, 296, 338. OE. for.

forgo, v. tr., *overlook, let pass:* inf. 276. OE. forgān. (forgan-gan).

forthe, adv., *forth,* 351. OE. forð.

forþi, conj., *therefore, for this reason,* 279. OE. forþȳ.

forwreste, v. tr., *wring, disturb,*

strike: pp. forwrast, 220. OE. for + wræstan.

fote, n., *lower part of a structure, base,* 42. OE. fōt.

fourme, n., in phrase, in fourme, *according to rules or prescribed methods,* 230. OF. fourme.

fourme, v. tr., *fashion, make:* pp. fourmyt, 46. OF. fourmer.

fourty, adj., *forty,* 230. OE. fēowertig.

fre, adj., *ready to grant, gracious,* 318. OE. frēo.

freke, n., *man,* 287, 323. OE. freca.

frende, n., *patron, helper,* 176. OE. frēond.

freshe, adj., *undecayed, unsullied,* 89. OE. fersc, perhaps influenced by OF. freis, fresche.

fro, prep., *from,* 12, 107, 116, 137. ON. frā.

frowarde, adj., *perverse, refractory,* 231. Early ME. fro (<ON. frā) + ME. -ward (<OE. -weard).

ful, adv., *exceedingly, full, very,* 1, 53, 55, 82; fulle, 1, 53. OE. ful.

fulfille, v. tr., *execute, perform:* inf. 176. OE. fullfyllan.

fulloght, n., *baptism,* 299. OE. full-wiht.

fulsen, v. tr., *aid, help:* imper. fulsen, 124. OE. filst + OE. -n(i) suffix of such verbs as fæstnian.

fundement, n., *foundation* (of a building), 42. Cf. OF. fonde-ment (<Lat. fundāmentum).

furre, v. tr., *line, trim, or cover with fur,* 81; *adorn or clothe with fur,* 252: pret. 3 pl. furrid, 252; pp. furrit, 81. OF. forrer.

fynde, v. tr., *find, come upon:* inf.,

156; pret. 3 pl. founden, 43, 46.
OE. findan.

fyndynge, n., *finding,* 145.

fyne, adj., *pure, righteous,* 173:
superl. fynest, 252. OF. fin.

fynger, n., *finger,* 145, 165. OE.
finger.

fyrre, adv., comp. of fer, 169, 293.
OE. fierra.

fyrst, adj., *first,* 331; in adverbial
phrases, on fyrst, 42, 144, 207:
fyrste, 207. OE. fyrst.

fyrst, adv., 197.

G.

gargel(e), n., *gargoyle:* pl. -es, 48.
Cf. OF. gargouille (gargoule,
gargole).

garnyshe, v. tr., *adorn, decorate,
ornament:* pp. garnysht, 48. OF.
garniss-, from garnir.

gate, n., *way,* 241. ON. gata.

gay, adj., *bright,* 75; *finely dressed,*
134. OF. gai.

geder, v. refl., *assemble, come together in a body:* pp. gedrid,
134. OE. gad(e)rian.

gentil, adj., *pagan, gentile,* 216.
OF. gentil.

gentil, adj., *noble,* 229. OF. gentil.

gete, v. tr., *bring a person out of a
certain position:* pret. 3 sg. gete,
241. ON. geta.

glent, v. intr., *deviate, turn aside,*
241: inf. 241. Cf. Sw. dial,
glänta.

glisne, v. intr., *glisten, glitter,
sparkle:* pres. p. glisnande, 78.
OE. glisnian.

glode, n., *bright space, painted
space (within the coffin),* 75.
Cf. ON. glaðr; OE. phrase,
sunne gǣþ tō glade.

glotte, n., *venom,* 297. OF. glette.

glow, v. intr., *call,* 171: pres. subj.
1 pl. 171. Cf. OE. gleowian.

go, v. intr., *go, walk:* pret. 3 sg.
ȝode, 198. OE. gān.

God, n., *God,* 325, 339: gen. sg.
Goddes, 316; Godde, 171, 282.
OE. god.

gode, adj., *good,* 230. OE. gōd.

golde, n., *gold,* 75, 78, 80, 248. OE.
gold.

golde, adj., *gold,* 51. OE. gold.
Adj. form usually golden.

goste, n., *spirit,* 192; *Holy Ghost,*
127, 319. OE. gāst.

governour, n., *governor, ruler,* 251.
OF. governeür.

gowne, n., *gown,* 78. OF. goune.

grace, n., *grace, favor, mercy,* 120,
126, 171, 276. OF. grace.

gracious, adj., *gracious,* 319. OF.
gracious.

graunte, v. tr., *grant,* 126: pp.
graunte, 126. Cf. OF. graanter.

grave, n., *grave,* 153. OE. græf.

gray, adj., *grey,* 48. OE. grǣg.

graythist, adj., *prepared, ready:*
superl. graythist, 251. ON.
greiðr.

grete, n., *grit, earth,* 41. OE. grēot.

grete, adj., *great,* 134, 141, 282: pl.
grete, 283. OE. grēat.

grete, v. intr., *cry, weep:* pret. 3 sg.
grette, 126. Cf. OE. grǣtan
(OM. grētan), and OE. grēotan.

gronynge, vbl. n., *groaning,* 282.
Cf. OE. grānian.

grounde, n., *ground, earth,* 41. OE.
grund.

grubber, n., *grubber, digger,* 41.
Cf. OE. *grybban.

grue, n., used with negatives. Not
one grue lenger, 319. Cf. OF.

Glossary

gru, *meal, grain.* Cf. Sir Gaw.
& Gr. Kht. 2251, Alexander 3270.
gurde, v. tr., *clothe with a garment:*
pret. 3 pl. gurden, 251. OE.
gyrdan.
gurdille, n., *girdle,* 80. OE. gyrdel.
gyfe, v. tr., *give,* 276: inf. 276;
pret. 3 sg. gefe, 282. Cf. ON.
gefa; OE. giefan, gefan.
gynful, adj., *deceitful, guileful,
treacherous,* 238. Cf. ME. gin,
aphetic form of OF. engin.
gynge, n., *company* (of clergy),
137. OE. genge.

H.

halde, v. tr., *hold,* 42, 166, 223, 249;
with prepositions to enlarge the
meaning: with to, 232: inf.
halde, 42, 166; holde, 232, 249;
2 sg. -s, 223. OE. healden,
hāldan.
halowe, n., *saint:* pl. -s, 23. OE.
hālga.
harde, adj., 40; pl., 288. OE.
heard.
harme, n., *injury:* -s, 232. OE.
hearm.
hathel, n., *man,* 198. OE. æþele,
or perhaps metathesis of OE.
hæleþ (Holthausen).
hatte, v. intr., *to be called, bear the
name.* The forms here given
are examples of pret. 3 sg. with
passive signification, 4, 25, 38.
OE. hātte (pret.) with passive
meaning.
have, v. tr., 17, 224, 312, 315; as
auxiliary, 7, 8, 26, 88, etc.;
forms, 2 sg. 187, 195, 340; 3 sg.
26, 98, 147, 157, 180, 266, 272,
etc.; 1 pl. have, 155; han, 300;
3 pl. has, 148, 271; pret. 2 sg.

hades, 224; 3 sg. had, 95, 207;
hade, 17, 100, 119, 126, 189, 312;
3 pl. haden, 8; hade, 88; pret.
subj. 2 sg., hades, 315; 3 sg.
had, 243. OE. habban.
he, pers. pro.: masc., he, 13, 15, 17,
23, etc.; hym (dat. or acc.), 89,
100, 109, 121, 138; reflex, 17.
129, 313; fem. ho, 274, 279, 308,
326; hyr, 280, 308, 337, 338.
Neut. hit, 7, 26, 47, 49, 54 (2
times); in phrase, to loke hit
by kynde, 157; redundant, 38;
with plural verb, 304; reflex.,
309; plural, þai, 9, 43 (2 times),
45, 46, etc.; hom (dat. or acc.),
9, 16, 214, 232; reflex. 53, 56.
OE. hē, hēo, hit, etc.
hedde, n., *head,* 281. OE. hēafod.
heere, v. tr., *praise:* 1 sg. heere,
339; pp. herid, 325. OE. herian,
hēran.
heghe, adj., *exalted, lofty, of high
rank,* 137, 241, 253; in phrases,
heghe God, 325, 339; heghe
masse, 129; superl. heghest, 253.
OE. hēah, hēh.
heghe, adv., *high,* 223. OE. hēah,
hēh.
heire, n., *circuit,* 211. AN. heire.
helde, v. intr., *depart, turn away,*
137; *bow,* 196: 3 pl. heldes,
196; pret. 3 sg. heldyt, 137.
OE. hieldan, hēldan.
helle, n., *hell,* 196. OE. hel(1).
helle-hole, n., *the pit of hell,* 291,
307. OE. hell + hol.
hemme, v. tr., *decorate with a
border or fringe:* pp. hemmyd,
78. Cf. OE. hem, n.
hende, n., *gracious,* 325; *of high
rank,* 58. Cf. OE. gehende.

Hengyst, prop. n.; gen. sg. Hengyst, 7. OE. Hengest.

hente, v. tr., *receive, suffer,* 232; *carry away, take away,* 291: pret. 1 sg. hent, 232; pret. 2 sg. hentes, 291. OE. hentan.

here, adv., 13, 146, 147, 157, etc. OE. hēr.

here, v. tr., *hear:* pret. 3 pl. herden, 310. OE. hīeran, hēran.

herghe, v. tr., *harry, spoil,* 291: pret. 2 sg. herghedes, 291. OE. hergian.

herken, v. tr., *hearken. hear.* 134; intr., *seek,* 307: inf. 134, 307. OE. hercnian.

hert, n., *heart,* 242, 257. OE. heorte.

hethen, adj., *heathen,* 7. OE. hǣðen, hēðen.

heven, n., *heaven,* 166, 196. OE. heofon.

hewe, v. tr., *hew, cut:* inf. hewe, 40; pp. hewen, 47. OE. hēawan.

highe, v. intr., *hasten, speed:* pret. 3 pl. highide, 58. OE. hīgian.

his, poss. pro., 5, 28, 65, 78, etc. OE. his.

hit, poss. pro., *its,* 309. See also **he.**

holy, adj., *holy,* 4; Holy Goste, 127, 319. OE. hālig.

home, n., *home,* 107. OE. hām.

honde, n., *hand,* 84, 223: pl. -s. 90, 166. OE. hond (hand).

hondequile, n., *an instant, a moment,* 64. OE. handhwīl.

honeste, n., *honesty, honourable character,* 253. OF. (h)oneste.

honge, v. intr., *hang* (a person): pp. hongyt, 244. OE. hangian, hongian.

honour, n., *honour,* 253. OF. honor, AN. honour.

hope, v. tr., *think:* 1 sg. hope, 4. OE. hopian.

hor, poss. pro., *their,* 17, 18, 61, 87 See also **he.**

houre, n., *hour,* 326; *prayers or offices pertaining to a canonical hour,* 119: pl. -s, 119. AN. houre.

how, adv., 95, 187, 258, 264, 284: qualifying verb in direct questions, 284; qualifying verb in indirect questions, 258, 264; qualifying adj. in indirect questions, 95, 187. OE. hū.

humme, v. intr., *hum:* pret. 3 sg. hummyd, 281. Echoic.

hundred, adj., *hundred,* 58, 208, 210: hundrid, 58. OE. hundred.

hungre, v. tr., *hunger:* pret. 3 pl. hungride, 304. OE. hyngran.

hungrie, adj., *hungry,* 307. OE. hungrig.

hurl, v. tr., *hurl:* pret. 3 sg. hurlyd, 17. ?Imitative; cf. LG. hurreln.

hyder, adv., *hither,* 8. OE. hider.

I.

I, pers. pron.: 4, 36, 122, 174, etc.; me (dat. or acc.), 124, 193, 195, 241, etc.; pl. we, 155, 156, 169 (2 times), 171, etc.; us (dat. or acc.), 185, 212, 294, 333, etc. OE. ic.

if, conj., 176, 274; even if, 271. OE. gif.

ilke, adj., *same,* 101, 193. OE. ilca.

in, prep., 1, 3, 5, 10, etc.; *into,* 56, 259, 260, etc.; *among,* 109, 217; *during,* 5, 7, 24, 212; *at,* 216; (?) *by means of, through,* 173; *in respect to, as regards,* 87; with verbs, 17, 288, 345; in phrases: in fonte, 299; in fourme, 230; in grete, 41; in his behalve, 181; in honde, 223; in mantel, 250; in my(n)de, 97; in no wise, 263; in route, 62; in sele, 279; in sorow, 305; in sounde, 92; in worlde, 186; expressing purpose, 124, 173(?); at end of clause, 149, 288, 326, 328: inne, 149. OE. in.

into, prep., 9, 12, 45, 115, etc. OE. intō.

inwith, adv., *within,* 307.

J.

James, prop. n., 22. OF. James.

jape, n., *evil trick, evil device:* pl. -s, 238. OF. *jape.

Jhesus, prop. n., 180: Jhesu, 22. Lat. Jēsūs.

joly, adj., *fair, proud, arrogant,* 229. OF. joli.

Jono, prop. n., *Juno,* 22. Lat. Jūno.

joy, n., *joy,* 180, 188. OF. joye.

joyne, v. tr., *appoint, order:* pp. joyned, 188. Aphetic for ajoyne (OF. enjoign–, from enjoindre).

Jubiter, prop. n., *Jupiter,* 22. Lat. Jūpiter.

juge, n., *judge,* 216. OF. juge.

jugement, n., *(judicial) decision, judgement,* 238. OF. jugement.

jugge, v. tr., *condemn, sentence,* 188; *decree, order,* 180: pp. juggid, 188; juggit, 180. AF. juger, OF. jugier.

justifie, v. tr., *administer justice, judge:* pret. 1 sg. justifiet, 229. OF. justifier.

justise, n., *magistrate, justice:* pl. -s, 254. OF. justise.

K.

kaghten, see cache.

keie, n., *key:* pl. -s, 140. OE. cǣg.

kene, adj., *learned, wise:* pl. kene, 254. OE. cēne.

kenely, adv., *eagerly, quickly,* 63. OE. cēnlīce.

kenne, v. tr., *make known:* inf. 124. OE. cennan, ON. kenna.

kepe, v. tr., *guard,* 66; *preserve,* 266: pret. 3 pl. kepten, 66; pp. kepyd, 266. OE. cēpan.

kest, see cast.

kidde, see kydde.

kithe, n., *country, region,* 98. OE. cȳðð.

knowe, v. tr., *know,* 285; *understand,* 74, 263: inf. 74; 1 sg. 263; pret. 3 sg. 285. OE. cnāwan.

kny3t, n., *knight,* 199. OE. cniht.

kydde, part. adj., *declared, made known,* 44; in phrase, kydde of Saynt Paule, well known as belonging to St. Paul, 113; *recognized,* 222; *celebrated, famous, renowned,* 254; kidde, 222, 254. OE. (ge)cȳðed.

kynde, n., *nature:* by kynde, *by nature, naturally,* 157. OE. (ge)cynd.

kynge, n., *king,* 98, 156, 212, 222, 254; (of the Lord) 267. OE. cyning.

kynne, v. intr., *be conceived, be born:* pp. kynned, 209. OE. cennan.

kyrke, n., *church,* 113: pl. -s, 16. ON. kirkja; cf. OE. cyrice.

L.

lacche, v. tr., *snatch, take up:* inf.
316. OE. læcc(e)an.

ladde, n., *serving-man:* pl. -s, 61.
Origin obscure.

Lady, n., *The Virgin,* 21. OE.
hlæfdīge.

laghe, n., *law,* 187, 200, 216, 245,
268, 287; *faith,* 34; *religious
system, belief,* 203: lawe, 216;
pl. -s, 287; lawes, 268. LOE.
lagu.

laite, v. tr., *look through, search
through, examine:* pp. laitid, 155.
ON. leita.

lake, n., *pit,* 302. OF. lac; Lat.
lacus.

large, adj., 72. OF. large.

lasshe, v. intr., *flash:* pret. 3 sg.
lasshit, 334. Probably onomato-
poetic.

last, v. intr., *last, endure,* 215;
continue fresh, 264, 272: inf.
264; pret. 3 sg. lastyd, 215. OE.
læstan.

later, adj., comp. of late; in phrase,
later ende, *concluding portion,*
136.

lathe, v. tr., *call, invite:* pres. subj.
3 sg. lathe, 308. OE. laðian.

lavande, pres. part., *flowing,* 314.
Cf. OE. lafian, OF. laver.

lay, v. tr., *lay, place:* inf. lay, 67;
pret. 3 pl. laide, 72; pp. layde,
149. OE. lecgan.

layne, v. tr., *keep silent:* imper. 2
sg. layne, 179. ON. løyna.

lede, man, 146, 150, 200, 315. OE.
lēod.

lege, adj., *liege:* pl. lege men,
vassals, 224. OF. liege + ME.
men.

lely, adv., *loyally, faithfully,* 268.
OF. leel + OE. -līce.

leme, n., *flash, gleam, ray* (of
light), 334. lēoma.

lene, v. tr., *grant,* 272, 315; *give,
bestow,* 192: pres. subj. 3 sg.
lene, 315; pp. lant, 192, 272.
OE. lænan.

lenge, v. intr., *abide, remain:* pret.
3 sg. lengyd, 68. OE. lengan.

lengthe, n., *length,* 205. OE.
lengðu.

lepe, v. intr., *run, rush, leap:* pret.
3 pl. lepen, 61. OE. hlēapan.

lere, n., *appearance, features, complexion,* 95. OE. hlēor.

leste, adj., with noun understood or
implied, *least, smallest,* 162.
OE. læst.

lethe, v. intr., *cease, end:* inf. 347.
ME. leþien formed on EME.
leð.

lette, v. tr., *hinder:* 3 sg. lettes,
165. OE. lettan.

lettre, n., *letter* (of alphabet), 51;
missive, 111: pl -s, 51, 111.
OF. lettre.

leve, n., *leave, permission,* in phrase,
by Goddes leve, 316. OE. lēaf.

leve¹, v. tr., *believe:* inf. 175; 1 pl.
leven, 183; 2 pl. leves, 176. OE.
līefan, lēfan.

leve², v. tr., *leave,* 292; *abandon,*
61: pret. 2 sg. laftes, 292: 3 pl.
laften, 61. OE. læfan.

lewid, adj., *unknown, unsatisfactory,* 205. OE. læwede.

librarie, n., *library,* 155. OF.
librarie.

liche, n., *corpse,* 146, 314: lyche,
146. OE. līc.

lidde, n., *lid,* 67: lydde, 72. OE.
hlid.

life, n., 192, 224, 236, 315, 347; in phrase, opon lyfe, 150: lyve, 236; lyfe, 192, 315; life, 224, 347. OE. lïf.

lighte, v. intr., *fall (upon), light:* pret. 3 pl. lighten, 322. OE. lïhtan.

liȝtly, adv., *quickly,* 334. OE. lēohtlïce.

Limbo, n., *Limbo,* 292. Lat. limbo (abl. sing. of limbus).

lippe, n., *lip:* pl. -s, 91. OE. lippa.

lire, n., *flesh,* 149. OE. lira.

liston, v. intr., *listen:* pret. 3 pl. listonde, 219. OE. hlystan.

litelle, adj., *little,* 160; in phrase, a litelle, 190. Comp. lasse, in phrase, þe more and the lasse, 247. OE. lȳtel.

litelle, adv., *little,* 165, 348; comp. lasse, 104, 320. OE. lȳtel.

lo, interj., 146. Cf. OE. lā and ME. lo (with close o).

lodely, adj., *hateful, horrible, loath-some,* 328. OE. lāþlic.

loffynge, vbl. n., *remnant,* 292. Cf. OE. læfan.

lofte, n., in phrase, o(n) lofte, 49; *above, over* (as one garment over another), 81. LOE. loft, ON. lopt. See olofte.

loghe, adj., in phrase, on loghe, 147. ON. lāgr.

loghe, adv., *low,* 334.

loke, v. intr., with 'to,' *look,* 313; with 'on,' *look, examine,* 68; in phrase, to loke hit by kynde, *appear, seem,* 157: inf. 68, 157; pret. 3 sg. lokyd, 313. OE. lōcian.

lome, n., *vessel, coffer,* 68, 149. Cf. OE. gelōma.

londe, n., *land, country,* 200, 224: pl. -s, 30. OE. land, lond.

London, prop. n., 1, 25, 34. Lat. Londinium.

longe, adj., *long* (of time), 150, 155; absol. as noun, upon longe, *at length,* 175. OE. lang, long.

longe, adv., *for a long time,* 97; preceded by advs. of comparison, 'as, how, so,' 95, 126, 147, 157, 187, 264, 316; followed by 'er,' 308; followed by adverb since, 1, 260; comp. in phrases, no lenger, 179; not one grue lenger, 319. OE. lange, longe.

longe, v. intr., *pertain, belong:* 3 pl. longen, 268. Cf. OE. gelang, adj.

lorde, n., *lord, noble,* 134, 138, 146; *The Lord,* 123, 175, 280, 288, 315, 349: lord, 175, 288, 315; pl. -s, 138, 146. OE. hlāford.

lore, n., *learning, science,* 264. OE. lār.

louse, v. tr., *let loose, set free,* 165; *give forth, utter,* 178: inf. 165; pret. 3 sg. loused, 178. Cf. ON. lauss (adj.), louss.

love, n., *palm* (of hand), *hand:* pl. -s, 349. ON. lōfi (wk. masc.).

love, adj., *dear,* 34. Cf. OE. lēof.

love¹, v. tr., *love:* 3 sg. loves, 268, 272. OE. lufian.

love², v. tr., *glorify, praise:* pp. lovyd, 288, 324. OE. lofian.

lovynge, part. noun, *praising,* 349.

lure, n., *loss, harm:* pl. -s, 328. OE. lyre.

luste, v. impers., with dative case of pers. pron., *please, choose, care:* 3 sg. 162. OE. lystan.

lye, v. intr., *lie,* 95, 147, 157, 186, 187, 264, 281, 314; *to be extended on a bier*, 179: inf. lye, 264; 2 sg. lies, 179; ligges, 186; 3 sg. lyes, 99; pret. 3 sg. lay, 281, 314; lyggid, 76; pp. layne, 95, 157, 187; layn, 147. OE. licgan; cf. ON. liggja.

lyftande, pres. part., *lifting, raising*, 178. Cf. ON. lypta.

lyinge, vbl. n., *state of being dead*, 205. Cf. OE. licgan.

lykhame, n., *dead body, corpse*, 179. OE. līchama.

lym, n., *limb*, in phrase, life ne lym, 224. OE. lim.

lyvye, v. intr., *live*, 298, 328: inf. 298; pp. levyd, 328. OE. (Angl.) lifian.

M.

macer, n., *mace-bearer:* pl. -s, 143. OF. maissier.

maȝty, adj., *mighty, powerful* (of Divinity), 27, 175, 283; *strong, able-bodied* (*powerful, influential*(?)), 143: maȝti, 143; maghty, 27; myȝty, 175. OE. mæhtig, mihtig.

Mahon, prop. n., *Mahomet*, 20. OF. Mahom.

maire, n., *mayor*, 65, 143. OF. maire.

make, v. tr., *construct, frame* (of material things), 50; *contrive, fashion* (of immaterial things), 238; *appoint, ordain*, 201; *cause*, w. following inf. 39, 298; w. prep. 'of,' *determine* (by calculation), 206; w. opon (tr.), 128: inf. 206, 238; pp. 39, 50, 201, 298; makyd, 128. OE. macian.

Maker, n., *creator*, 283.

malte, v. intr., *melt, disappear*, 158:

inf. 158. Cf. OE. meltan and OE. mieltan.

manas, n., *threat*, 240. OF. manace.

maner, n., *behavior, manners:* pl. -s, 60. AF. manere, OF. maniere.

manerly, adv., *becomingly, properly*, 131.

mantel, n., *mantle*, 81, 250. OF. mantel.

marbre, n., *marble*, 48, 50. OF. marbre.

marcialle, n., *marshal*, 337. OF. mareschal (marescal).

Margrete, prop. n., *Margaret*, 20. OF. Margarete.

martilage, n., *necrology, burial register of a cathedral*, 154. Med. Lat. martilogium, martilagium.

mason, n., *mason*, 39. OF. masson.

masse, n., *mass*, 129, 131. OE. mæsse.

mate, v. tr., *overcome, render powerless:* pp. matyd, 163. OF. mater.

matens, n., *matins*, 128. OF. matines (fem. pl.).

Maudelayne, prop. n., *Magdalene*, 20. OF. Madelaine.

may, v. pret. pres., *can, may* (pret. sometimes has present force): 1 sg. may, 194: 3 sg. 151, 261, 293, 305; 2 pl. 175; pret. myȝt, 1 sg. 316; 3 sg. 94, 97, 258, 264, 276, 284; 3 pl. 74, 166. OE. mæg -(meahte) mihte.

mayster-mon, n., *chief, leader*, 201. OF. maistre + OE. man(n), mon(n).

mayster-toun, n., *master-town, metropolis*, 26. OF. maistre + OE. tūn.

maystrie, n., *force, superior power,* 234. OF. maistrie.

meche, adj., *great, much,* 220, 350; *large,* 81; *long* (of a lapse of time), 206; comp. more, in phrase þe more and the lasse, 247; mo (of numbers), 210. OE. mycel.

mecul, *great,* 27, 286. OE. micel (mycel); cf. ON. mykell.

mede, n., *corrupt gain,* 234; *virtue,* 270: pl. -s, 270. OE. mēd.

medecyn, n., *medicine, remedy,* 298. OF. medecine.

meele, n., *repast:* pl. -s, 307. OE. mǣl.

meere, n., *mare* (horse), 114. OE. mẽre.

mekest, adj., superl. of meke, *courteous, gentle,* 250. ON. mjūkr.

melle, v. tr., *mingle, mix:* pp. mellyd, 350. OF. meller.

memorie, n., *memory,* 158; *record,* 44. OF. memorie.

mende, v. tr., *cure, heal:* pp. mendyd, 298. Aphetic form of OF. amender.

mene¹, v. tr., *mean, signify,* 54; tr., *remember,* 151: inf. 54, 151. OE. mǣnan.

mene², v. tr., *lament, mourn:* pret. 3 pl. menyd, 247. OE. mǣnan.

menske, n., *courtesy, honour,* 337. ON. mennska.

menske, v. tr., *grace, favor,* 269; *honour, reverence,* 258: 3 sg. menskes, 269; pret. 3 pl. menskid, 258.

menskefully, adv., *gracefully, fitly,* 50.

menyver, n., *miniver,* 81. OF. menu vair.

merciles, adj., used adverbially,

---

obtaining no mercy, 300. OF. merci + OE. lēas.

mercy, n., 284, 286. OF. merci.

meritorie, adj., *deserving of reward, praiseworthy,* 270. OF. meritoire.

merke, v. tr., *note, write:* pp. merkid, 154. OE. mearcian.

mervaile, n., *marvel, wonder,* 43, 65, 114, 125; in phrases, hit is mervaile, 160; mervayle hit were, 158: mervayle, 43, 114, 158. OF. mervaille.

mery, adj., *mirthful,* 39. OE. myr(i)ge.

meschefe, n., *harm, injury,* 240. OF. meschef.

mesters-mon, n., *artificer, craftsman,* 60. ME. mesters, gen. case (<OF. mester) + ME. mon (<OE. mon(n)).

mesure, n., *amount, degree,* 286. OF. mesure.

mete, v. tr., *meet:* pret. 3 sg. mette, 337; pret. 3 pl. metten, 114. OE. mētan.

metely, adv., *meetly, fitly, fittingly,* 50. OE. gemetlīce (?).

metropol, n., *metropolis,* 26. OF. metropole.

meynye, n., *retinue, suite, train,* 65. OF. meyné.

ministre, n., *assistant priest:* pl. -s, 131. OF. ministre.

Moder, n., *mother,* 325. OE. mōdor.

moght-freten, adj., *moth-eaten,* 86. OE. moððe + OE. freten (pp. OE. fretan).

molde, n., *earth,* in phrase, on molde, *on earth, in the world,* 270; in pl. *clods, lumps of earth,* 343. OE. molde.

mon, n., *man,* 58, 97, 140, 143, 151, 258; *man* (as distinct from God), 160, 163, 234, 240, 264, 266; indef. *one,* 206; in general sense, referring to whole species, 125, 269, 270: gen. sg. monnes, 163, 234, 240, 264, 266; pl. nom. men, 58, 125, 140, 143. OE. man(n), mon(n).

monlokest, superl. adj., *most humane,* 250. OE. mon + OE. -līcost.

mony, adj., *many,* 11, 55, 58, 143; with article (indef.) before following sb., 39, 60, 79, 134, 296; with sb. in sg. without article, 41; absol. 53, 63, 114, 220; in phrase mony one, 214; pl. 55, 153. OE. manig, monig.

more, adv., comp. *more,* 230; in phrase, more ne lasse (with neg.), *at all,* 104; no more, 341; superl. moste, 269. OE. māra.

morowen, n., *morning,* 306. OE. morgen.

mote, n., *blemish, spot:* pl. -s, 86. OE. mot.

moulynge, n., *mould, mouldy growth,* 86. Cf. ON. *mugla.

mounte, v. intr., *amount to:* 3 sg. mountes, 160. OF. monter.

mournynge, part. n., *mourning, lamentation,* 350. OE. murnung.

mouthe, v. tr., *say:* inf. 54. Cf. OE. mūþ.

m(u)kke, v. tr., *shovel:* pret. 3 pl. mukkyde, 43. ON. moka.

murthe, n., *gladness, joy,* 335: myrthe, 350. OE. myr(i)gð.

muse, v. intr., *be at a loss to discover:* pret. 3 pl. muset, 54. OF. muser.

my, poss. pron., 123, 184, 226, 228; myn, 235, 253: pl. myn, 194. OE. mīn.

mydelle, n., *middle, waist,* 80. OE. middel.

myʒt, n., *might, power* (human), 163; (of God), 162, 283: myghtes, 283; pl. -es, 162, 283. OE. miht.

myʒty, see **maʒty.**

mynde, n., *memory,* 151; *record,* 154; *mind, reason, 'wits,'* 163. Cf. OE. gemynd.

mynne, v. tr., *mention, record:* pret. 3 sg. mynnyd, 104. ON. minna.

mynnynge, n., *remembrance,* 269. ON. minning.

mynster, n., *minster, cathedral,* 35; *temple* (pagan), 27. OE. mynster.

mynster-dore, n., *minster-door:* pl. -s, 128.

mynte, v. intr., *point (with a finger):* pret. 3 sg. mynte, 145. OE. myntan.

myny, v. intr., *dig, excavate:* pret. 3 pl. mynyde, 43. OF. miner.

mysse, v. tr., *be without, lack:* pp. myste, 300. OE. missan.

mysterie, n., *mystery,* 125. AF. *misterie.

N.

na(i)te, v. tr., *recite, repeat:* pp. naityd, 119. ON. neyta.

nakyde, adj., *bare, naked,* 89. OE. nacod.

nay, adv., 265. ON. nei.

ne, conj., *nor,* 102 (twice), 103, 149 (twice), 152 (twice), etc.; ne . . . ne, *neither . . . nor,* 240, 262; with omission of preceding negative, 104. OE. ne.

Glossary

neven, v. tr., *name:* pp. nevenyd, 25, 195. ON. nefna.

never, adv., *never, at no time,* 166, 199, 235, 237, etc.; emphatic neg., 156, 226; never so, 72, 239. OE. nǽfre.

New, adj., *new,* 25, 38. OE. nēōwe, nēwe.

new, adv., *newly, anew,* 6, 37 : newe, 14. OE. nīwe.

no, adj., 148, 150, 170, 184; no mon, no monnes, 240, 266; in phrase, in no wise, 263; with comparatives, fyrre, 169, 293; no lenger, 179; no more, 341 : pl. no, 238, 243. OE. nān (nōn).

noble, adj., 38, 227. OF. noble.

noȝt, n., *nothing,* 208; in phrase, aboute noȝt, *fruitlessly, in vain,* 56: noght, 101. OE. nōwiht.

noȝt, adv., 1: noght, 261. OE. nōwiht.

nombre, n., *number,* 206; *number of people,* 289. AN. numbre, OF. nombre.

nome, *name,* in phrases, in Christes nome, 16, in þe Fader nome, 318 : name, 28, 195: pl. -s, 18. OE. nama, noma.

non, adj. pron., *no one;* absol. 241, 289: pl. none, 101. OE. nān.

non, adv., *by no means, not at all,* 157. OE. nān.

nones, in phrase, for þe nones, *expressly,* 38, but often used in ME. poetry as metrical tag or stop-gap. ME. for þan anes, for OE. for þǽm ānes.

not, adv., 74, 97, 185, 319; not bot, *only,* 194. See noȝt.

note¹, n., *structure, piece of work,* 38. OE. notu.

note², n., *explanation,* 101; *notes* (of music), 133; *fame, reputation,* 152: pl. -s, 133. OF. note.

note, v. tr., *set down* (in writing) : pp. notyde, 103. OF. noter.

noþer, adv. (conj.), *neither,* with following, ne, 102, 152; used to strengthen a preceding neg., 102, 199: nothyre, 199. OE. ne + *ōðer (<OE. ōhwæðer).

nourne, v. tr., *speak, say,* 101, 152; *name, call after,* 195: inf. 101, 152; pp. nournet, 195. Origin obscure. Peculiar to *Gawain*-poet; but cf. Swed. dial. norna, nyrna, *inform* (*secretly*).

now, adv., *now, at this time,* 19, 25, 169, 332; with imperative, or introducing clause, temporal meaning being weakened or effaced, 33, 179, 325. OE. nū.

noy, n., *trouble, woe,* 289. Aphetic form of OF. anoi.

noyce, n., *clamor, din,* 62; noice, 218. OF. noise, noyse.

nyȝt, n., *night,* 117, 119. OE. niht, neaht (Angl. næht.).

O.

of, prep., *of,* 203; indicating separation, 167; with out, 158, 241, 292; indicating agent or doer, 24, 127; indicating material or substance of which anything is made, 47, 48, 50, 71, etc.; indicating subject-matter of thought, feeling or action, 57, 106, 174, 273, etc.; with verbs, 120, 152; expressing the relation of the objective genitive, 145, 156, 173 (twice), 206, etc.; indicating that in respect of which a quality is attributed or a fact is predicated, 30, 60, 87, 172, etc.; in partitive expressions, 29, 63, 135, 162, etc.; in the sense belonging or pertaining to, 19 (twice), 21, 28, 33, etc.; in phrase, in fourme of, 230. OE. of.

ofte, adv., *oft, frequently*, 135, 232. OE. oft.

olofte, see on.

on, prep., *on, upon*, 2, 46, 68, 83, etc.; *to*, 138; expressing manner, on . . . wise, 77, 132, 229; on benche, 250; on erthe, 198, 237; on fyrst, 42, 207; on lofte, 81; on loghe, 147; on molde, 270; on a quile, 105; on row, 52; one speche, 152; olofte, 49. OE. on.

one, num. and pron., *a single*, 156, 319, 323; after dem. and pronom. adj., 6, 214; with superl., 198. OE. ān.

ones, adv.; at ones, 352.

one-under, prep., *under, beneath*, 70. OE. on + under.

openly, adv., *clearly, plainly*, 90. OE. open + -līce.

opon, adj., *open:* pl. opon, 128. OE. open.

opon, adv., *upon*, 125.

opon, prep., *upon*, 76, 171; with phrase, opon slepe, 92; opon lyfe, 150. OE. upon.

or, conj., *or;* followed by elles, 121. OE. ōðer.

oþer, adj., *other*, 346: pl. othire, 32, 59; absol. as pron. 93. OE. ōðer.

oþer, conj., *or*, 20, 22, 188, 255: oþir, 86. Adv. oþer . . . oþir, either . . . or, 86. OE. ōðer.

oure, poss. pron., *our*, 154, 155, 169, 295, etc.: of the body of Christians, 21, 280, 315, 324, etc. OE. ūre.

oute, adv., 9: out, 158; owte, 191; with of, 167, 292; out of, 241. OE. ūt.

overdrive, v. intr., *pass:* pret. 3 sg., overdrofe, 117. OE. oferdrīfan.

oye(r), n., *commission of Oyer and Terminer*, 211. AF. oyer, OF. oir.

P.

palais, n., *palace*, 115. OF. palais.

Paradis, n., *paradise*, 161. OF. paradis.

parage, n., *lineage, rank*, 203. OF. parage.

parte, v. intr., *depart, go away:* pp. partyd, 107. OF. partir.

passe, v. intr., *go, pass*, 115, 138, 141, 351; tran. *transcend, exceed*, 163: pret. 3 sg. passyd, 115, 141; passide, 138; 3 pl. passyd, 351; pp. passyde, 163. OF. passer.

Paule, prop. n., *Paul*, 113: gen. sg., 35. OF. Pol.

payne, n., *torment*, 333. OF. peine.

paynte, v. tr., *color, wash:* pp. payntyde, 75. OF. peindre.

paynym, n., *heathen, pagan*, 285; gen. pl. -es, 203. OF. paienime.

pepul, n., *people*, 10, 109, 217, 296: pepulle, 217, 351. AF. poeple, OF. poeple.

perle, n., *pearl*, 79. OF. perle.

pervert, v. tr., *turn from correct to false belief:* pret. 3 pl. pervertyd, 10. OF. pervertir.

pes, n., *peace, quietness*, 115. OF. pais.

Petre, prop. n., *Peter*, 19. OE. Petre (<dat. or acc. case Lat. Petrus).

picchit, part. adj., *set, placed,* 79. Cf. OE. *picc(e)an.

pinche, v. tr., with adverb, *get into some position by pinching or pressing:* pret. 3 pl. pinchid. 70. ONF. *pinchier.

place, n., *country,* 10; *city, town,* 228; *religious edifice,* 144, 153. OF. place.

plane, v. tr., *dress (with a plane), smooth:* pp. planede, 50. OF. planer.

plante, v. tr., *establish:* pret. 3 sg. plantyd, 13. OE. plantian.

playn, adj., used as a noun, *flat surface* (i. e. church pavement), 138. OF. plain.

plite, n., *the Everlasting Covenant,* 285. OE. pliht.

plye, v. intr., *bend in reverence, bow:* pret. 3 pl. plied, 138. OF. plier.

plyȝtles, adj., *without covenant, having no part in the Messianic dispensation,* 296. OE. pliht + lēas.

pontificals, n. (used in plural), *episcopal robes,* 130. L. pontificālis.

pope, n., 12. OE. pāpa.

porer, adj., comp. degree, with noun implied, *poorer:* pl. 153. Cf. OF. povre (poure).

powdere, n., *dust, remains of decomposed matter,* 344. OF. poudre.

power, n., *authority, jurisdiction,* 228. OF. poër.

poysne, v. tr., *poison, pervert, corrupt* (morally) : pp. poysned, 296. OF. poisonner.

prayse, v. tr., *praise, extol, laud:* pp. praysid, 29. OF. preisier.

prece, n., *multitude, throng,* 141. OF. presse.

preche, v. tr., *preach, proclaim, declare* (something sacred or religious) : pret. 3 sg. prechyd, 13. OF. prechier.

precious, adj., 79. OF. precios, precious.

prelacie, n., *clerical attendants,* 107. AF. prelacie.

prelate, n., 130, 138. OF. prelat.

prestly, adv., *quickly,* 130. OF. prest + OE. -lice.

primate, n., *bishop of London,* 107. OF. primat.

prince, n., *monarch, ruler,* 203 : (of God), 161. OF. prince.

prise, n., *an instrument used for prizing, lever:* pl. -s, 70. OF. prise.

procession, n., *procession,* 351. OF. procession.

providens, n., *providence, prescience, far-seeing care* (of God), 161. OF. providence.

psalmyde, part. adj., *composed as psalms, in the form of sacred poetry,* 277. OE. sealmian.

pure, adj., *pure, free from error,* 13. OF. pur.

putte, v. tr., *put, place, lay, set,* 70, 153; with phrase, in power, 228 : pret. 3 pl. putten, 70; pp. putte, 153, 228. LOE. putian.

pyne, n., *grief, trouble,* 141; *suffering, torture* (of Hell), 188. Cf. OE. *pin (<Lat. pœna) ; cf. ON. pina, OE. pinung.

Q.

quat, rel. pron., *that, which,* 68. OE. hwæt.

74 St. Erkenwald

quaynt, adj., *carefully elaborated, artfully designed*, 133. OF. queinte.

queme, adj., *pleasing*, 133. OE. gecwēme.

quen, conj., *when, as soon as*, 57, 65, 128, 163, etc.; *whenever*, 162; *at which time*, 182, 246, 291; *since*, 302. OE. hwanne, hwænne.

quere, n., *choir*, 133. OF. cuer.

quere, adv. (interrog.), *where*, 274. OE. hwǣr, hwēr.

quere, conj., *where, in which place*, 279. OE. hwǣr, hwēr.

quest, n., *baying (of hounds), hence with reference to the singing of the choir*: pl. questis, 133. OF. queste.

queþe, v. tr., *say*: pret. 3 sg. quoþ, 146, 159, 193, 225, etc. OE. cweðan.

queþer, adv., *yet*, 153. OE. hwæðere.

queþer, conj., correl. with oþer, 188. OE. hwæðer, hweðer.

quil, conj., *while*, 215, 217. OE. hwīl, n.

quile, n., *short time*, in phrase, on a quile, 105. OE. hwīl.

quontyse, n., *example of cunning, marvel*, 74. OF. cointise.

quy, adv. (interrog.), *why*, 223; introducing indirect quest., 186, 222. OE. hwȳ.

qwo, interrog. pron., introducing indirect quest., 185, 197; neut. quat, 301; introducing indirect quest., 54, 94, 186, 187: quo, 197. OE. hwā.

R.

radly, adv., *quickly*, 62. OE. hrædlīce.

ratte, n., *rag, scrap*: pl. -s, 260. Etym. obscure.

rayke, v. intr., *go, make one's way, proceed*: pret. 3 sg. rayked, 139. ON. reika.

reame, n., *realm*, 11, 135. OF. reame.

reche, v. tr., *give, hand to one*, 256; *bestow, grant*, 280, 338: pret. 3 sg. raȝt, 280, 338; 3 pl. raght, 256. OE. rǣcan.

rede, adj., *red*, 91. OE. rēad.

rede, v. tr., *guide, govern, rule*: 3 sg. redes, 192. OE. rǣdan, rēdan.

redeles, adj., *without counsel, having no resources*, 164. OE. rǣdlēas, rēdlēas.

redy, adj., with prep. of, *dexterous, expert*, 245. Cf. OE. rǣde.

refetyd, pp., *refreshed with food*, 304. OF. refet, variant of refait, pp. of refaire.

regne, n., *reign, period of a sovereign's rule*, 212. OF. regne.

regn, v. intr., *reign, rule*: pret. 3 sg. regnyd, 151. OF. regner.

reken, adj., *straightforward, upright*, 245; *elegant*, 135: superl. pl. used absolutely, rekenest, 135. OE. recen.

relefe, n., *relief, alleviation*, 328. OF. relief.

remewe, v. intr., *depart from*: pret. 1 sg. remewit, 235. OF. remeuv–, stressed form of remouvoir.

renaide, pp., *apostate*, 11. Cf. OF. renier.

rend(e), v. tr., *tear:* pp. rent, 260.
OE. rendan.

renke, n., *man*, 239, 275 : pl. -s, 271.
OE. rinc.

renne, v. intr., *run:* pret. 3 pl.
ronnen, 62. OE. rinnan, ON.
renna.

repaire, v. intr., *resort to:* 3 pl.
repairen, 135. OF. repairer.

reson, n., *sentence, saying*, 52; *intellectual faculty*, 164; *wisdom*,
267; with phrase, by reson, 235 :
pl. -s, 164; resones, 52. OF.
reson.

restorment, n., *restorement, resti-
tution*, 280. OF. restorement.

reule, v. tr., *govern, exercise
authority over:* inf. 231 ; pret.
3 sg. rewlit, 212. OF. reuler.

revele, v. tr., *disclose, make known:*
inf. 121. OF. reveler.

reverence, n., *reverence, respect*,
338; in phrase, for reverens
sake, 239: reverens, 239. OF.
reverence.

revest, v. tr., *array in ecclesiastical
vestments:* pp. revestid, 139.
OF. revestir.

rewarde, v. tr., *reward, recom-
pense:* 1 sg. rewardes, 275; pret.
1 sg. rewardid (*regarded?*), 256.
ONF. rewarder, reguarder, re-
garder.

rialle, adj., *royal, splendid*, 77.
OF. rial.

riche, adj., *exalted, powerful*, 212,
239, 267; *of great value, splendid*, 77, 83, 280. Cf. OE. rīce,
OF. riche.

riche, adv., *richly*, with p. partici-
ples, 139. Cf. OE. rīce, OF.
riche.

richely, adv., *richly*, 304. OE.
rīclīce.

riȝt, n., *right* (as distinguished from
wrong), *righteousness*, 232, 235,
241, 256, etc.; *justice*, 275; in
pl. *deeds of justice*, 269: right,
304; ryȝt, 241; pl. -es, 269.
OE. riht, ryht.

ringe, v. intr., *resound, ring:* pret.
3 sg. ronge, 117; pres. part.
ryngande, 62. OE. hringan.

rise, v. intr., *ascend, mount up:* 3
sg. rises, 344. OE. rīsan.

rode, n., *rood, cross*, 290. OE. rōd.

rode, n., *redness, ruddiness*, 91.
OE. rudu.

ronke, adj., *violent*, 11 ; *abundant,
copious*, 91 ; *foul, loathsome*,
262: pl. 11, 262. OE. ranc, ronc.

rose, n., *rose*, 91. OE. rose (rōse),
OF. rose.

rote, n., *rot, decay*, 262. Cf. OE.
rotian, v., and Norwegian and
Icel. rot, n.

rote, v. intr., *rot, decay:* pp. rotid,
260. OE. rotian.

roten, part. adj., *rotten*, 344. Cf.
OE. rotian, v., ON. rotinn.

rottok, n., *decayed or musty thing*,
344. Etym. unknown.

route, n., *gathering, crowd*, in
phrase, in route, 62. OF. route.

routhe, n., *compassion, pity*, 240.
Cf. OE. hrēow, and for the ending ON. hryggð.

row, n., in phrase, on row, *in order,
in succession*, 52. OE. rāw (?),
var. of rǣw.

rowme, n., *a particular place
assigned to one*, 338. OE. rūm.
Cf. *Richard II*, v. v. 108: 'Go
thou and fill another roome in
hell.'

roynyshe, adj., *strange, uncouth:*
pl. 52. Cf. OE. rȳne.

ry3t, adv., 301(?), with now, 332.
OE. rihte, ryhte.

ry3twis, adj., *righteous,* 245. OE.
rihtwīs.

ryve, v. tr., *tear asunder:* inf. 262.
Cf. ON. rīfa.

S.

sacre, v. tr., *consecrate:* pp. sacrid,
159. OF. sacrer.

sacrifice, n., *sacrifice:* pl. -s, 30.
OF. sacrifice.

sacryd, adj., *sacred, holy,* 3.

sadde, adj., *grave, solemn,* 324; *important, weighty,* 202: sayd, 202.
OE. sæd.

sake, n., in phrase, for reverens
sake, 239. Cf. OE. sacu, ON.
sok.

same, adj., 204. ON. same.

Sandewiche, prop. n., *Sandwich,* 12.

Sathanas, prop. n., *Satan,* 24. OF.
Sathanas.

Savyoure, n., *Saviour,* 324. OF.
savëour.

sawe, n., *command,* 184. OE. sagu.

Saxon, prop. n., *Saxon:* pl. -es, 8,
24. OF. Saxon.

Saxon, adj., pl. 30.

say, v. tr., *say, speak,* 100, 122, 189,
273, etc.; with reference to
church service, *repeat,* 136; with
phrases, say soþe, 159, 197: inf.
100, 197; pres. 2 sg. says, 159;
3 sg. says, 277; imper. sg. 273,
279; pret. 3 sg. sayde, 122, 282;
sayd, 273, 324; pp. sayde, 136,
189. OE. secgan.

sayd, see **sadde.**

saynt, n., *saint,* 4, 12, 19, 20: pl. -es,
17. OF. saint.

sayntuare, n., *sanctuary,* 66. OF.
saintuarie.

schewe, v. tr., *make manifest:* pp.
schewyde, 180. OE. scēawian.

se, v. tr., *behold, see,* 293, 308; *per-
ceive,* 170; intr., *see,* 293: inf.
293; 2 pl. 170; pres. subj. 3 sg.
308; pp. sene, 100. OE. sēon.

seche, v. tr., *try to find,* 170;
explore, 41; inf. 41, 170. OE.
sēc(e)an.

sege, n., *seat, espiscopal chair,* 35.
OF. sege.

segge, n., *man,* 100, 159, 189, 204,
etc. OE. secg.

sele, n., *happiness, bliss,* 279. OE.
sǣl.

selfe, intens. pron., in cpd. pronouns,
oureselfe, 170, þiselwen, 185;
often with no meaning as compound pronoun and equivalent to
a simple pronoun, myselfe, 197,
300: from original oblique case,
þiselwen, 185. OE. self.

seme, v. impers., *seem, appear:*
3 sg. semes, 98. ON soema.

semely, adj., *fair,* 84. ON.
sōēmiligr.

semely, adv., *in an imposing
manner,* 35. ON. sōēmiliga.

sende, v. tr., *send,* 8, 12, 111, 172:
inf. 172; pret. 3 sg. sende, 111;
pp. sende, 8, 12. OE. sendan.

septre, n., *sceptre,* 84, 223, 256:
septure, 84. OF. sceptre.

Ser, n., *Sir,* 108, 118, 213 (twice),
225. Abbrev. form of sire.

serve, v. tr., *render obedience to:*
pp. servyd, 275. OF. servir.

service, n., 136. OF. service.

sese, v. tr., with prep. in, *endow,*

Glossary 77

possess oneself of: pp. sesyd, 345. OF. seisir, saisir.

sette, v. tr., *appoint, establish, dedicate,* 21, 24; *place,* 84, 332: pp. sett, 21, 24, 84; sette, 332. OE. settan.

seven, adj., *seven,* 155. OE. seofon.

sewe, v. tr., *follow, attend upon:* pret. 3 sg. sewide, 204. AN. suer, suire, OF. sivre.

sextene, n., *sacristan,* 66. Cf. AN. segerstaine, OF. secrestein.

shal, v., 174; with omission of be of passive inf., 255: 1 sg. 174; 3 sg. shalle, 347; pret. 3 sg. shulde, 54, 255; shuld, 42. OE. sculan.

shape, v. tr., *cut out, fashion* (of clothing), 88; reflex., *set oneself, prepare,* 129: pret. 3 sg. shope, 129; pp. shapen, 88. OE. scieppan, pret. scōp, pp. sc(e)apen.

shedde, v. tr., *shed* (tears or blood) : pres. 2 sg. sheddes, 329; pret. 3 sg. schedde, 182. OE. scēadan.

shewe, v. intr., *be seen, be visible:* pret. 3 pl. shewid, 90. OE. scēawian.

sike, n., *sighing;* in phrase, sorow and sike, 305. Cf. OE. sīcan.

sitte, v. intr., *sit,* 35; *abide, dwell, remain,* 293, 305; with preposition, sytte upon, *sit in judgment on,* 202: inf. 305; sytte, 202; pres. 3 sg. -s, 293; syttes, 35. OE. sittan.

skelt, v. intr., *hasten:* pres. 3 pl. skelton, 278. Origin obscure. See note.

skilfulle, adj. (used as noun),

following reason, righteous: pl. 278. ON. skil + OE. full.

sleke, v. tr., *relieve, remove* (pain) : pret. 3 sg. slekkyd, 331. Cf. OE. sleccan, Icel. slökva.

slent, n., *splash, sprinkling,* 331. Cf. ON. sletta. Cf. Björkman, *Scand. Loan Words,* p. 219.

slepe, n., *sleep;* with prep. opon slepe, 92. OE. slǣp, slēp.

slide, v. intr., *glide, flow:* pret. 3 sg. slode, 331. OE. slīdan.

slippe, v. intr., in phrase, opon slepe, *fall asleep, sink into sleep:* pp. slippide, 92. MLG. slippen.

so, adv., at beginning of sentence with continuative force, sometimes preceded by 'and,' 23, 75, 169; as intensive, often meaningless, 45, 95, 157, 223, etc.; so . . . þat, denoting result, 63, 126, 174; with never, 72, 239; to *that extent, to that degree,* 258; so longe, 150, 264; *thus,* 158, 303. OE. swā.

sodanly, adv., *suddenly,* 92, 342: sodenly, 342. Cf. OF. soudain.

solemply, adv., *formally, ceremoniously, in an impressive manner,* 129, 336. OF. solempne + OE. -līce.

solempne, adj., *of great dignity, of great importance,* 30; *grand, sumptuous,* 303: superl. degree, solempnest, 30. OF. solempne.

sone, adv., *soon, forthwith, straightway,* 58, 72. OE. sōna.

Sonne, n., *sun* (as divinity) : gen. s. Sonne, 21. OE. sunne.

soper, n., *supper,* 303, 308, 332. OF. soper.

sorow, n., *grief, sorrow,* 305; *lamentation, mourning,* 309; *suf-*

fering, 327; sorowe, 309, 327.
OE. sorh, sorg.
sothe, n., *truth,* 170, 197. OE.
sōð.
sothe, adj., *true, having no false-
hood:* pl. 277. OE. sōþ, sōð.
soþe, adv., *truly, truthfully,* 159.
OE. sōðe, sōþe.
soule, n., *soul,* 273, 279, 293, 300,
etc.; saule, 273. OE. sāwol.
soun, n., *sound, speech,* 324, 341:
sowne, 341. AN. soun, OF. son.
sounde, n., *soundness, health,* 92.
Cf. OE. gesund.
soupe, v. intr., *sup, eat supper:*
pres. 3 pl. soupen, 336. OF.
souper.
Soverayn, n., *sovereign,* 120. OF.
soverain.
space, n., *time, opportunity,* 93, 312.
OF. espace.
spakly, adv., *quickly, rapidly,
briskly,* 312, 335. ON. spakliga.
spar(r), v. tr., *fasten, secure (with
bolt or bar):* pret. 3 pl. sparde,
49. Cf. OHG. sperran, OE.
gesparrian.
speche, n., *speech, speaking, words,*
in phrase, one speche, 152, OE.
spǣc, spēc.
spede, n., *success,* in phrase for . . .
spede, 132. OE. spēd.
spedeles, adj., *ineffectual, unavail-
ing,* 93. OE. spēd + OE. lēas.
speke, v. intr., *speak:* inf. 312;
pret. 3 sg. spake, 217. OE.
sp(r)ecan.
spelunke, n., *tomb,* 49; *space around
the tomb enclosed by the cloister,*
217. (Cf. note.) OF. spelunque.
sperle, n., *bolt, bar,* 49: pl.
sperle(s). Cf. W. Flemish
spèrel, sperrel.

Spiritus Domini, n., *Mass of the
Holy Spirit,* 132.
sprent, v. intr., *leap:* pret. 3 sg.,
sprent, 335. Cf. Early Scand.
*sprenta (ON. spretta).
spryng, v. intr., *spread, extend:*
pret. 3 sg. sprange, 217. OE.
springan.
spyr, *inquire, ask,* with objective
clause introduced by interroga-
tive pronoun: inf. 93. OE.
spyrian.
spyrit, n., *soul, spirit,* 335. AN.
spirit, OF. esperit.
stable, v. tr., *establish, institute,* 2;
install, settle, 274: pret. 3 sg.
stablyde, 2; pp. stablid, 274.
Aphetic form of estable<OF.
establir.
stadde, part. adj., *placed, fixed,*
274. ON. steðja, pp. staddr.
stille, adj., *still, immovable,* 219.
OE. stille.
ston, n., 47, 219: pl. -es, 40. OE.
stān.
stonde, v. intr., *be inscribed, be set
down,* 52; *stand,* 73, 219; *be,
remain,* 164; with phrase in
my(n)de, *continue, flourish,* 97:
pres. 3 sg. stondes, 164; pret. 3
sg. stode, 97; pret. 3 pl. stoden,
52, 73, 219. OE. standan
(stondan).
stounde, n., *time, hour:* pl. -s, 288.
OE. stund.
strange, adj., *singular, unknown,
unheard of,* 74. OF. estrange.
streȝt, adv., *justly, uprightly,* 274.
ME. streȝt, adj. use of pp. of
strecchen (<OE. streccan).
suche, adj., 178; suche a, 97, 104,
110, 146, 151: pl. 178. OE.
swylc.

suffre, v. intr., *suffer:* pret. 3 sg.
suffride, 2. OF. suffrir.

summe, adj., *some,* 100, 276:
sum, 192. OE. sum.

sutile, adj., *mysterious, miraculous,*
132. OF. sutil.

swarve, v. intr., *deviate, turn away:*
pres. 3 sg. -s, 167. OE. sweor-
fan.

swete, adj., *precious, benignant,* 120;
fresh, unspoiled, 342. OE.
swēte.

swynde, v. intr., *vanish, disappear:*
pret. 3 sg. swyndid, 342. OE.
swindan.

syke, v. intr., *sigh:* pret. 3 sg.
syked, 189, 323. Cf. OE. sīcan.

Synagoge, n., *synagogue,* 21. OF.
sinagoge.

synge, v. tr., *sing:* inf. 129; pp.
songen, 128. OE. singan.

sythen, adv., *ago,* 1; *before now,*
260. Cf. OE. siððan, ON. siðan.

sythen, conj., *from the time that,*
2; *since, seeing that, inasmuch
as,* 180, 185, 222: sithen, 185,
222. Cf. OE. siððan, ON. siðan.

T.

table, n., *table,* 332. OF. table.

take, v. tr., *undertake,* 168; *catch,*
297; with tome, *allow sufficient
time,* 313; intr., *with to, proceed,
reach,* 57: inf. 168; pret. 3 sg.
toke, 313; 3 pl. token, 57; pp.
take, 297. LOE. tacan, ON.
taka.

tale, n., *tale, story,* 102, 109. OE.
talu.

talent, n., *desire, longing,* 176. OF.
talent.

talke, v. intr., *with to, address:* 3
sg. -s, 177. Cf. E. Fris. talken.

tecche, n., *blotch, spot,* 85. OF.
teche.

teche, v. tr., *teach, make known:*
3 sg. -s, 34. OE. tǣc(e)an.

telle, v. tr., *say, tell,* 36, 109, 114;
reckon, 31: inf. 114; pret. 1 sg.
tolde, 36; pret. 3 pl. tolden, 109;
pp. tolde, 31. OE. tellan.

teme, v. intr., *attach oneself, belong:* pret. 3 pl. temyd, 15. OE.
tīeman, tēman.

temple, n., 5, 28, 31, 36: pl. -s, 15.
OE. templ, OF. temple.

tene, n., *grief, woe,* 331. OE.
tēona.

tere, n., *tear:* pl. -s, 314, 322. OE.
tēar.

tethe, n. (pl.), *teeth,* 297. OE. tēð.

thar, v. pret. pres., *dare:* 3 pl. 262.
OE. þearf.

thenke, v. tr., *intend, mean, purpose:* 1 sg. 225. OE. þenc(e)an.

thre, num. adj., *three,* 49. OE. þrī.

threnen, adj., *three times,* 210.
LOE. þrinna.

thrid, adj., *third,* 31. OE. þridda.

throghe, n., *coffin,* 47. OE. þrūh.

thryvandly, adv., *excellently,* 47.
ON. þrīfa-sk + OE. -līce.

thykke, adj., *thick,* 47. ON. þykkr;
cf. OE. þicce.

thynke, v. impers., *seems:* 3 sg.
thynkes, 259. OE. þync(e)an.

til, conj., *until, till,* 12, 136; with
negative in principal clause, 313:
tille, 136. ON. til.

tithynges, n. (pl.), *tidings,* 57.
ON. tīðindi, pl.

title, n., *title,* 28; *inscription,* 102.
OF. title.

so . . . þat, 126, 151, 175. OE.
þæt.

þat, dem. pron., *that,* 3, 4, 5, 10,
etc.; used absolutely, 160, 173,
299, 300; after þat, 207; before
þat, 209; by þat, 113; with þat,
69. OE. þæt.

þat, rel. pron., indecl., *that, who,
which,* 8, 10, 15, 36, etc.; þat . . .
his, *whose,* 154. OE. þæt, dem.

þe, def. art., 5, 8, 9, 10, etc.: the, 34,
343. LOE. ðe.

þen, adv., *then, at that time,* 11, 13,
37, 73, etc.; *thereupon, upon
that, after that, afterwards,* 137,
177, 273, 281; *in those circumstances, such being the case,* 324
(?); correl. with 'when,' 165;
ere þen, 118: then, 177. OE.
þænne, þanne.

þen, conj., *than,* 230, 270. OE.
þænne, þanne.

þer, adv., *there, in that place,* 39,
52, 56, etc.; introducing verb, 3,
53, 93, 138, 150; *then, on that
occasion,* 334; as conj., *where,*
304, 306, 314, 336; þere as, *in
that case in which, where,* 167:
ther, 3, 94. OE. þær, þēr.

þerafter, adv., *afterwards,* 189.
OE. þæræfter.

þerinne, adv., *therein, in it,* 27.
OE. þærinne.

þerof, adv., *because of that,* 339.
OE. þærof.

þeron, adv., *thereon,* 79. OE.
þæron.

þeroute, adv., *out of that place,
forth from thence,* 291. OE.
þærūt(e).

þertille, adv., *thither,* 69. OE.
þær + ON. til.

þerto, adv., *thither,* 59; *to it,* 70.
OE. þærtō.

þi, poss. pron., *thy, thine,* 124, 193,
261, 263 (twice), etc.: thi, 283,
285, 290; þin, 330. OE. þīn.

þider, adv., *thither,* 58, 63, 64, 135.
OE. þider.

þiderwarde, adv., *in that direction,
thither,* 112. OE. þiderweard.

þiderwardes, adv., 61.

þis, dem. pron., 33, 98, 125, 153,
etc.; þis ilke, 193; in phrase,
wyt this, 341: this, 11, 341; pl.
þes, 155, 317. OE. þis, neut.

þou, pers. pron., *thou* (abbrev. þu),
159, 179, 181, 183: þow, 186;
þe (dat. or acc.), 225, 318, 339;
the, 197, 326; pl. ȝe, 175, 176,
297, 298; ȝee, 170; ȝow (acc.),
174. OE. þū.

(þre), adj., *three,* 210. OE. þrēo.

þritty, adj., *thirty,* 210. OE.
þrītig.

þurghe, prep., *through, because of,*
123; *by the action of,* 192:
thurghe, 123. OE. þurh.

þus, adv., *thus, in this way, like this,*
96, 99, 179, 186, etc.; *accord-
ingly, and so, consequently,* 248.
OE. þus.

U.

uche, adj., *each,* 204; with indef.
art. uche a, 275, 348; in phrase
uch on, 93. OE. (Merc.) ylc.

ughten, n., *early morning,* 118.
OE. ūhta.

unchaungit, part. adj., *unaltered,
unchanged,* 95. OE. un-¹ + OF.
changer.

unclose, v. tr., *open:* pret. 3 pl.
unclosid, 140. OE. un-² + OF.
clos-, stem of clore.

under, prep. *under, beneath, below;* in phrase, under heven, 166; denoting subordination, 203, 227. OE. under.

unhappen, adj., *unfortunate, unblessed, unhappy:* superl. degree, unhapnest, 198. OE. un–¹ + ON. heppinn.

unknawen, adj., *unknown*, 147. OE. un–¹ + OE. cnāwen.

unlouke, v. tr., *unlock, unfasten:* inf. 67, 162. OE. unlūcan.

unpreste, adj., *ignorant, unknowing*, 285. OE. un–¹ + OF. prest.

unsaȝt, part. adj., *fierce, warlike:* pl. 8. OE. un–¹ + LOE. sæht.

unskathely, adj., *innocent*, 278. OE. un–¹ + ON. skaði + OE. -līce.

unsparid, part. adj., *unrestrained*, 335. OE. un–¹ + OE. sparian.

unwemmyd, part. adj., *unspotted, unstained*, 96, 266, OE. unwemmed.

unworthi, adj., *unworthy*, 122. Not found in OE. Cf. OS. wirþig, ON. verþugr, OE. unweorþ.

up, adv., *up*, 178; *up* (from bed), 118. OE. ūp.

uphalde, v. tr., *uphold:* pp. uphalden, 349. OE. ūp + OE. healdan.

upon, prep., *upon, on*, 290, 317; with verbs, sytte upon, 202; in phrases, upon longe, *at length*, 175: opon, 76; opon slepe, 92. OE. upon.

use, v. tr., *practise, employ, follow*, 187, 270; with londe, *inhabit, make one's home*, 200; 3 pl. usen, 270; pret. 2 sg. usyt, 187; 3 sg., usit, 200. OF. user.

V.

vayle, v. intr., *profit:* 3 sg. vayles, 348, OF. vail, vaill, 1st pers. pres. indic. (or vail–, vaill–, subj. and part. stem), of OF. valoir.

vayneglorie, n., *vainglory*, 348. OF. vayneglorie, Med. Lat. vāna glōria.

verray, adj., *true, exact, precise, lifelike:* pl. 53. AF. verrai, OF. verai.

verrayly, adv., *verily, truly*, 174. OF. verai + -līce.

vertue, n., *power*, 286; *mighty work, miracle*, 174: pl. -s, 174. OF. vertu.

vigure, n., *figure:* pl. -s, 53. OF. figure.

visite, v. tr., *make a visitation:* inf. 108. OF. visiter.

vouche-safe, v. tr., *condescend, deign*, 121: inf. 121. OF. voucher + OF. sauf.

W.

wagge, v. tr., *wag, shake:* pret. 3 sg. waggyd, 281. Cf. OE. wagian, Mod. Swed. wagga.

waken, v. intr., *arise, be stirred up, be aroused:* pret. 3 sg. wakenyd, 218. OE. wæcnan.

wale, n., *choice, choosing*, in phrase, to wale, *at one's choice, in abundance*, 73. ON. val.

wale, v. tr., *choose one's way, betake oneself:* pp. walon (?), 64. Cf. ON. valinn, pp. of ON. velja.

Wales, prop. n., *Wales*, 9.

warpe, v. tr., *pronounce, utter:* pret. 2 sg. werpe, 329; 3 sg. warpyd,

321. ON. varpa; cf. OE. weorpan.

water, n., *water,* 316; *tears,* 329, 333. OE. wæter.

wede, n., *dress,* 96; pl. *clothes, garments,* 77, 85. OE. wǣde, wēde.

weghe, n., *man, person,* 96, 186: pl. wehes, 73. OE. wiga.

welde, v. tr., *rule, govern:* 3 sg. weldes, 161. OE. wieldan, weldan.

wele, n., *prosperity, good fortune,* 233. OE. wela.

wele, adv., *well, fully,* 183: comp. better, 18; superl. best, 272. OE. wel.

wele-dede, n., *righteous deed, 'good works,'* 301. OE. weldǣd.

welneghe, adv., *very nearly, very nigh,* 119. OE. wel + OE. nēah.

wemles, adj., *spotless, stainless:* pl. 85. OE. wamlēas.

wende, v. intr., *proceed, go:* pret. 3 pl. wenten, 69. OE. wendan.

wepe, v. intr., *weep:* pret. 3 pl. wepid, 220; wepyd, 310; pres. part. wepande, 122. OE. wēpan.

were, v. tr., *wear* (a crown): 2 sg. weres, 222. OE. werian.

werke, n., *construction, building-process,* New Werke, 38 (see note); *occupation,* 61. OE. weorc.

werkemon, n., *workman:* pl. werkemen, 69. OE. weorcmonn, wercmonn.

werre, n., *war,* 215. NF. werre, OF. guerre.

weshe, v. tr., *wash:* 3 pl. weshe, 333. OE. wæscan.

wete, n., wete of eghen (*tears*), 321. OE. wǣte, wēte.

wille, n., *will, desire,* 226. OE. willa.

winne, v. tr., *gain, win:* pret. 1 pl. wan, 301. OE. winnan.

wise, n., *way, manner, guise, procedure, fashion,* 77, 132, 229; in phrase, in no wise, *in no way, by no means,* 263. OE. wīse.

witere, v. tr., *inform:* imper. sg. 185. ON. vitra.

with, prep., *in company with, along with,* 107, 131, 143; *together with,* 65, 299; denoting means, 40, 48, 51, 71, etc.; denoting manner, 62, 91, 191, 289, 314, etc.; denoting cause, 301, 335; *at* (temporal), 321; *accompanied by,* 133; denoting possession, 55, 79, 82, 133, etc.; with nouns denoting in a vague sense combination or conjugation, 141; in phrases, with þat, 69; wyt this, 341: wyt, 165, 341. OE. wið.

within, adv., 68, 75; prep., 252; of time, 64; withinne, 68, 252. OE. wiðinnan.

withouten, prep., *without,* 85. OE. wiðūtan.

wonder, n., *amazement, astonishment,* 73, 220; *marvel,* 99, 106. OE. wundor.

wondre, v. intr., with opon, *marvel, wonder:* 3 pl. wondres, 125. OE. wundrian.

wonne, v. intr., *abide, dwell:* 3 sg. wonnes, 279. OE. wunian.

wonte, v. intr., *be lacking, be deficient:* pret. 3 pl. wontyd, 208. ON. vanta.

woo, n., *woe,* 310. OE. wā.

worde, n., *word,* 56, 178, 191, 218, etc.: pl. 56, 178, 191, 310, etc. OE. word.

worlde, n., *world, earth,* 186; in phrases, alle þe worlde, 64; in al þis worlde, 218. OE. weorold, worold.

worm(e), n., *worm:* pl. -es, 262. OE. wyrm.

worthe, v. intr., *become, be:* inf. 258; imper. sg. worthe, 340; pp. worthyn, 330. OE. weorðan.

wothe, n., *danger, harm,* 233. ON. váði.

wrakeful, adj., *ruinous, destructive,* 215. Cf. OE. wraecfull and OE. wracu + OE. full.

wrange, n., *wrong:* pl. -s, 243. Cf. ON. (v)rangr.

wrange, adj., *wrong, unjust,* 236. ON. (v)rangr.

wrathe, n., *anger, wrath,* 215, 233. OE. wræððo.

writte, n., psalmyde writtes, *the Psalms:* pl. -s, 277. OE. (ge)-writ.

wyȝt, adj., *strong:* pl. wyȝt, 69. ON. vīgr.

wyl, v., *wish,* 68: pret. 3 pl. wolde, 68. OE. willan.

wynter, n., *winter* (for year): pl. 230. OE. winter.

wyrke, v. tr., *do, perform, bring about,* 226, 301 (?), intr., *work, labor,* 39; *act, behave,* 274, 301 (?): inf. 39; pret. 2 sg. wroghtes, 274; 1 pl. wroghtyn, 301; pp. wroght, 226. OE. wyrcan.

wyt, v. pret. pres., *know:* 2 sg. wost, 183: 1 pl. wot, 185. OE. witan.

wyterly, adv., *certainly, surely,* 183. ON. vitr + OE. -līce, ON. vitrliga.

Y.

ydol, n., *idol:* pl. -s, 17, 29. OF. idole.

ylka, adj., *each, every,* 96. ME. (North dialect) ilk (<OE. ylc) + ME. a (<OE. ān), indef. art.

yrne, adj., *iron,* 71. OE. īren.

Ȝ.

ȝea, adv., *yea, indeed, well then,* 273. OE. ȝēa.

ȝeme, v. tr., *govern, rule:* pret. 1 sg. ȝemyd, 202. OE. ȝīeman, ȝēman.

ȝepely, adv., *quickly, recently,* 88. OE. ȝēaplīce.

ȝere, n., *year:* pl. ȝere, 208, 210; ȝeres, 11. OE. ȝēar, ȝēr.

ȝet, adv., *still, to this day,* 44; *furthermore, besides, in continuation, still,* 210, 257; with negatives, 199. OE. ȝīet, ȝēt.

ȝet, conj., *for all that, nevertheless,* 148.

ȝisturday, adv., *yesterday,* 88. OE. gystrandæg.

ȝode, see go.

ȝorde, n., *enclosure;* here the reference is to St. Paul's Churchyard, 88. OE. geard.

ȝoske, v. intr., *sob:* pret. 3 sg. ȝoskyd, 312. OE. geocsian.

ȝour, poss. pron., *your,* 173, 176, 209. OE. ēower.

BIBLIOGRAPHY

This bibliography is select, containing only the more important works on each subject.

I. EDITIONS

De Erkenwalde, in Horstmann's Altenglische Legenden, Neue Folge, pp. 265-274. Heilbronn, 1881.

St. Erkenwald, an Alliterative Poem, written about 1386, narrating a Miracle wrought by the Bishop in St. Paul's Cathedral. Edited by Sir Israel Gollancz. London, 1922. Reviewed by Holthausen, Anglia Beiblatt 34. 17-8. H. S. V. Jones, Journal of English and Germanic Philology 24. 284-5; P. G. Thomas, Year's Work in English Studies, 1922, pp. 39-40.

II. TRANSLATIONS

Sir Israel Gollancz, edition of St. Erkenwald (see above under I), pp. viii-xii. Metrical paraphrase of lines 343-352 on p. xii.

III. METRE AND ALLITERATION

F. Rosenthal, Die Alliterierende Englische Langzeile im 14. Jahrhundert (Anglia 1. 414-459).

J. Schipper, Englische Metrik 1. 195-212. Bonn, 1881.

J. Fuhrmann, Die Alliterierenden Sprachformeln in Morris' Early English Alliterative Poems und im Sir Gawayne and the Green Knight. Hamburg, 1886.

K. Luick, Die Englische Stabreimzeile im XIV., XV., und XVI. Jahrhundert (Anglia 11. 392-443, 553-618; especially pp. 584-5).

M. Kaluza, Strophische Gliederung in der Mittelenglischen rein Alliterirenden Dichtung (Englische Studien 16. 169-180; especially p. 174).

J. Lawrence, Chapters on Alliterative Verse, pp. 89-99. London, 1893.

M. Trautmann, Zur Kenntniss und Geschichte der Mittelenglischen Stabzeile (Anglia 18. 83-100).

B. Kuhnke, Die alliterierende Langzeile in der Mittelenglischen Romanze Sir Gawayn and the Green Knight (Studien zum Germanischen Alliterationsvers, Vol. 4). Berlin, 1900. Reviewed by Fischer, Anglia Beiblatt 12. 65-76, and Luick, ibid. pp. 33 ff.

J. Fischer, Die Stabende Langzeile in den Werken des Gawaindichters (Bonner Beiträge zur Anglistik 11. 1-64). Bonn, 1901. Reviewed by Luick, Anglia Beiblatt 12. 33-49. Compare further Fischer and

Mennicken, Zur Mittelenglischen Stabzeile (a reply to Luick), pp. 139-154 of Bonner Beiträge 11.
M. DEUTSCHBEIN, Zur Entwicklung des Englischen Alliterationsverses. Halle, 1902.
K. LUICK, in Paul's Grundriss der Germanischen Philologie, 2d ed., 2. 2. 160-8. Strassburg, 1905.
J. THOMAS, Die Alliterierende Langzeile des Gawayn-Dichters. Coburg, 1908.
M. KALUZA, Englische Metrik in historischer Entwicklung (Normannia 1. 183-197). Berlin, 1909.
K. SCHUMACHER, Studien über den Stabreim in der mittelenglischen Alliterationsdichtung (Bonner Studien zur Englischen Philologie, Vol. 11). Bonn, 1914.
O. F. EMERSON, Imperfect Lines in *Pearl* and the Rimed Parts of *Sir Gawain and the Green Knight* (Modern Philology 19. 131-141).
W. E. LEONARD, Beowulf and the Niebelungen Couplet (University of Wisconsin Studies, No. 2, pp. 99-152). Madison, Wis., 1918.
W. E. LEONARD, The Scansion of Middle English Alliterative Verse (University of Wisconsin Studies, No. 11, pp. 58-104). Madison, Wis., 1920.

IV. LANGUAGE

R. MORRIS, Preface to Early English Alliterative Poems (Early English Text Society, Vol. I, pp. xxi-xl).
F. SCHWAHN, Die Conjugation in Sir Gawayn and the Green Knight und den Sogenannten Early English Alliterative Poems. Strassburg, 1884.
W. FICK, Zum Mittelenglischen Gedicht von der Perle, eine Lautuntersuchung. Kiel, 1885.
F. KNIGGE, Die Sprache des Dichters von Sir Gawain and the Green Knight, der Sogenannten Early English Alliterative Poems und De Erkenwalde. Marburg, 1885.
J. FISCHER, Die Stabende Langzeile (see above under III), pp. 48-64.
M. KULLNICK, Studien über den Wortschatz in Sir Gawayne and the Grene Kny3t. Berlin, 1902. Reviewed by Thomas, Englische Studien 47. 250-256.
K. SCHMITTBETZ, Das Adjectiv in 'Sir Gawayn and the Grene Kny3t' (Anglia 32. 1-60, 163-189, 359-383).
H. BATESON, Introduction to Patience (see below under IX), pp. xxxii-xxxvii.
H. BATESON, The Text of 'Cleanness' (Modern Language Review 13. 377-386).
I. GOLLANCZ, 'The Text of "Cleanness"' (ibid. 14. 152-162).

O. F. EMERSON, Middle English Clannesse (Publications of the Modern Language Association 34. 494-522).

MABEL DAY, The Weak Verb in the Works of the Gawain-Poet (Modern Language Review 14. 413-5).

J. R. HULBERT, The "West Midland" of the Romances (Modern Philology 19. 1-16).

I. GOLLANCZ, Introduction to St. Erkenwald (see above under I), p. v.

O. F. EMERSON, Some Notes on the Pearl (Publications of the Modern Language Association 37. 52-93).

R. J. MENNER, Sir Gawain and the Green Knight and the West Midland (Publications of the Modern Language Association 37. 503-526).

O. F. EMERSON, Notes on Sir Gawain and the Green Knight (Journal of English and Germanic Philology 21. 363-410).

F. HOLTHAUSEN, St. Erkenwald (Anglia Beiblatt 34. 17-8: a review of Gollancz's edition).

K. SISAM, The English Language in the Fourteenth Century (Fourteenth Century Prose and Verse, pp. 265-292).

V. SOURCES

C. HORSTMANN, Altenglische Legenden, p. 528. Heilbronn, 1881.

G. NEILSON, 'Huchown of the Awle Ryale,' the Alliterative Poet. A Historical Criticism of Fourteenth Century Poems ascribed to Sir Hew of Eglintoun, pp. 105-16, 127-9. Glasgow, 1902.

G. H. GEROULD, Saints' Legends, p. 238. Boston, 1916.

J. R. HULBERT, The Sources of St. Erkenwald and the Trental of Gregory (Modern Philology 16. 485-9).

L. A. HIBBARD, Erkenbald the Belgian: A Study in Medieval Exempla of Justice (Modern Philology 17, 669-678).

I. GOLLANCZ, Preface to St. Erkenwald, pp. xii-lv. London, 1922.

VI. DATE, AUTHORSHIP, AND RELATIONSHIP TO OTHER POEMS

M. TRAUTMANN, Ueber Verfasser und Entstehungszeit einiger Alliterirender Gedichte des Altenglischen. Halle, 1876. Also published with sub-title Habilitationsschrift.

M. TRAUTMANN, Der Dichter Huchown und seine Werke (Anglia 1. 109-49).

C. HORSTMANN, Altenglische Legenden, pp. 266, 527. Heilbronn, 1881.

M. TRAUTMANN, Anglia Anzeiger 5. 23-5 (review of Horstmann's Altenglische Legenden).

M. C. Thomas, Sir Gawayne and the Green Knight. A Comparison with the French Perceval, preceded by an Investigation of the Author's Other Works. Zürich, 1883.

F. Knigge, Die Sprache des Dichters von Sir Gawain and the Green Knight, der Sogenannten Early English Alliterative Poems und De Erkenwalde, pp. 1-10. Marburg, 1885.

J. B. Henneman, Untersuchungen über das Mittelenglische Gedicht "Wars of Alexander," pp. 30-5. Berlin, 1889.

I. Gollancz, Introduction to edition of Pearl (see below under IX), p. xlv, note 2. London, 1891.

G. Neilson, 'Huchown of the Awle Ryale,' the Alliterative Poet. A Historical Criticism of Fourteenth Century Poems ascribed to Sir Hew of Eglintoun. Glasgow, 1902.

J. T. T. Brown, Huchown of the Awle Ryale and his Poems, examined in the Light of Recent Criticism. Glasgow, 1902.

C. F. Brown, The Author of the Pearl, considered in the Light of his Theological Opinions (Publications of the Modern Language Association 19. 115, note 1; 126, note 2).

C. G. Osgood, Introduction to edition of Pearl (see below under IX); especially p. xxviii, note 2; p. xlix, note 5.

C. Reicke, Untersuchungen über den Stil der Mittelenglischen Alliterierenden Gedichte Morte Arthure, The Destruction of Troy, The Wars of Alexander, The Siege of Jerusalem, Sir Gawayn and the Green Knight: Ein Beitrag zur Lösung der Huchown-Frage, pp. 8-15. Königsberg i. Pr., 1906.

H. N. MacCracken, Concerning Huchown (Publications of the Modern Language Association 25. 507-534).

R. M. Garrett, The Pearl: an Interpretation (University of Washington Publications in English, Vol. 4, No. 1). Seattle, 1918.

H. Bateson, Introduction to 2d. edition of Patience (see below under IX); especially p. xi, note 2; p. xxxii.

I. Gollancz, Introduction to edition of Pearl (see below under IX), p. xlv.

I. Gollancz, Introduction to edition of St. Erkenwald.

J. E. Wells' Manual of the Writings in Middle English 1050-1400, New Haven, 1916; First Supplement, 1919; Second Supplement, 1923; should be consulted for further bibliography of the Gawain-poet and of the separate alliterative poems.

VII. HISTORICAL BACKGROUND

Bede, Historia Ecclesiastica, Bk. IV, cap. 6. Edited by J. A. Giles. London, 1843.

Acta Sanctorum, Aprilis 30, Vol. III, pp. 790-6. Parisiis et Romæ, 1866.

W. STUBBS, 'Erkenwald' (Dictionary of Christian Biography 2. 177-9).
W. HUNT, 'Erkenwald' (Dictionary of National Biography 17. 390-1).
W. DUGDALE, History of St. Paul's. London, 1658.
H. H. MILMAN, Annals of St. Paul's Cathedral. London, 1868.
Documents Illustrating the History of S. Paul's Cathedral. Edited for
the most part from original sources, by W. Sparrow Simpson (Camden
Society, New Series, Vol. 26). London, 1880.

VIII. GENERAL

TEN BRINK, Early English Literature (translated by Kennedy) 1. 337-351.
New York, 1883.
A. BRANDL, in Paul's Grundriss der Germanischen Philologie 1st ed., 2.
661-3. Strassburg, 1893.
W. H. SCHOFIELD, The Nature and Fabric of the Pearl (Publications of the
Modern Language Association 19. 154-203).
F. J. SNELL, The Age of Chaucer (especially p. 28). London, 1901.
C. G. OSGOOD, Introduction to the Pearl (see below under IX).
I. GOLLANCZ, Introduction to Pearl (see below under IX).
I. GOLLANCZ, Cambridge History of English Literature. Vol. I, chap. 15.
London and New York, 1907.
W. H. SCHOFIELD, Symbolism, Allegory, and Autobiography in the Pearl
(Publications of the Modern Language Association 24. 585-675).
K. SISAM, Fourteenth Century Prose and Verse, pp. xviii-xxi. Oxford,
1921.
P. G. THOMAS, English Literature before Chaucer, pp. 128-141. London,
1924.

IX. EDITIONS OF WORKS BY THE AUTHOR OF ERKENWALD AND OTHER ALLITERATIVE POEMS FREQUENTLY CITED

Sir Gawayne, a Collection of Ancient Romance-Poems. Edited by Sir
Frederic Madden. London, 1839.
Sir Gawayne and the Green Knight. Edited by Richard Morris (Early
English Text Society, Vol. 4). London, 1864. Revised by I. Gollancz
in 1897, and further in 1912.
Sir Gawain and the Green Knight. Edited by J. R. R. Tolkien and E. V.
Gordon. Oxford, 1925. (Edition cited.)
Early English Alliterative Poems in the West-Midland Dialect. Edited by
Richard Morris (Early English Text Society, Vol. I). London, 1864;
revised edition, 1869.
Pearl, an English Poem of the Fourteenth Century. Edited with a Modern
Rendering by I. Gollancz. London, 1891.

The Pearl, a Middle English Poem. Edited by Charles G. Osgood. Boston and London, 1906. Reviewed by Hulbert, Modern Philology 18. 499-501.

Pearl, an English Poem of the Fourteenth Century. Edited, with a Modern Rendering, together with Boccaccio's Olympia, by Sir Israel Gollancz. London, 1921. (Edition cited.)

Patience, a West Midland Poem of the Fourteenth Century. Edited by Hartley Bateson. Manchester, 1912. Reviewed by Emerson, Modern Language Notes 28. 171-180; Ekwall, Anglia Beiblatt 24. 133-6; Macaulay, Modern Language Review 8. 396-8; Brandl, Archiv für die Neueren Sprachen 129. 516; Athenæum, October 26, 1912; Liljegren, Englische Studien 49. 142-3. 2d edition, recast and partly rewritten, Manchester, 1918. Reviewed by Emerson, Journal of English and Germanic Philology 18. 638-641; New York Nation 108. 991. (Edition cited.)

Patience, an Alliterative Version of 'Jonah' by the Poet of Pearl. Edited by I. Gollancz. London, 1913. Reviewed by Ekwall, Englische Studien 49. 144-6; Fehr, Anglia Beiblatt 26. 105; Brunner, Archiv für die Neueren Sprachen 132. 184; Athenæum, July 18, 1914; Grattan, Modern Language Review 9. 403-5. 2d edition, revised. London, 1924.

Purity, a Middle English Poem. Edited with Introduction, Notes, and Glossary by Robert J. Menner (Yale Studies in English, No. 61). New Haven, 1920. Reviewed by Binz, Literaturblatt für Germanische und Romanische Philologie 42. 376-9; Archiv für die Neueren Sprachen 141. 309; Emerson, Journal of English and Germanic Philology 20. 229-241; F. Holthausen, Anglia Beiblatt 34. 136-8. (Edition cited.)

Cleanness, an Alliterative Tripartite Poem on the Deluge, the Destruction of Sodom, and the Death of Belshazzar, by the Poet of Pearl. Edited by Sir I. Gollancz. London, 1921. Reviewed by Menner, Modern Language Notes 37. 355-362.

The Wars of Alexander, an Alliterative Romance. Re-edited by W. W. Skeat (Early English Text Society, Extra Series, Vol. 43). London, 1886.

The Vision of William Concerning Piers Plowman. . . . Edited by W. W. Skeat (Early English Text Society, Vols. 28, 38, 54, 81). London, 1867-84.

The Parlement of the Thre Ages, and Wynnere and Wastoure. Edited for the Roxburghe Club by I. Gollancz. London, 1897.

The Parlement of the Thre Ages, an Alliterative Poem on the Nine Worthies and the Heroes of Romance. Edited by I. Gollancz. London, 1915. Reviewed by New York Nation 102. 172; Bright, Modern Language Notes 31. 127-8. (Edition cited.)

Winner and Waster, an Alliterative Poem on Social and Economic Problems in England in the year 1352 (with Modern English rendering). Edited by Sir I. Gollancz. London, 1920. Reviewed by Steadman, Modern Language Notes 36. 103-110; Hulbert, Modern Philology 18. 501-3; Holthausen, Anglia Beiblatt 34. 14-6; Lee, Year's Work in English Studies 1919-1920, p. 39.

The Romance of William of Palerne (otherwise known as the Romance of William and the Werwolf). Re-edited by W. W. Skeat (Early English Text Society, Extra Series, Vol. 1). London, 1867.

The Gest Hystoriale of the Destruction of Troy. Edited by G. A. Panton and D. Donaldson (Early English Text Society, Vols. 39, 56). London, 1869, 1874.

Death and Liffe, with Introduction by W. W. Skeat, in Bishop Percy's Folio Manuscript, edited by Hales and Furnivall, 3. 49-75. London, 1868.

Death and Liffe, an Alliterative Poem. Edited by James H. Hanford and John M. Steadman, Jr. (North Carolina Studies in Philology, Vol. 15, No. 3). Chapel Hill, N. C., 1918. Reviewed by Carleton Brown, Modern Language Notes 34. 63-4. (Edition cited.)

Scottish Alliterative Poems. Edited by F. J. Amours. 2 vols. (Scottish Text Society, 1897.) Includes the texts Golagros and Gawayne, Awntyrs off Arthure, Pistill of Susan, Buke of the Howlat.

Sege of Jerusalem. Herausgegeben von G. Steffler. Emden, 1891.

Morte Arthure. Edited by E. Brock (Early English Text Society, Vol. 8). London, 1871.

Morte Arthure. Herausgegeben von E. Björkman. Heidelberg. 1915. Reviewed by J. D. Bruce, Modern Language Notes 32. 127; Archiv für die Neueren Sprachen 134. 467; Koch, Englische Studien 51. 115-121; Imelmann, Deutsche Literaturzeitung 38. 453-7; Binz, Literaturblatt für Germanische und Romanische Philologie 40. 227-9; Holthausen, Anglia Beiblatt 34. 91-3. (Edition cited.)

X. FACSIMILES

Pearl, Cleanness, Patience, and Sir Gawain, reproduced in facsimile from MS. Cotton Nero A. x in the British Museum. With an introduction by Sir I. Gollancz (Early English Text Society, Vol. 162). London, 1923.

DATE DUE